MARTIN GREEN

First published in 2020

EMPIRE PUBLICATIONS

1 Newton Street, Manchester M1 1HW

© Martin Green 2020

ISBN: 9781909360792

CONTENTS

THANKS TEAM GREEN

For a writer my inability to spell and punctuate is remarkable so I'd like to big up Lady Helen Murphy who has been proofreading the book a chapter at a time during lockdown. Thanks Helen, see you on the other side! I'm convinced the best times are coming your way. My English really is that bad I'd also like to thank Tara Page and Ashley at Empire Publications for rubber stamping Helen's corrective recommendations.

KINDNESS

I'm not a rich guy in a monetary sense. I'm just a worker-wanker like the next worker-wanker so there has been no advance payment or lucrative publishing deal surrounding this book in fact two weeks away from print I've still not seen a contract at all.

For this reason it's a real good job that the flow brought the right people my way at the right time so I could make it happen. Fabulous artist Amy Davis came forward to do the artwork for the book in exchange for a charitable donation to Johnny Spangles' charitable organisation in Urmston.

The only two Celeb opinions that I really wanted from day one were two of my heroes growing up: Clint Boon and Bez. I wanted Clint's King of the Manc music scene opinion and I wanted Bez's mad Manc energy endorsement. All the way through writing the book I had those two Manc legends in mind. I didn't know them, I've been to their gigs and ran past Clint on the Manc 10k, but that was it. When the book was almost done I put out some feelers and tracked them down. Being genuine Greater Mancs they knew exactly who the Rats were and what they stood for and both agreed to check out the book. When good vibes came back I asked Clint Boon to do the Foreword and Bez to do a bit of Promo. No mither was their shared response.

Clint's fee was a bottle of Rioja and Bez's was a small donation to his favourite charity - Coffee for Craig - who I came to know when feeding the homeless on Piccadilly back at the start of the project. So what a fitting end. That is proper not-London etiquette, both guys were genuinely delighted to support and champion The Rats. Thank you so much.

If you enjoyed this book I have my own life story out and about. Search for *The Balloon - We All Know One* by MJ Pinkie (That was my pen name when I used to be embarrassed about my past!)

Look out for *The Further Adventures Of The Balloon* that is coming down the pipe soon.

Thank you to The Rats for letting me right into their mischief.

AJ aka ADRIAN DRUMMOND HILL

Spending time with the Rats is always barmy and dysfunctionally good. Their feral vibe and visually astonishing appearance attracts a lot of attention from arty creative types looking to take inspiration from drawing, photographing or filming the band. One such art buff that was drawn in by the allure of their startling genuinity  is now known as the band's Official Photographer.

Adrian Drummond Hill, or A.J as he is affectionately known, is a man done good having made a career with BAE Systems in Saudi Arabia. He helped teach the Saudi Air Force how to use BAE's hardware in his previous life as a war games man. Gaz has AJ in at about number seven on the UK Rich List claiming that the air-con unit in his gaff costs more than the rest of the band's assets put together.

AJ's passion for photography initially blossomed as a twitcher as he became a skilled and accredited bird photographer (feathered not porn) during a forty-year stretch in the Middle East. On his return to the UK he switched his attention from birds to rats as street photography became his favoured focus area. The band have lit up his long lenses ever since he first wandered into their world back in 2011. Now in his 70s, A.J likes to turn up unannounced and capture genuine live shots of the band, sometimes appearing and disappearing with the goods on film without even being spotted by his misfit friends. Over the years he has accompanied the band on some of their most colourful adventures and he has most certainly become emotionally attached to them along the way. He is freelance and free, having never asked for a payment in return for any of his work.

A.J's value to the band is unquestionable. His photographs have been exactly the publicity required to realise Gary and Ray's mad plans to sensationalise the band and make them famous. His images have captured each and every one of their wonky steps to greatness. His work is plastered all over the internet and has been featured in many of the country's leading newspapers.

Examples of AJ's work can be found in the picture section of this book.

FOREWORD

Rock & Roll is for anyone. Rock & Roll is for everyone.

You don't have to be young, working class and angry to start a band. You can be rich or poor. You can be young or old. You can be skilled or… you can be shit. Over the last 40 years, there have been three bands that have stood out to me for their pure 'street' realism.

One was called 'The Worst', a three piece Manchester based band who I had the pleasure of witnessing at the Electric Circus a couple of times towards the end of the 70s. The drum kit was part Chad Valley kids gear and part… the spare wheel of a car. They were dirty, angry and 'street' in every sense of the word.

The second band were 'The Young Offenders Institute'. They were from Moston. I stumbled across them around 2004. As with The Worst, the spirit of the street oozed out of the pores of these young men. So many bands strive to look that way, act that way, sound that way, and then retreat to their nice homes and lives. Lots of us have been guilty of that over the years.

Seeing the way the Piccadilly Rats story has unfolded over the last decade has been a joy to witness. Not only bringing happiness to the hearts of thousands of Mancunians (and visitors to our wonderful city) but also always reminding me of that genuine, no bullshit 'street' vibe which only once in a while, comes along in a Rock & Roll band.

It's fair to say that over recent years, The Piccadilly Rats have become as intrinsic a part of Manchester's modern fabric as any of it's football teams or the symbolic Manchester Bee. Reading The Rat's Tales will take you on a journey which is at times hilarious, sometimes inspiring and, occasionally, tragic. To me, a band like The Piccadilly Rats is as important and relevant to our culture as any world famous, household name band or artist.

Rock & Roll is for anyone. Rock & Roll is for everyone.

Clint Boon
Manchester,
August 2020

INTRODUCTION

Soundtrack: The Jam – *That's Entertainment*

Please excuse me for using this introduction to tell you how I came to be personally associated with the extraordinary characters who are 'The Piccadilly Rats'.

The Rats are without doubt Great Britain's most infamous street busking band. Since their formation in 2008 they have burrowed their way into the everyday consciousness of thousands of Mancunians, shrewdly building their nest on the Piccadilly corner plot of Lever Street on the main rat run between Manchester's largest train station and the vibrant pedestrian shopping district of Market Street. Anyone visiting the city by public transport is likely to have had their eyes and ears assaulted by a drum-playing rat, an old man in a police hat who appears to be having a wobble fit and another milky-white pensioner stripped naked to the waist accessorised with 'Men in Black' shades, a medallion and a pair of black gloves that were responsible for consistently flipping some very funky t'ai chi Disco moves. The band's line up freak-quently changes but the band's front-man, Gaz, is always stood at the back, strumming his guitar and bringing vibrant soulful vocals to a mixture of rock 'n' roll and Manc covers. The band has become synonymous with a visit to Manchester City Centre. The madcap nature of their street theatre performance regularly attracts the attention of the city's leading publication, the *Manchester Evening News*.

Reporters at the paper have recognised the public interest in the band and have printed numerous stories about the misadventures of The Rats, many of which have made it into the national tabloids. The massive personalities of the elderly band members have also caught the attention of TV producers leading to appearances on some of the country's top television shows.

So just who the hell are these turbo-powered, bus pass-wielding street vermin?

Well, my earliest personal recollection of meeting any member of the band was way back in 1989 when I used to partake in under age drinking activities at the famous Sinclair's Oyster Bar in Shambles Square down by Victoria Station. Back in the 1500s a 'shambles' was a drainage system for a butchery. Picture the scene: lots of butchers hacking up dead livestock on tables in the middle of the square with all the blood, guts and animal juices running off into 'The Shambles'. Sinclair's always felt like a shambolic meat market to me. Ayingerbrau Pilsner was the pub's loopy juice offering. The outstanding quality and value for money of the brew attracted a very colourful drinking collective. Five pints of Ayingerbrau was said to have a similar effect on the human body as drinking eight pints of Stella and dropping an acid tab so an afternoon in Sinclair's was always a massive win. There are wonderful hazy recollections of Saturday afternoon piss-cannery that still bring a wry smile to my face over thirty years on.

As you would expect when consuming mock lager LSD, funny things happen and extraordinary characters tend to appear. Two fellas in particular stick in my mind. They used to come to Sinclair's most Saturday afternoons to help entertain the revellers that would gather on the pub benches in the square courtyard of the pub. They came on business to extract a few bob from the crowd.

Act One was a large-framed West Indian gentleman called Anthony. I believe he was a bus driver by trade and a do-gooder boozer when he wasn't working. He used to carry a large mirror, it was an oversized hand-held mirror, the kind of mirror that makes your head looks massive. If you already have a massive head to start with then you really have to love your own reflection to appreciate an accessory like this. Anthony loved his mirror and everything that was in it. He also carried a giant plastic yellow karaoke microphone which he would boom his massive voice into. He would arrive at Sinclair's alone and leave the place alone but, in between, his voice seemed to resonate and reverberate over all three floors of the pub and in every room of the building. Somehow he managed to be in everybody's company, all of the time. He had a gargantuan laugh that was always triggered by his own jokes that in truth weren't really jokes; more like insults delivered with a Barry White/ Brian Blessed deep throated chuckle. He had next-to-no actual comedic act or content, but he had a serious if funny face. He would scowl at you before revealing his friendly gleaming white teeth which soothed the interaction. He would happily trade reflective insults with anybody who wanted a banter war via the mirror. Then he'd skilfully deploy the teeth again to pressure you into making a charitable donation. Anthony was a typical 'UFC' - an Unexplained Funny Character. He told us that he gave every penny that he ever extracted from us young pissheads to a worthy children's charity. He had a certificate saying something similar and I think he probably did but we didn't really give a fuck. He was just quality.

The other regular act in Shambles Square was the very same milky-white dance machine as described above. A future Piccadilly Rat, no less! Ray Boddington was Mancunia's Eminem long before Eminem's mam ever got the keys for their van. Ray wore colourful shell suits and trackies, lop-sided caps and other street bling including a Beastie Boys-esque chunky chain and a medallion. He wore Stevie Wonder-style shades which suggested that he wasn't quite playing off a full deck.

Up close he looked at least 40 years too old for his clothes. He had peroxide straw-coloured hair, cut into a straight cropped bowl-head, like Jim Carrey in *Dumber and Dumber*. He had very high, protruding, almost Somalian cheekbones and a look of cute mischief in his eyes. When he got close, he spoke softly and warmly and was very engaging. He almost whispered to draw you in then talked extremely quickly without stopping to draw breath. Ray was completely consumed by his mission to bring his music to the world. He'd reel off all his recent achievements, all his plans and dreams in relation to his act and his career trajectory regarding this and, even at my tender age, I was intrigued by the man's flow. He was on a mission to become famous and even though he'd clearly been pursuing his dreams for about sixty years, he was still absolutely convinced that his talent warranted a record deal and a world tour. I just couldn't work out if he was serious or if he was taking the piss.

Once he had pre-lubed everyone up with Ray Boddington promo-foreplay chat, he'd call everyone's attention and press the magic button on his Ghetto Blaster. His Saturday Afternoon Matinee performances were absolutely supersonic mixing Mick Jagger style energy with sincerity and humour. Ray rapped and sang over cassette tapes on his significantly giant boom box. He wrote his own songs and his cornucopia of a street theatre presentation included some pretty dynamic dance moves for a senior citizen. He somehow blended old school Pierrot silent miming moves with modern street and break-dance.

To summarise, Ray was a feast for the senses. His rapping should have been shite but his timing was so good that he really made you listen to what were, under the surface, pretty meaningful lyrics. He did melancholic pain served with a ridiculous rebellious punk smile. His singing voice was vulnerable and again it drew you in. He was sincere. He believed in himself but it was his 'not quite right' teenage boy in an old man's body, a mix of youthful energy and exuberance that very nearly made it all make sense. That missing 1% was the key to the striking power of the performance. In a nutshell, Ray balanced tragic and ridiculous with sincerity and fun.

Underneath the act, Ray was a cool guy. He loved himself. He had an open heart and he was able to radiate that out to his audience. Even so, audience reaction to Ray was a mixed bag. He connected with good people very easily. Less kind and uneducated people would try to be cruel but Ray deflected that kind of negativity with a skilful wit. He was much too smart for the average bully.

MY POST-JUVENILE DRINKING CAREER

My next interaction with a Piccadilly Rat came some 26 years later when I was out and about in Manchester as the Tory Austerity era took hold. Parts of Manchester City Centre had become uncomfortable places to visit. Like any city in the capitalist world there are rich people and there are poor people. The Uber-rich don't really come into contact with the really poor people, but us workers co-exist with street-folk every day. Working in the city I, like many others, noticed a steep rise in displaced people begging for a living. The half-a-mile route from Piccadilly Station down to Piccadilly Gardens had in no time at all become an uncomfortably tragic Beggars Alley..

On my way to work in the early mornings I noticed people sleeping rough, really fuckin' rough. Shockingly, the new drug on the street, Spice, seemed to give people the ability to just crash out face down on freezing cold pavements for long periods of time without dying. Seeing homeless folk sleeping tucked up in doorways under cardboard and sleeping bags is one thing but this new wave of dehumanisation was something that I found very hard to come to terms with. When people start stepping over unconscious people in the street and accepting this as the norm, when that's okay in our city, then I think we have just about had it as a species.

Seeing this shit situation develop as I walked to work every day, I couldn't help but take an interest in the state of Manchester. I wanted to ask the unfortunate people living out these numbed existences how and why they came to be living like this. I started facilitating a soup walk every Monday night where I'd take a different volunteer out every week and carry a giant, red hot pan of soup around the Piccadilly area to help feed and engage with the street-folk. I'd make approximately one hundred portions of soup that would hold its temperature for around two hours which was usually enough time to get around and engage all the folk on the circuit.

On one of the soup walks I met Heath. He was a well-spoken polite musician who was clearly of posh Southern descent. On a bitterly cold winter's evening I found him sat on the floor on the corner of Lever Street tuning up his guitar. He had a really pleasant way about him. He declined soup but I asked him about his situation and he was very open with his reply. He explained to me that his lifestyle and his life situation had changed dramatically and very quickly in recent times. He was living out a completely different life to his previous one. Some might say that before he fell on hard times, Heath had everything going for him. He had a high-flying job, a big house, a fast car and his life partner was a successful businesswoman. He basically wanted for nothing. Unfortunately, it all went tits up for him. Depression, drink and a few bad decisions caused him to lose everything almost immediately. Before he knew it, his relationship was over. He no longer had any material possessions of note and circumstances soon led him to be of no fixed abode. He explained to me, in a very nice way, that this experience could happen to anyone. He'd been lucky. He'd come through it and he had just been set up in a flat by Manchester City Council. He was out grafting (busking) to earn money for his electric. I sensed he was also out for conversation and company. We discussed this briefly and Heath explained that Manchester had been a refuge for him. He had made friends with some of the other buskers and they sometimes teamed up to play together. He told me proudly, "I'm a Piccadilly Rat now. Please look out for us if you're ever passing here in the afternoon. You'll see what I mean."

I didn't really understand what he was telling me but I was pleased that he had some friends. I wished him all the best and, as I walked away, I felt an instant respect for a man who was clearly working through a low point in his life with great dignity.

Less than two weeks later I wandered aimlessly into my first taste of a Rats' gig and got to witness first hand why Heath was buzzing off being part of the band. As I approached the scene I could tell from his posture that Heath had traded his guitar and was clearly the adult sized rodent playing the drums in a lively four-piece where the guitarist and the drummer's music seemed to encourage lots of mad energy from their seemingly less talented associates. The scene was overwhelming. Like watching your first porno as a kid (dads had VHS collections in the 80's!). There was so much stuff to take in that you'd never ever seen before!

The band's singer somehow managed to look cool as fuck in Rupert The Bear pants and a fur coat. Then it hit me like a *Back To The Future* lightning bolt – I could not feckin' believe what I was seeing; my old hero, Ray from Sinclair's in 1989, was in the mix. He was even madder than before with his feckin' top off, absolutely ruling the pavement stage. His dance moves were still supersonic but a bit less acrobatic. Strangely my eyes were drawn to his offensive nipples that were sticking out like rubber bullets. Tucked away behind Ray was the cutest, dumpy, little furry-faced man dressed as a Copper. He wobble danced in a very funny special-needs kind of way. Together they were an all-out attack on the passers-by's senses. I stood there for twenty minutes taking in their performance and buzzing off the skilful way that they engaged the crowd. I had an Oasis style coat on and when they broke into *Wonderwall* and the singer gestured for me to join the fray. I Stretford-strutted in and Ian-Browned it on the spot for the rest of the tune. It went on a little bit too long for me to stay feeling totally comfortable but the small crowd didn't seem to mind me being there so I made it all the way to the last line of the song: "You're gonna be the one that saves me!". It's a poignant line and as soon as the singer Garry dropped it I knew that I would forever feel energised whenever I saw them play. I didn't even know them but already they had made me feel like I was actually in the band. If somebody had taken a Polaroid picture of the small crowd facing them then they would have captured a lot of happy faces. The characters, music and street theatre provided by The Piccadilly Rats does that to folk and it brightened up my day no end.

The people offered up a sprinkling of change and my first and last gig in a band was over. The singer in the Rupert the Bear pants turned out to be the band's leader Gaz Stanley. He stepped forward, patted me on the back and said, "Nice One". He never asked me to join.

The band seemed to break into an interval where the old men dancers chatted easily with people of all ages and I took the opportunity of trying to book them to play at a small charity festival that I was organising on behalf of The Riff Raff Society Charity in South Manchester. Gaz told me that as long as it's genuine then Tommy the Policeman will do anything for a pint and a butty. That confirmed the booking and started my association with the United Kingdom's best-known buskers but enough about me…

THE LINE UP

Soundtrack: The Who – *Who are You?*

GAZ STANLEY

Born: 1957
Place of Birth: Manchester
Raised in: Harpurhey
Roles: Lead Vocals, Lead Guitar, band Leader, Visionary, Creative Publicist, Decision Maker, Band Strategy Co-Manager, Accountant, Philanthropist, Dysfunctional Team Co-ordinator.

RAY BODDINGTON

Born: 1941
Place of Birth: Levenshulme
Raised in: Salford
Band Roles: Vice Captain, Harmonica, Vocals, High Octane Street Performance Dancer, Stripper, Storyteller, Creative Publicist, Decision Maker, Band Strategist.

TOMMY TROUBLE

Born: 1942
Place of birth: Monkey Town
Raised in: Heywood
Band Roles: Baton Wielding Fake Police Officer, Wobbly Dancing, Incoherent Drifting, Fan Interaction/Engagement, Deaf as a Postness, Super Strong Special Strength, Human Money Tree.

RABCAT

Born: 1960's
Place of Birth: Wavertree
Raised in: Liverpool
Band Roles: Snarling Drums in a rat mask, Maverick, Manc-Scouse
Peace Ambassador, Genuine Talent, General Disdain for People, No
Swearing Policy Monitor (Rabcat can't tolerate bad language)

HEATH

Born: 1966
Place of Birth: Sefton Park Hospital, Liverpool
Raised in: Cheadle, Norwich
Band Roles: Guitar, Bass Guitar, Drums in a Rat Mask, Vocals, good manners, intellect, calming influence.

DAVE THE RAVE

Born: 1960's
Place of Birth: Manchester
Raised In: Manchester
Band Roles: Amateur Drums, Additional Rat Mask Dancer and Keith Richards-esque Posturer Dancer, Tobacco Enthusiast and General Fire Hazard

SHIRLEY

Born: 1940's
Place of Birth: Lancs
Raised: Lancs
Band Roles: Percussion Section, Gurning

ALAN

Born: Salford
Place of Birth: Salford
Band Roles: Percussion, Art & Design, Harmonica, Vocals

1: COMING TOGETHER

Soundtrack: The Beatles - *Come Together*

There are various ways to comprehend this life and all that we are and everything that we do. Some people regard everything as written, so all coincidences, experiences and life's general path is mapped out by a higher force. God's plan if you like. Others believe that each of us completely creates and controls our own destiny through the power of thought and mind and then there are people that believe that they simply can't avoid any of the chaos that comes their way. Life has no plotted course; it is what it is and they deal with their day-to-day crap one turd at a time.

The creation and formation of the nation's most notorious busking band has its roots in all of the above. From the outside looking in, the band appear to be a group of completely chaotic characters that have somehow been brought together to create something quite unintentionally sensational but in real life the truth is much more calculated. Gaz Stanley has always been driven to make a noise, to shock people, to get noticed and to make his mark in The People's Republik of Mancunia and beyond.

This chapter is just a short overview of how the characters in the band came together. Scattered throughout the story of the band's rise to fame are the extraordinary stories of the incredible journeys taken by some of them that led them to be involved in the group.

Gaz Stanley is an unlikely saint. In my opinion, he's a genius. The Manchester street scene isn't just a collection of homeless addicts. Many dysfunctional people gather in the city centre. Most of these people would be sad and lonely if they didn't congregate in this way. They would almost certainly spend their days at home alone watching shite daytime telly and wasting electricity that they probably cannot afford. Gaz has given some of these people opportunities beyond their wildest dreams. He has given all of Manchester's street people a band that is a symbol that even 'they' can be great. Just as importantly he has used his creative energy to make tens of thousands of people take a minute out of their day to stop, smile and feel love. That's what The Rats do.

Manchester City Centre is a melting pot, a true rat race. Every type of person imaginable passes through town from smartly dressed office workers to naive teenagers out shopping and mooching with their friends. Everybody remembers their first trip to town, the first time in the city centre without their parents. It's a worrisome time for those parents because, at the other end of the spectrum are the hustlers, addicts and even the paedophiles. If you're not streetwise any of the above can cause you grief.

When he's working in town and not performing, I've noticed that Gaz is very reserved and cautious around every dodgy character that comes into his space. He's super careful bordering on paranoid which makes his ability to engage wacky characters all the more extraordinary. Gaz really does make sure that he identifies who the good guys are before he takes them into his inner circle. He's very Capricorn in this respect. While he evaluates people, he gives very little of himself away but once you're in, you're in. If he's decided that your intentions are good, then you're pretty much in the band either as a supporter or if you look and act mad enough as a performer. He has the ability to reach out to special, dysfunctional people and to sell them the performance stage that is The Piccadilly Rats. He does it in a genial, mindful, understated way. Gaz always sees comedy in the behaviour of others and himself but as the straight man of the band it's his job to highlight how mental the rest of his band mates are.

He's forever making funny comments to reiterate this:

"Fuck sake, have you seen this lot?"

"They were that shit, they were brilliant."

"We were electric today. Tommy even faced the right way for the last song."

"I thought Ray Boddington had left the band today then he came back with a Steak Bake."

Garry is very observant and appreciative in regards to the mayhem that surrounds him but still a tiny bit embarrassed by the madcap shenanigans of the band which really endears him to people because, despite having to manage the un-manageables, his stock position is always a wry almost embarrassed smile.

His ability to provide an income for this very fluid band (basically anyone can jump on the tambourine) has earned him an almost Mother Teresa level of credibility on the streets of Manchester.

So again, how did Mother Garry Stanley come to form the band?

In brief, the band was formed in Gaz's creative

mind well before he could even really play music. Gaz is performer, a gifted character actor and these days he's a gifted self-taught musician. He's blessed with a great voice and a magical eye for street performance. His understanding of the concept of surrealism is unmatched and his eye for 'no talent' spotting is legendary.

So how do you get from having an idea that you really believe in to actually delivering the none-sense in your head to the world. Well, Gaz knew that he could sing but to do music semi-seriously first he had to teach himself to play the guitar properly. Gaz got a guitar as a kid and fiddled with it a bit but he never actually sat in a music class or got close to being in a real band.

He turned to music after he had an anti-epiphany when he realised that whilst most of his acting associates were picking up sizeable cheques and contracts doing TV and film work, the only thing that he was picking up on a regular basis was litter around Piccadilly Gardens. He decided to stop auditioning for TV adverts and small parts in TV dramas and start investing all of his spare time learning to play guitar in a bid to give birth to his brainchild, which at that time was no more than a desire to do some kind of musical street theatre. Little did he know that the creative seed in his mind would one day become The Piccadilly Rats.

At that time Gaz was an out of work actor picking up just enough scraps of employment to feed his family but rather than commit full-time to a factory job or something as equally soul destroying as that, he somehow had to earn enough coin in a way that retained enough spare time to improve his guitar skills and increase his showmanship.

Gaz's main income came from collecting unused

copies of the *Manchester Evening News*. He landed a part-time role with the MEN cleaning department collecting the unsold papers all over town. He supplemented this by holding up an advertisement board for Pizza Hut each weekday lunchtime on Market Street. Both of these jobs involved spending long periods of time around Piccadilly Gardens and this enabled him to build a network of interesting, colourful and, in some cases, semi-skilled street folk contacts that could possibly one day come to be part of his street theatre vision. First though, Gaz had to test his own performance acumen and actually play music in public for the first time. If he could supplement his income from playing music publicly then that would become a justified cycle of improvement. Play and get paid for learning – that was the plan that kept resonating in Gaz's mind.

Matthew 7:7-8 says "Ask, and it shall be given you; seek, and ye shall find; knock, and it shall be opened unto you" and that is pretty much how a most unlikely opportunity presented itself to Gaz.

A bit like Ray always had been, Garry was now consumed by his mission to bring street theatre to Manchester City Centre. He shared his vision with everyone that he thought would buzz off the concept.

One such person was Paul Herstell, manager of Empire Exchange (Record & Collectables Shop) on the corner of Newton Street and Piccadilly. Paul listened intently to Gaz's plans and right out of the blue made him the most extraordinary offer. He offered Gaz use of an unused premises where, among other things, he could practice his guitar skills. Initially there was no rent to pay. The guy just gave him an unconditional leg up and a chance to develop himself.

On the back of just a few short conversations Paul presented Gaz with the keys for a lock-up on Back Piccadilly, a shady back street that runs behind all the main bars and restaurants on the Ancoats side of Piccadilly Gardens. Behind a sturdy metal shutter and up four flights of steep 'Anne Frank' style stairs, Gaz walked into the most Bohemian-looking band practice lounge in town. It was dark, dusty and lit like a brothel. An Art Deco black and white checked dance floor backed onto a small performance stage where Gaz would spend many an hour jamming on his own. This was one of those 'meant-to-be' blessings that make a man think that a higher force is opening doors for him. That is exactly what happened on Back Piccadilly. Thanks to Paul a door was opened and Gaz wasted no time at all and began teaching himself to play track after track. He still couldn't read sheet music. He learned to play tracks using Tablature, which is a form of musical notation that charts which fingers to place on which frets of the guitar.

For a man in his fifties he learned quickly and retained chords and whole songs easily. This was another sign that he was in line with his higher calling. He couldn't remember where he'd put his keys and bus pass in the morning but he suddenly had the power to learn and retain tracks like *The House of the Rising Sun* by The Animals without too much effort at all. Everything was falling into place.

In between guitar practice and insignificant manual work tasks, Gaz kept a close eye on the street performing scene. One of the main characters on the City Centre street-folk smorgasbord was Ray Boddington. Gaz realised that Ray was unique from day one. As a street performer, Ray had the impressive ability to draw and

6

hold the interest of a large crowd. Every time Gaz saw a large huddle of people gathered around on Market Street, nine times out of ten he would know that Bez's great granddad Ray was doing a bit. When Gaz discussed Ray's act with him he was always fascinated and amused by his extreme visions of grandeur. Ray spoke about himself to everyone that would listen; a rambling rock 'n' roll rhetoric delivered by Albert Steptoe in Hip-Hop fatigues.

Gaz was amused by Ray's delusional state but also intrigued by the man's undeniable self-confidence. When somebody one hundred percent believes that they have made it, then they actually already have. Gaz saw the power in Ray's unquestioned faith in himself. Without ever discussing it, he felt the same. Gaz was Rock Star already. He dressed like and walked like a rock star, and now he was putting the graft in to start playing like one too.

Watching Ray perform on his own, Gaz couldn't decide if the crowd were laughing with him or at him. Gaz didn't see this as a particularly bad thing as it was far more important that Ray had the ability to hold the crowd's attention. The bare-chested elderly street-dancing loon had clearly already cracked the code of how to attract and entertain a crowd and get paid for it.

Gaz looked on as Ray did his thing – it was notable that Ray always kept an eye on what was current either in music or whatever was in the public interest at the time. So, for example, if the football World Cup was on Ray might have some part of an England kit on performing his take on Fat Les's *Vindaloo*. That was his thing - pushing a series of happy trigger buttons in people's minds all at once to grab their attention.

Imagine the scene on a damp Manc Monday; a young fella walking up Market Street with *Vindaloo* banging out of a ghetto blaster. First smile trigger - great England football song. Second smile trigger - 70 year old man with his face painted with a St George's flag and his top off. That manages to stop the passer-by for a "What the Fuck?" emergency stop. Third smile trigger - Ray would then catch the onlooker's eye and throw in some white-gloved dance moves, a funny comment or a rap that would convince the passer-by that the performance was specifically for them. Before they could come to comprehend the whole unexpected entertainment offer, Ray would also have subliminally convinced them that he needed their lunch money more than they did. He connected with people just like the snake did in the old *Jungle Book* film. If he caught your eye then you were fucked. You would have no other option other than to respect the performance and make a donation as a thank you for sharing that moment with him. This was his key skill.

Ray was a genius in terms of selecting what tracks and humour to go with. Theresa May, Jedward and One Direction all featured at times when they were in the news and relevant. Gaz sussed this early doors and started to bang heads with Ray in relation to what songs they could perform together and what costumes would grab public attention.

Their first outing in 2008 saw Gaz playing instrumental guitar and Ray dancing out in front. People stopped and looked on with interest. Having a decent musician alongside Ray, someone who believed in him, definitely had an impact on the crowd. There was definitely less laughter and more looks of genuine interest. It was an important first step which rubber-stamped Gaz's intentions to develop the act further.

Yet while the band was starting to come together in town, back home in Blackley Gaz's family took the news that he was on the verge of becoming a street performer very badly. His wife and kids were horrified that their old man was becoming a busker. The wife was particularly straight with him, "go through with this and you're out". His girls both had office jobs in Manchester and were equally adamant. "No dad of ours is gonna embarrass us like this". Of course Rock 'n' Roll Gods can't be dictated to like this and after the very next afternoon performance Gaz was declared homeless.

By this time Gaz had jammed with a few different chaps on the circuit and he almost considered them to be his band. He called together Ray, Heath and a fella called Kenny Weaver who had been pretending to play bass, to explain his situation. He had to prove to his family that his wish to do street performance was a credible occupation and not only credible but more profitable than litter-picking – so he asked that they all spend the following day performing and try and make a few quid.

Gaz had been constantly searching for a gimmick that would identify the band. Something beyond being old and energetic. All along he knew that the right theme would present itself, but he didn't quite know when, where and how it would come. The verbal lashing that he took from his wife and kids was the spark to finding this. He walked through town the next morning thinking about nothing but how wrong his family were to be embarrassed by his actions.

Silently wittering his way through Manchester

Arndale Centre, Gaz was drawn to the window of 'Luvyababes' fancy dress shop where an angry-looking rubber rat mask called out to him. The Rat represented his current lowly status and the feeling of rebellion in his gut. The stern-looking rat meant business and so did Garry. He entered the tackiest of shopping emporiums and purchased two rat masks.

Later on that day Gaz met up with the lads and introduced them to The Rats. He tried playing a set in the mask but he couldn't handle being trapped inside it. Gaz has many phobias and wearing the mask incorporated most of his fears. It wasn't for him so a lad called Heath was summoned to give it a try whilst playing on a tiny toy-like drum kit. Instantaneously, a large crowd gathered and dancer Ray looked even cooler again in front of a drumming rat and Gaz in a fur coat and FILA trackie bottoms. After a few songs Ray noted that the crowd were intrigued but a bit scared by the rat who did a great job staying in time with Gaz. Ray blamed the rat for the lack of money thrown into Gaz's empty guitar case. He suggested trying a different kind of mask or softening the rat's appearance and, after a short break for lunch, Ray returned with a giant dickie bow for the rat.

The small costume change brought about a dramatic change in the way the crowd received the performance. Shocked faces were replaced by smiling, loving ones. The rat had become a thing of beauty and the guitar case started filling up quickly. Being free of the rat mask, Gaz saw his future unfolding before him. This was undoubtedly it.

They played the same four songs all day, over and over and Gaz took his share of the spoils home and left

£50 on the mantelpiece before going to stay with a friend. He convinced the lads to meet again the very next day straight after his cleaning shift and they played again for about four hours.

The street theatre vibe Gaz had been searching for clearly struck a chord with the everyday Manc. Passers-by were really buzzing off one of the unlikeliest rock line-ups of all time. People stopped, smiled, took loads of photos and some even danced. Most importantly for Gaz, his girls must have heard that the band were making outrageously good noises. When they walked by and he saw their smiles it showed that the family war was almost over. Crucially for Gaz's marriage, the busking income had dropped in again. This time, the wife was in when Gaz got home to present his takings saying "The girls said that the rat is hilarious and you looked and sounded really cool." The Piccadilly Rats had taken their first steps to stardom and, after 36 hours in exile, Gaz proudly walked back into his family home as a respected dad, husband and *musician*.

GARRY STANLEY'S TALE

1: STANLEY'S SON

Soundtrack: Gilbert O'Sullivan - *Nothing Rhymed*

Garry Stanley Smith was born on the nineteenth of December in 1957 in the midst of a proper winter with snow and other cold stuff. In 1961 Garry's family made the short move from Middleton to Harpurhey and he attended Harpurmount School from the age of four. A year later the family were devastated when dad Stanley passed away aged thirty-one. He had outlived his estimated life expectancy by ten years or so as he was born with complications and spent his whole life battling with the restrictions placed on him by his birth defects. Garry never really understood the seriousness of his father's medical situation until he passed away, but he did know that he had issues with his stomach. He remembers him as being a kind man with a sense of humour. Garry remembers looking down on his Dad from his bedroom window, his Dad wasn't very tall or strong, so he'd climb into the bin outside in the yard and jump up and down in order to flatten all the cardboard boxes. Garry remembers his Dad smiling up at him when he noticed his boy looking down and laughing at him. He had the ability to see the humour in his own situation and this was definitely a life trait that he passed down to his son.

Getting on for sixty years later Garry recognises that

his father's death has continually triggered insecurities and fears that have manifested in many ways throughout his life. Garry has been held back in many ways by his fears regarding travel, planes, trains, enclosed spaces, lifts, toilets, dogs, ferrets and much more. Here and now these afflictions make for mildly amusing lighthearted reading but to have actually lived through being terrified by all of this stuff can't have been easy. Garry has a high intelligence, as an actor, a musician and a leader of people. Unfortunately for him the restrictions he puts on himself because of his childhood experience inhibited his life experience. He has turned down lots of opportunities throughout his life based on fear.

Following Dad's death Garry was removed from school and received one to one tuition, or at least he was supposed to. His only memories of this specialised tuition was collecting leaves in the park to make arty pictures with. This type of non-schooling went on for six months before Garry re-joined his classmates who had all progressed a lot within that six-month time frame. This led to feelings of frustration and inadequacy. Gaz was made to feel like the class dunce.

The authorities must have diagnosed him with depression (no shit!) as he was made to attend sunlight treatment sessions in Central Manchester where a room full of boys dressed only in their underpants and black swimming goggles all had to stand around and gawp at a big sun lamp. Nobody explained the process and what was hopefully an attempt to beat depression through light therapy. It just freaked out Garry and made his life that extra bit shit. He dreaded going there and interacting with the creepy fuckers that facilitated it.

2: CHILD'S PLAY

Soundtrack: Blur – *Song 2*

Garry's house was on the same street as his grandparents' but they lived a bit closer to school and he has great memories of going there at home time and stuffing his face with sweets and pop (Tizer/Calypso Cola) as he was suitably spoilt there on a regular basis, almost every day in fact.

When Garry's younger brother by two years, Rob, was old enough, he used to love going to his Nan and Granddads too. This enabled Mum to work various part time jobs and bring in enough income to always make the boys' birthdays and Christmases magical and Garry still treasures those memories to this day. Garry's best ever present was an electric guitar that he received when he was either six or seven. He tinkered about with that thing for years.

Kathleen was a very selfless loving mother. She remained single for five years after Stanley's death before she met and married Terry. They went on to have three sons together in quick succession and Garry warmed to Terry at first and his happiest childhood times were his last year or so at Primary School and into the six weeks holidays. Younger brother Rob was a bit of a tearaway and loved knocking about with Gaz around the Estate. Mum or Terry must have had a contact at the Council or at least the swimming baths as Gaz and Rob had complimentary passes for Harpurhey Pool and would spend a lot of time there messing about. The sixties summers seemed to go on forever and the brothers shared a real childhood spent getting up to absolutely everything that a pair of young scamps should and shouldn't do. Their aunts and uncles and cousins all lived locally too so there was always somewhere to go and a biscuit barrel to be raided.

By the time he hit High School Garry started getting into scraps. Living on an estate with many large Catholic families meant that there was always plenty of scope for playing and scrapping with multiple sets of rough and tumble brothers. He remembers rucking with two sets of brothers in particular: the Wynn's and the Cahill's. Footy in the summers or collecting wood for the Bonfires in the winters always started off friendly enough but the competitiveness of boys often triggered scraps that could sometimes get out of hand but in those days things were always resolved in the moment, grudges were never carried over and life skills were enhanced through such experiences.

Garry used to love the Bonfire night experience. Every lad on the estate would gather everything that was not screwed down ready for burning. A couple of memories stand out in Garry's mind. He remembers playing a game similar to tig or tick but instead of touching somebody to handover responsibility to deliver the next tig you'd chuck stones at them. He remembers him and Rob trudging across a battlefield to load the bonfire with a pair of internal doors strapped to their backs. They got hijacked and got absolutely pelted with house bricks that loudly thudded into their internal door defences, scaring them shitless.

As Rob progressed to High School age Gaz started falling out with Terry who was becoming more and more domineering as Garry's teenage juices started to flow. The pair of them started to Stag off regularly over Garry's sudden lack of respect for Terry and his complete lack of interest in school. He never quite caught up from being taken out of the system as a five-year-old, his confidence was always shot in that respect. Rob was naughtier than Garry and would often get caught wagging it off school, but Terry had decided to draw a line in the sand and exert his authority over his eldest step son in particular. Garry didn't understand that so sooner or later it was going to go right off.

Garry and Rob's antics started to get out of hand and on Bonfire Night in 1970 they got a practical joke spectacularly wrong and when they posted a banger through a neighbour's letterbox. Their net curtains caught fire instantaneously and only the fast actions of the inhabitants of the property stopped the house burning down. The Police were fantastic and instantly believed in the remorse of the boys, the stupidity of the incident and the innocent nature of what could have been a very serious crime. They both received an official Police Caution and the shame that came with a Police Van bringing them back to the family home. Mum Kathleen stood their corner and they both got away with a long grounding rather than a beating off Terry.

This over-long cooling off period failed to bring stepfather and son any closer together and they didn't have to wait too long though before the man, and the almost man of the house, came to blows.

In an argument over the mis-treatment of a Bob Marley record at a family party of thirty or so revellers, most of whom were related to the pair, looked on as teenage Garry lost his shit with his stepfather's lack of respect for his record collection, he picked up and smashed a long handled wooden broom in half over Terry's head. Terry must have had an extremely hard head because he didn't even flinch, and he shot out of the house after Gaz with very bad intentions having been made to look a right twat in front of everyone. Luckily for Garry the old bugger wasn't as fit as he was hard, and he gave up half way up the road, coughing his lungs up.

Mum managed to negotiate non-violent peace talks between Garry and Terry that put Garry firmly in his hierarchical place in the family home. Fortunately, he had enough about him to realise that just keeping the peace and staying out of the way as much as possible was a fair trade for the decent life that his Ma had provided for him from birth. He didn't want to upset her but Bob Marley was Bob Marley and he was glad to have got up and stood up to Terry. He knew that he just needed to stay cool and busy until he was old enough to make his Exodus.

Shortly after the signing of the Island Records Peace Treaty an unexpected move of school and house meant that Garry keeping his head down wasn't that easy. His settling in period involved having four settling-in fights at his new school to establish his new place in that particular pecking order. Even though Garry was tall and reasonably strong he's always been a lover, not a fighter and his new school scrapping record reflected this, 4 fights, 3 losses and a spirited draw.

Garry wasn't too disheartened because by making a decent show of himself in these scraps meant that the middle of the road bullies knew that he would stand up for himself so 3.5 fights was just about the right introduction for him to establish where his new friend set was gonna be. Garry's place was never knocking around with the most popular kids in school and that suited him as they were all rather dull. As in most schools the interesting kids tend to be the geeks and the freaks and without holding a recruitment event it didn't take Gaz long to attract a few arty types to knock around with.

Gaz was a decent looking lad and at this time in his life being the new decent looking, stand up for himself, interesting kind of guy that he'd become started to make an impact with the ladies. He went with this unexpected spike in interest and became a bit of a player enjoying numerous romantic interactions with some of the best totty on the scene.

As Gaz moved into his last year at High School, City and United who had both had amazing sides up until this time, both started to go into decline. Gaz was a Blue but his new mates talked more music than football so that's where he started to get his kicks. He started going to gigs and loved the buzz of live music. Gaz had self-taught himself a few bits on the guitar growing up but he'd never had proper lessons or played in a band or anything like that. His only experience of playing with other kids was in a music class at school. The posher kids in his year had instruments of their own and could read music so music lessons were based around the privileged kids. Gaz liked the vibrations of the instruments and always listened to the instructions given to the chosen few but he only ever got to partake in the odd shake of a tambourine or ping on a triangle if he was lucky, that was until one day when the teacher had to leave the room to take an important call. Gaz bravely got up, walked over and picked up a an electric guitar and started giving it a bit of the famous rift from The Rolling Stones - *Satisfaction*, without hesitation the two posh kids in place on the bass and drums started to appreciatively play along. Like many an ill-fated mission it only lasted thirty seconds or so but in just that short period of time Gaz got the respect of his class along with a bollocking from his less than inspirational teacher on his return.

Gaz took Saturday morning jobs on the market to finance his vinyl collection and his visits to youth clubs and discos. Garry's musical taste was eclectic, growing up in the sixties he was all about rock 'n' roll; The Beatles and the Stones, Gerry and The Pacemakers, The Searchers, The Tremeloes but his song writing hero was always Irishman Gilbert O'Sullivan whose songs were often played around all the Irish houses including his own on the estate. Later on he buzzed off the visually stunning T-Rex and he was also a big Bowie Fan.

Gaz left school empty handed in terms of qualifications and money so he wasn't able to follow a recurring vision that kept coming into his thought canal. He was a big fan of the London music scene and although he could only play a few chords on his guitar his day-dreams kept taking him there. He ignored his sixth sense and signed up for a factory job on the line at Barr's Soft Drinks. A few months later the Punk Rock explosion of the Seventies hit London and he felt pig sick as his limited guitar knowledge certainly wouldn't have held him back in the three-chord world of Punk Rock.

Instead Gaz was involved in making pop of a different variety to go in the famous glass bottles that he had spent half of his youth running around the estate collecting.

3: THE GOLDEN EGG

Soundtrack: John Lennon - *Woman*

Gaz had become a good talker and he made new friends at Barr's easily. Young lads Mal, Col and Dave were his new crew and away from work they started going to North Manc boozers like The Shirdale in Harpurhey and The Golden Lion in Blakeley. Post-school his good looks and long hair continued to attract plenty of female attention and the lad's first Saturday night trip to Belle Vue's Danceland Club paid dividends with Gaz copping for Anne from Beswick. She was tidy but they never made it past a drink in town on the following Tuesday.

A week later Danceland turned out to be the goose that laid the golden egg as Gaz met the love of his life for the first time. Three well-fit birds walked past his four strong crew and Gaz caught the eye of the fittest one. Gaz was renowned among his peers as a decent talker but he still had shit chat up lines like everyone else and when the opportunity arose this is how it went...

'Hiya, you alright?'

'Don't you wanna know?'

This almost Shakespearean reverse psychology was always going to fill the shopping basket of a man in his absolute prime and it triggered a short walk to the bus-stop and a bit of a nibble before the flame of passion was extinguished when she got on the 216 to Droylsden.

Gaz knew instantly that she was shit hot and he set up a date for the very next day. He took Diane to the Lake Hotel in Mitten. The lake had an act on every night and their first date was noisy and joyful. They both liked a drink and the live music but more importantly she looked even fitter than she had in the dark.

Their first few dates were all around the Belle Vue area that they met in. Gaz knew how to treat a lady and he didn't hold back. Half a dozen pints and a meat and potato pie out of the pie machine in the Cheshire Hunt Pub ticked both of their good night out boxes. Conversation came easy and they were a 'meant to be' from the start.

Young people in love would queue for hours back in those days while other young people in love spoke to other young people in love in phone boxes. Gaz played a bit of that game but much preferred to do face to face and from the start the two of them were inseparable.

Getting two buses to Belle Vue was a right ball ache for Gaz though so the pair started meeting in town in other great northern boozers like The Grenadier, The Castle and the City Inn Pub in Ancoats.

They weren't going out for long before the Barr's lads suggested taking all their chicks to see The Rolling Stones play a gig in Bingley, West Yorkshire. Gaz was a big fan and was super excited to take Diane along. The Stones didn't let anyone down but the minibus that they went in did and the eight pretty young things spent the night huddled together creating a memory that would stay with them forever. They didn't have an orgy or anything, they just froze their tits off and shared the togetherness that comes with not taking home four eighteen-year-old girls to their dad's without letting them know.

Diane's dad was a unit, he looked like John Wayne

and he had hands that could choke a Rhino. She was supposed to be home by 11.30pm but the cat dragged her in just under twelve hours later. Luckily, the Rhino-choker was a Stones fan and he bought the whole "I didn't do anything officer explanation".

It wasn't long before they did do everything. Petite with big boobs, Diane was as amazing in the buff as she was in personality and Gaz was never ever gonna give her up. As soon as they'd had a few pants-off dance-offs the soft sod was down on one knee and they tied the knot at the tender age of twenty. Gaz is Di's toy boy by three months.

Gaz used his job at Barr's to fund making a family and after three blissful years of marriage Di popped out their sprogs, girl, boy, girl. At twenty-five Gaz got the best normal job of his career working for British Rail in the post section at Piccadilly. He loved that job but when they privatised the Railway they made him a redundancy package offer that he simply could not refuse and he paid off most of his mortgage while he was still only in his early thirties. Clever lad.

After leaving the railway Gaz flitted from crap job to crap job without ever really finding himself anything close to a credible career path in terms of financial abundance, development opportunities, or even something that was even mildly interesting.

4: THE ACTING GAME

Soundtrack: Basement Jaxx – *Where's Your Head At*

So when his friend Steve told him that he was making serious lolly as an extra on the telly, Garry's ears pricked up like those of a hungry Doberman. Steve said that on good jobs he was taking home up to £700 a day.

"How the fuck do I get into that, Steve?"

"All the jobs come through the Studio Gaz, you should come down."

The Studio was actually 'The Actors Studio' successfully managed by Andy Divine who played Shadrach Dingle in the famous Yorkshire Soap *Emmerdale Farm*. Andy was a right character, a man with funny bones and a face like a shaggy dog, Andy was a people person and an open book when it came to considering raw acting talent that were real characters like himself. Andy's own career was a great example to show that great northern characters just like Garry really could find a relevant way in the fake and phoney environment of the entertainment industry even though, if truth be told, Andy was actually a Southerner who did a great job pretending to be a loveable droopy dog faced northern rogue.

At the Studio Andy facilitated acting workshops to develop the attendee's skill sets in line with the acting work opportunities that came forward from the TV companies that recognised the nationwide appreciation of northern humour and grit. Andy took weekly subs off the Attendees of the Studio and a small cut of any TV or Film income obtained by his troops through association with The Studio.

Gaz was encouraged by Andy and his esteemed acting luvvie friends to be himself so, reassured, he learned to develop and perform in line with his own often raw and cynical dry wit. Garry has a really interesting Rod Stewartesque Glam Rock hair cut best served up in Granville style working class uniform like a janitor's coat, warehouse overalls or mining fatigues.

It was easy to exaggerate Garry's free spirited hair against a gritty working class backdrop, costume or set. It identified him as a comical but rebellious free spirit trapped in a piss poor existence up north. So it shouldn't have been too difficult for him to replicate what was his exact real life situation.

Shadrach's contacts led to Gaz's first paid work as an extra on Emmerdale. Gaz got paid £180 for a week for messing about on set which was close to double his railway salary before he took the pay out. The cast were kind and Gaz liked the kudos of being on the telly. He was on the verge of being onto something very good.

From time to time The Studio would put on showcases to match the needs of the Casting Directors that would come and cherry pick the characters that they needed to fit into their northern soaps, sitcoms and films.

Beverley Keogh, who put the hilariously raw Channel 4 Sitcom *Shameless* together, came and identified Gaz as a fit or more accurately a suitable misfit. Gaz was invited to audition for a part on the show. He failed twice but on his third try out he landed a part as a shoplifter.

In the Green Room Gaz got into character by explaining to actor John Henshaw (the landlord in *Early Doors*) that he was having a meltdown remembering his lines. John was initially kind and sympathetic but Gaz went on and on about how he was going to fuck this up and how difficult a situation he had been put in. Eventually Mr Henshaw asked to see Garry's script and with supreme comic timing Gaz whipped out a tiny piece of paper out of his shirt pocket that contained the whole two lines of his television acting debut. Mr

Henshaw shook his head and blurted out an exasperated: "Are you taking the fuckin' piss?" as he revealed his own bible thick script commitment for the day ahead.

In Gaz's scene he got nicked for shoplifting before being incarcerated in a cop shop cell. Thankfully the makeshift cell wasn't real and it had no roof on it as it was a set built prop. Gaz would have struggled to participate if it was real because he cannot bare enclosed spaces. Unfortunately his phobias didn't stop at claustrophobia he also couldn't deal with dogs, lifts, public toilets, revolving doors or being away from his family at all which probably made spending a day on set trying to convince him to do all of the above a bit of an unnecessary test from the point of view of a time-is-money TV or Film Director.

There is no doubt in my mind Gaz would have made an excellent Jack Duckworth or Les Battersby in *Coronation Street* but his inability to beat his phobias and work is probably what stopped him progressing.

There were reasons why Gaz didn't like things, he wasn't just choosing to be an awkward cunt. He was a naturally funny slapstick comedian in the same vein as Frank Spencer but again he was just being himself. He was always getting stuck in the enclosed spaces that he'd come to fear so much. He was the man who was trapped for over an hour in the rotating entrance door to Debenham's because a lady got her handbag wedged against the wall on the opposite side. After 40 minutes in solitary confinement he'd turned a milky shade of white and was ready to puke and shit himself. Things just always happened to him. The catch on a train toilet door once snapped off from the inside on him and he got trapped on a moving throne with a queue of desperate people baying for his blood stood outside the toilet door. Whenever shit happened. Shit happened to Gaz.

Later in the book you'll read about Gaz's amazing ability to think things into existence. For example he dressed like a Rock Star, thought like a Rock Star and slowly learned to play and sing like a Rock Star. No surprise he became a Rock Star in his own underpants. Unfortunately the same thing happens when he focuses on negatives. So when he travelled to London by train he would fixate on the act of breaking toilet doors and it would actually happen. Spindle locks were the worst; he'd see one and start sweating profusely, he cursed every one that he came across. One such toilet security negative mind-trick situation was when attending an interview with Take That's Super Agent Nigel Martin Smith who had Showbiz contacts eating out of his hand at the time. Gaz turned up frantically frazzled at 11.40am forty minutes late for a meeting about a part in *Coronation Street* because the Spindle lock in Nigel's posh bog had decided to become mystically charmed by Garry's pre-destined mental capacity to reverse Houdini each and every locking device that he ever came across. The lock clicked and clicked and turned and turned and forty-four minutes later the lock sprung back into life unlike Gaz's Cori-Casting experience. Nigel Martin Smith copped for a ten minute rant about toilet locks and this swearing infested interview technique got Gaz absolutely nowhere nearer a semi-permanent role on the box.

The truth of the situation was that Garry was more than capable of becoming a skilled, funny northern character actor worthy of an era defining role in a sitcom or film but unfortunately he was not capable of going to the toilet, having dinner, staying in a hotel or getting in a lift. As much as his personality turned people on, his phobias turned people off. Indoors and on set he was a difficult cup of tea to make. So Casting Directors tended to go with less refined tea in their bags. People that were prepared to be ordered around and plunged into boiling water without leaving a bitter taste in the mouth. Garry was the Lapsang-Souchong acting tea bag in the range. Lovely, smokey, a little bit odd and just like the infamous Chinese brew; he would remain relatively untried and undiscovered as an actor.

That's a shame because the opportunity to find his niche trade was there right in front of him as was the chance to get his hands on the silly money that attracted him to the acting game in the first place. Just the Prison Cell Scene on its own including his whole three lines: 'Hey mate I shouldn't be in here, I've done nothing wrong, It's true!' These Shakespearean cries for freedom alone generated two cheques of £700 and £300 a few days later when the TV company sold a repeat episode.

Gaz thought that he'd made it and was more than happy to drift back into shit litter picking jobs around Heywood where he'd made his home while he waited for the big acting opportunities to come.

Gaz's finances were generally kept on an even keel as whatever money came in pretty much went out straight away. It's funny that as it seems that once your mind sets a frequency at which your rich-o-meter vibrates, circumstances line up to keep you at the same level. A good example of this was the way the way the Grand Garry generated doing the Prison Break Scene on *Shameless* evaporated a few days after he had received it when an idiot youth on a Quad Bike rear ended his daughter's parked car causing £800 of uninsured damage. Dad did what dad's do and Gaz was back to square one on the life's a bitch-o-meter.

At this time in his fledgling acting career more work and good money was definitely there for the taking. Unfortunately for Gaz his everything-a-phobias had already been registered with Shadrach and the luvvie inner circle, so the quality of the work coming his way was already on a downward trajectory even after just two jobs.

Out of the blue Garry's agent called him with a job that would turn out to be the beginning of the end of his Thespian days although at the time Gaz could not believe his luck. His agent informed him that an easy job had come in; Heinz Salad Cream wanted to make an advert up on the Moors; "Only thing is that it's just a thousand pounds for the day. What d'ya think?" Gaz bit his hand off and was informed that. "There is another auditioning for the part but as you're the only person that has been invited you'd have to really fuck it up for you not to get the gig."

So on the day Gaz met a Casting Director at Granada Studios and the bastard met Gaz with a huge knowing grin on his face: "'Ah Garry, pleased to meet you.'"

"Why are grinning at me like a fuckin' Cheshire Cat?"

"Well if you don't know the answer to that question then your agent probably hasn't been one hundred percent honest about the details around this job."

"For fuck sake what am I here for?"

"Mr Stanley please let me explain." The smug bastard of a Casting Director then pulled a pair of socks out of his top drawer and suggested that Garry put the socks down his pants.

"What's this all about?"

"Listen Garry, if you want the part and the good money on offer Heinz are doing a big series of funny adverts this could be the making of you. Please take this the right way. You look funny. You're a classic grumpy working class straight man."

"Go on then what's with the socks?"

He handed Garry the rolled together pair of sports socks. "Right stick them down there but don't hesitate and be sure to go straight down ya leg, don't give them socks the chance to bite ya cock off chuckle, chuckle."

"Bite my cock off?"

"Yes Garry, when you're on set the socks will be replaced by a ferret if you can deal with that the part is yours."

"Oh that's alright then you just want me to stick a Sabre-toothed rodent down my kecks, for fuck sake."

For the first time in his fledgling acting career Gaz didn't want a job but he knew that if he was ever gonna break the cycle of not doing stuff because of his many phobias then sticking a cock hungry ferret down his pants for a thousand pound was a pretty sound testing arena to see if he could ever break the self inflicted cycle of negativity that he'd imposed on himself. Gaz knew he wasn't easy to accommodate and to succeed in this acting game he also knew that he would have to change. So he decided to give it a whirl and shook the smarmy fucker's hand in the strangest contract agreement of his life so far.

On the job Gaz was completely out of his comfort zone and not just because he was about to feed his bollocks to a ferret. He has a phobia which turns into anxiety regarding being separated from his family and his home, he also can't be doing with spending time in the close proximity of strangers. So when the Director of the Heinz Salad Cream adverts rang to tell him that he was booked into a hotel in Sheffield and he would be sharing a room with the two extras that would also be in the advert he was already beginning to question his suitability for the role.

It's funny that Gaz considers himself almost allergic to strangers because as soon as he makes a connection with a stranger he stops considering that person to be a stranger and, you guessed it, he makes those connections seemingly effortlessly, usually by cracking a funny line about a shared observation. Garry's experience in travelling to Yorkshire and meeting his new room-mates was testimony to his wonky mindset and unjustified lack of confidence in certain situations. Before he even went to bed the night before he completely over-thought the looming nice bits of the experience that laid in front of him. People free of any serious negative mental thought patterns would think "Nice trip over the Pennines by train, ooh yes sit back relax take in the view." Same for the free hotel and meals. Such things aren't seen as significant hurdles to overcome to most people but the possibility of getting stuck in the loo on the train over to Sheffield lingered long in Garry's brain and on the day of the trip he awoke feeling anxious and chose to abstain from enjoying his usual numerous morning cups of tea and instead both at home then on train he sat long-faced and dehydrating like a nil by mouth granny waiting to have a hysterectomy.

In reality it wasn't that bad, Gaz chose not to risk

the loo on the train so he arrived in Sheffield crossed-legged and desperately in need of a visit to the Little Boys Room and he braved the Gents on the station without too much fuss where he attempted to break the Guinness World Record for a piss. Then he risked a quality cup of Yorkshire Tea before getting a taxi to the hotel to meet his lovely new room-mates who were really nice and nothing like the monster strangers that he'd spent all week demonising in his head. As normal it was Gaz that broke the ice by asking which animal the others had been asked to shove down their pants at their interviews. This rhetoric obviously led to a lively introductory explanation and once again he'd instantly and effortlessly made friends of strangers. Not that he'd ever recognise his own people skills.

Things got even better when Hugo, the larger than life Director of the Advert, turned up and invited the actors downstairs for a freebie Dinner and half a dozen beers on Heinz. Gaz feared foreign spicy food but Yorkshire and the Showbiz way of life seemed to take away all of Garry's barriers to a good time. He claimed a VIP Pie 'n' Chips, Tetley Bitter and shared plenty of his daft stories before falling into bed in a rather sensational mood.

Unfortunately day two in Yorkshire-dom was more of a challenge. Hugo insisted that they all had to leave early and so they missed out on a civilised non spicy breakfast. He bundled all three actors into his ramshackle Ford Escort Van before René Arnouxing it all over the Yorkshire Dales. Gaz spent the entire journey with his white knuckles clamped to the dashboard cursing and protesting for Hugo to slow the fuck down. This kind of *Last of the Summer Wine* northern misfit character acting was right on point in Hugo's head. He had no idea that Garry wasn't messing around at all and by the time they arrived on set Garry had gone well and truly under.

Having crawled his way out of the vehicle Gaz took in the scene. A bleak house on a hill and nothing else for miles and miles. In Garry's mind it was the real life Hammer House of Horrors. He'd arrived at his end of days.

Hugo was having a great time and took great joy in presenting Gaz with his health and safety kit for the day. Garry was instantly drawn to the cricketer's box – a hard plastic protector for his crown jewels. "What the fuck is this Hugo?" "That, Garry, is your Family Life Insurance Policy. It will remove any chance of our ferret friend tucking into your personal equipment. It's not complicated just shove it down ya pants, so stick it in, see how it feels."

Garry huffed and puffed and followed Hugo's instructions. Unsurprisingly he'd never played cricket and his walk around to see how it felt quickly developed into slapstick comedy gold as Gaz didn't realise that the protective box should have sat tightly inside his underpants instead his face told the story of the ill fitting as his ferret protection box slipped down his left leg his face followed suit slipping down to the left like he was having a stroke and the more the box slipped the faster and more exaggerated Gaz's shuffle to the left got until he was doing the full John Cleese mad sideward crab. Hugo lapped up his barmy display and fuckin' loved him and couldn't wait to capture the magnificence of his eccentricity on film.

Right on cue the duty Rodent Handler arrived

carrying an oversized caged containing not one but two cock hungry ferrets.

Gaz challenged him on arrival without even saying hello: "Are these Ferrets tame?"

"Oh no this one here nearly had my finger off this morning!"

"Are you shitting me? What the fuck are you telling me that for?"

"Well you did ask mate."

As you can probably imagine the whole ferret down the pants scene was never going to go well. For some reason he can't quite recall, the punchline for Heinz Salad Cream campaign was supposed to be the release of a ferret into Garry's trousers. Hugo and the Rodent Handler tried and tried to get Garry to go hands free and just let the animal run down his trousers. Gaz wouldn't have it and insisted on making it a much more intimate experience than it needed to be. He made the handler teach him how to hold the animal by the shoulders which in real life was a bit of an achievement by itself because Gaz just wouldn't ever consider handling a ferret before he decided that learning to do so was much better option than not doing so.

So after a prolonged period of swearing, sweating and deliberating on who was gonna be allowed to pull Gaz's pants back so he could finally release the beast, Hugo finally lost his rag with him and somehow managed to set the ferret on his way. Rather than let it ferret its way out naturally Gaz clamped it down against his leg and a hostage situation developed where he refused to let the rodent move. The handler informed Garry that this was the worst thing to do as the animal could go into defence/battle mode. "Garry it's much safer if you just let him run down ya leg." Garry had no negotiation left in him and kept the ferret pinned down until it decided to release ice cold piss down his leg. Now the game was reversed and Garry was trying to force the ferret out while it changed its mind and decided to start heading upwards. Garry began to scream which seemed to make the ferret panic. This manifested in the rodent depositing more ice cold piss as well as a cherry on the cake; much warmer and much more disgusting turd which was Game Over for everyone.

Garry now had full on Post Traumatic Ferret Stress Disorder kicking in and Hugo called an end to the chaos. The TV crew took over and de-ferreted and de-robed Gaz in double quick time and bundled him into a shower in the house.

Hugo had arranged for fresh farmer type clothes to be presented to Gaz as he came out of the shower so he was ready for Take Two.

When he re-appeared Hugo read him the riot act in a nice way: "You're being paid more than enough money to make this advert Garry, now forget about everything that just happened we just need you to put a chicken on your head. It's just a joke Garry. The punchline is 'Your letting that Bird walk all over ya!' So just look bewildered. No practice Garry just fuckin do it." Gaz entered a state of bewilderment and didn't make a sound until the bird was on his head and the necessary footage was in the can.

The Heinz Salad Cream – "It's all going on!" advertising campaign was a massive success and Gaz's advert was shown religiously in the middle of Emmerdale Farm for at least six months. Unfortunately it was the beginning of the end of Gaz's acting career as he just couldn't face being compromised again. Being around people on their terms was just far too stressful for him.

To be a success he'd have to write his own script.

2: ENHANCED FREQUENCIES

Soundtrack: Electric Six - *High Voltage*

So by 2008 Garry Stanley had created a template of what The Rats looked like and his vocals and guitar gave the band a recurring sound base. Gaz was the only band member that was essential to making a performance happen. Everyone else involved at the start interchanged music and performance responsibilities, a bit like the great Ajax team of the '70's where Cruyff would drop back to fullback when defender Ruud Krol fancied his chances up front. It was the same with The Rats. If Heath, the drummer, had to go and sort his benefits out Gaz would grab someone else to fill in.

The band were beyond fluid which was a good thing because it meant that as long as Gaz was in the mix then it was always Showtime. Organising chaos was a key skill for him; from the first time that he asked Ray to gig with him, Gaz was fully aware that chaos was his new currency. Like most things in life, the more you put in, the more you get back out. The same rules applied here for Gaz but it's quite an odd and exciting dynamic to be fishing for co-performers that are, at the very least, crackers, especially when you're quite a guarded character. Yet he could see that the basic formula of Straight Man Singer + Nutcase + Rat = Long Term Stardom and legendary Manc Status.

At this point, Ray (Nutcase 1) & The Rat (Heath) were all building towards Garry's vision but he was always looking to up the ante and add more chaos and kudos to the production. He recognised that for the band to go where he wanted it to (unrivalled chaos) then he would have to wander far from his own comfort zone. The street magic trick was for him to become the almost invisible, unbreakable back bone in a body of bedlam.

Band performance times fitted in with Garry's litter picking and pizza advertising commitments which meant that the daily Rat-Jam took place late afternoon when most office workers were heading home. The Lever Street corner Gaz had picked to set up the Rats' Nest was the perfect spot for catching the most possible public views. Equally as important, this paved pedestrian area was big enough to hold a crowd without any health and safety concerns. As you can imagine, The Rats were all over the relevant health and safety legislation!

Gaz's plan for the band was to get into the consciousness of as many Mancs as possible. That was the common-sense grafter's route to becoming famous. There are approximately three million people in Greater Manchester and, apparently, approximately sixty or so million registered human beings in Britain so if The Rats got to be known just by a majority of Mancs alone then they would be embedded in the consciousness of almost one in twenty Brits – which isn't a bad starting place in terms of becoming famous. Gaz demanded structured consistent performance times so The Rats played four weekday afternoons and lunchtime on a Saturday. Ray and Gaz saw these performances as part of a bigger picture but, at this time, the rest of the performers just turned up for the buzz and to get money for chips and gravy, gas and electric and all that. Gaz wasn't at all precious or business savvy when it came to sharing out the busking dividend. If you contributed you got a split, regardless of talent or even application. In Gaz's mind any performance was significant.

Heath on drums was known to suffer from depression so quite often he would disappear and go into self-imposed isolation. One such afternoon Gaz was playing away without a drummer when a character called Dave Copeland came out of Wetherspoon's which is right next to The Rats' Nest. Dave was known to Garry only because he often rolled out of Wetherspoon's, Dave was always respectful and clearly buzzed off The Rats. On this occasion Dave let on to Gaz giving him the customary Manc upwards tilt of the chin. Then his eyes focused on the lack of numbers in the band's line up. He politely waited for Gaz to stop singing *Blue Moon* before he asked, "Where the fuck is the rat?" adding "Why is nobody playing those drums?" he said it like he felt offended and somewhat short changed.

Gaz was surprised at Dave's precise observation skills, "He goes walkabout every now and then, Dave."

"Really?" Dave replied. "Well, I can do a bit. I've just gotta nip back to the yard then I'll come straight back. Ten minutes, don't pack up."

Nine and a half minutes later Dave sat down and accepted the rat mask. He wore it in his own very unique way, almost like a flat cap with the rat's face pointing up to the sky so he could manage to smoke at the same time. Gaz didn't like that rat mask style at all but people could still just about make out the rat character as Dave was sat down drumming at a lower level than the onlookers and he did okay on percussion tip-tapping away on the drums like he always had been. Gaz realised straight away that Dave wasn't musically gifted at all but both he and Ray couldn't deny the guy was a cool looking character and, more importantly, he was undoubtedly another 'meant to be' brick in The Rats' wall.

It turned out that Dave was a part-time employee and friend of Mr Arthur Donnelly, who is reputed to have been the brains behind the Quality Street Gang who reigned over a large part of Northern England in the 60's and 70's. After a well-documented and colourful life, Mr Donnelly ran a successful scrap metal yard close to town which was, of course, the one that Dave had to nip back to on his first day in the band.

Dave soon became an appreciated fully-fledged member of The Rat Family and, after two weeks of happy jamming, Heath returned from the doldrums and, without any need for discussion, Dave understood how things were and stepped aside to welcome Heath back on the sticks. Rather than leave the band, he nipped home and came back dressed as Keith Richards, resplendent in electric blue skinny pants, a waistcoat and a bandana. He looked like a human rock 'n' roll scrapbook: A little bit 'Who', a little bit 'Clash' and quite a lot of Keef all squeezed into an unlikely renegade Manc.

Clearly Dave wanted to stay in the band and completely unexpectedly he had a very clear plan to do so. Without any need for a team meeting, he just strutted in and started freaky dancing alongside Ray Boddington. Ray didn't blink and everyone else grinned on in respectful acceptance. Dave oozed rock 'n' roll. Gaz kept asking him to wear the rat mask properly but the cigarette that hung out of the corner of Dave's mouth never seemed to go out. He was the funkiest fire hazard in town and definitely not a very good example to the juvenile onlookers but this was Manchester and the kids seemed to like him the best out of everyone. Dave was more than happy dancing and the ultra-enthusiastic way he took to his new role in the band earned him his nickname, 'Dave the Rave'. A week later, when Dave never showed for the Saturday lunch Rat Jam, Gaz rang Arthur Donnelly's yard to see if he was there. Mr Donnelly always referred to Dave as David.

Gaz: "Hi, is Dave Copeland there, please."

Arthur: "No. What is it that you want David for, please?"

Gaz: "He does some drumming and dancing for our band."

Arthur: "I hope you're not trying to wind me up here?"

Gaz: "No, Arthur. David is a man of many talents. He's definitely in the band."

The new band formula was now a flat back four of straight-man and rat drummer and two mad dancers. Dave's presence elevated the band's street theatre offering to another level and the word of mouth reviews that must have been happening in the boozers round town landed the band a few low level pub gigs as landlords started to visit The Rat's Nest to request their services. Most times they just got paid in sandwiches and beer and not Rock 'n' Roll Coke (a-Cola) for Ray and Heath but Gaz convinced the lads that to start building a bigger profile they must start getting known as a bookable act rather than just a busking group and these were their first small gigging steps to world domination and rat infestation. They were definitely starting to grab the attention of the city. Iconic photos of The Rats starting appearing on the social media feeds of almost everyone who ever passed through town. They were a vibration that simply could not be walked past or ignored. Conversations were happening in offices, coffee shops and now in pub music venues all over the city...

"Have you seen The Rats?"

Gaz and Ray hoped for one specific kind of reply, something like, "Yes, they are mental". Clearly such conversations were happening. The Rats' plan was manifesting nicely.

The band's line-up was looking more and more visually stunning and the fluidity of the set up meant that there was still room for more development in the act. If a band member went missing then their replacement always had the opportunity to add something extra to the mix. It wasn't too long before another opportunity to experiment arose as Heath sadly once again went walkabout as more depression and trauma entered his consciousness.

As sad as Heath's plight was, the band never questioned it, probably because they all had their own shit going on. He'd come back like the band boomerang when he was good and ready. As previously discussed some things are meant to be so when Heath dipped out the Universe coughed up the next appropriate nutter for Garry to coax into the chaos. So in true sliding-door fashion just at the right time an oriental-looking scouser walked right up to The Nest and introduced himself to Garry as 'Martin'.

Martin claimed to be a proper drummer. He spoke like an intellectual and plugged into the arty side of the street theatre offering. He respected what he had seen of Garry and Ray's creativity and offered to play with the band if he could find the time. The next time

Gaz saw Martin he said: "Hey, Martin, we still need a drummer. We've played a couple of gigs in pubs this week, Mother Mac's and The Unicorn. Have you ever played in Manchester?"

Martin replied, "Yeah we supported Motörhead at The Apollo."

"Fuckin Hell, I'll get my coat!" said Gaz, in astonishment.

Martin didn't blink - he clearly wasn't a bragger. He explained that the best known band that he had played in was Goldblade where he took over on drums in from a fella called Rob Haynes and helped them write a few tunes back in the day. These days he was a freelance; a free spirit who spent his time doing music and journalism. Gaz suspected that he was probably some kind of political activist as well, as he spoke really passionately about his revulsion at local political figures and their actions or more accurately their inactions.

Whenever a conversation started about politics, it usually ended in Martin expressing his angst against some kind of authority. He definitely had all the hallmarks of a real punk. The only thing that didn't seem to fit in with his anti-establishment edge was his stage name. Martin informed Gaz that whenever he played drums he became "Buster Rabcat". Another light bulb went off in Garry's head. Anyone answering to that name must have something special going on.

The Rabcat definitely passed Gaz's 'Interesting Character/Good Guy' interview criteria and, with Heath needing time out, Gaz couldn't wait to hear him play. Buster Rabcat was a serious but very enthusiastic rat from the very first moment that he took the drummer's chair. He was fully committed to the project and his heart was entirely invested into the pure street theatre experience that Gaz Stanley had sold to him.

In their first Rat Jam, Buster Rabcat in Garry's words was "Fuckin' Dynamite". He insisted on not playing any of what he categorised as 'Musical Cheese' like Oasis's *Wonderwall* or Smokie's *Who The Fuck Is Alice* and preferred Gaz to stick with Rock 'n' Roll, Mod and punk Classics. Rabcat was clearly a skilled drummer and wearing the rat mask was not a problem to him at all. This made Gaz happy and backed up his suspicion that the rat disguise was just the type of escape mechanism that Martin needed to feel comfortable. It was another perfect match.

The Jam, Eddie Cochrane, and early Beatles tunes were all significantly enhanced with Rabcat on the drums. The other rats sensed a real shift in momentum because, after a sensational first afternoon performance, Rabcat offered to take control of the band's social media to see where it might take them. Martin wasn't always available for the daily Rat Jams but Garry knew that he must pin him down and roll him out for the more elaborate gigs that he knew were just around the corner. Rabcat would be a key player in terms of gaining musical credibility and interest as his energy was dangerously good and very high voltage.

Rabcat often made the effort to come into Manchester and star in the daily Rat Jam and it really did take the band's performances up a few levels. The highly strung nature of his drumming was matched by his awkward highly strung anti-everythingness. He possessed an OCD perfectionist, slightly negative view on most things which made his inclusion in the band sometimes tricky. He was definitely not one for unrehearsed curve ball changes and that is a thin ice starting position if you decide to join a band like The Rats who were always beyond unpredictable. One such act of unpredictability submerged Rabcat right under the frozen lake of what was acceptable in his head. Heath was back on the scene swapping Drums for Bass Guitar and in an epic act of un-wisdom "Dave the Rave" decided to whip Rabcat's rat mask off his head and replace it with the new monkey mask that Heath was wearing on the Bass. This happened mid-set, without pre-discussion, and without stopping to consider what seismic consequences that this dramatic change of species might have on the band and the animal kingdom as a whole.

Rabcat is real with everything that he thinks, says and does so when he's doing street performance, he is 100% in character. He's not messing around so he just went with the animal character change and immediately got straight into his new found demonic monkey mask role. Part way through the next track, the newly crowned evil drum monkey attacked the innocent bystander Heath Rat. In true street theatre slapstick style, Buster Rabcat exerted just enough street violence onto the Heath Rat to reclaim the mask and the drums. Invisible backbone Gaz predictably just kept playing while the fight and mask swap progressed and, as ever, Heath took it on the chin and by the end of Eddie Cochran's *Come On Everybody*, he had absorbed the beating and had started monkeying around again on the bass.

Unexpectedly, when Rabcat reclaimed the Rat mask, the feel-good happy go lucky Rat, all cute and lovable with its dickie bow, seemed to have undergone a character transformation and another phase of the band began. Rabcat Rat became sinister and evil once again.

He took on a darkened persona and started to thrash the drums as if they were representative of the ignorant, dumbed-down society that he'd grown to detest. His core punkness started to flourish and as Gaz says, "he became fuckin' electric. Smashing the drums like a righteous firing squad at a Tory Party Conference."

Everyone perceives art and entertainment differently. A performance can mean something different to every member of the crowd. At this point in time, every onlooker must have at least though, "Fuck me, that Rat can play the drums." More in-tune onlookers realised that this mob of madcap surrealist jammers were sending a higher message. Rabcat was expressing himself in fine style, in an angry wood on metal 'fuck everything' kind of a way.

Even though they were only playing covers, the appearance and rebel energy of the band had really started to carry a message.

The Piccadilly Rats, at this point, had become dynamic and thought-provoking to say the very least. Not only were they starting to hit the Manc psyche they had also become Manchester's number one must-see tourist attraction.

3: THE UNMANAGEABLES

Soundtrack: The Stone Roses - *Fools Gold*

The band's line up was now at its optimum level, a divinely gathered six-pointed hell raising hexagon. When everybody showed up this was pretty much the dream line up. Unfortunately for everyone concerned, but especially Garry, getting them all to turn up at the same time was always an ongoing drama.

Gaz would usually arrange for all six of them to meet him at the bottom end of Market Street as most of the band lived on the North side of Manchester and if they weren't already in town it was likely that they would commute in through Victoria Railway Station. On gig days Gaz demanded that they all meet him by the Hot Dog Stand that is now called the 'Porky Blinders Sausage Stall' just in front of the tram tracks on Cross Street at the foot of the Market Street pedestrian shopping area. Gaz would time this for the end of his Pizza Hut advert board carrying shift, ready to make the short walk together to collect the band's equipment from the top end of Market Street on Back Piccadilly.

Every week at least one of The Rats wouldn't show up and almost every week it was a different Rat with a different and often ridiculous excuse for their absence. As both Mother Hen and Mother Theresa Gaz would check their traceability by ringing round on his bottom of the range hand-held Rat Tracking Device. His super deluxe Alcatel eight quid Bat Phone was everyone's check in point if they had a 'Gaz I've shit going on' excuse to make.

Regardless of if they all turned up at once there was always the possibility that one or more of them could go missing on the short walk up through town to collect their instruments. Gaz even suggested bringing a rope along for the band to hold onto for guidance like tiny tot children do in nursery situations but he decided that he couldn't even trust them to do that. It would just turn into a slapstick Tug of War display. It would take them all day just to make it up to their residential nest and Jam-spot. Gaz soon sussed out that the best policy was to just go with whatever God gave him on a daily basis and deal with any crazy situations that arose in the moment. If he took it all too seriously and started to fall out with The Rats for being late or absent, he'd be a one-man band in no time at all.

Garry soon became a skilled manager of the unmanageables. He felt in his heart that he'd started to live out his vocation. Life was never dull.

4: THE BIERKELLER FACTOR

Soundtrack: Buddy Holly – *Rave On*

Gaz has a hazy recollection of meeting Tommy Trouble somewhere previously. One day, without an invite or even a pre-conversation, Tommy decided to stand on the end of the band line-up facing the crowd on Rats' Nest Corner. Out of the corner of his eye Gaz clocked an elderly, dumpy and messy haired version of Manuel off *Fawlty Towers* – and thought "ay up, who the fuck is this?"

A trigger went off in Gaz's head, so he spent the rest of the band's performance of *All My Lovin'* by The Beatles intently watching Tommy's movements. First his fingers started clicking not really in time with the beat of Rabcat's drum, then his whole right arm started popping out like he was having an "I'm a Little Tea Pot" fit and, by the end of the song, he added a kick of an invisible football to his routine. Gaz bought Tommy's unscheduled and faultless audition and when the band broke for a brew Tommy flipped their mystery past meeting on its head by telling Garry that, "Yes, I remember you, must be fifteen years ago. I seen ya in Monkey Town, Heywood. That's my town. I'm surprised to see you're still alive if I'm honest." Gaz's face was a picture and the man that would go on to become everyone's favourite talentless wobbly copper had just literally walked into the band.

The Rats was now stacked with mad characters. Each set they performed became completely unpredictable and a hell of a lot of fun. Dave the Rave continued to be great value. At the Rats Nest, he had claimed a particular paving slab as his own and he busted all his deep meditation-type rude moves in that one square foot of raving slab. It was as if that raving slab radiated an energy from the Rock 'n' Roll centre of the earth that Dave managed to channel in his own marvellously Bohemian style.

Every now and then the Rock 'n' Roll energy subsided, just enough for Dave to bugger off, usually unannounced, mid-track. Not that it mattered as Ray and Tommy were just as entertaining. Twenty minutes later he'd return with his weekly food shop, lay it down and get straight back into it rocking on his raving slab. When all three of them were in the groove, onlookers just didn't have enough eyes to take it all in. The musicians were just as captivating with Rabcat smashing the shit out of everything in the rhythm section, Heath the unflappable Bass Pimp looking the business either as Elvis or a Monkey depending on his mood. While Gaz sang with the excited energy of a teenager proud to show off to his mad mates.

The mad energy of the band kept a steady trickle of offers from interested passers-by to play gigs in and around town. A lot of the time, nothing came out of these interactions but every now and then Garry or Ray would decide it was worth the effort to lug all the gear somewhere. The band has never had transport, so logistics have always been a barrier to them doing stuff.

One of their first gigs as a six-sided hell-raising hexagon was absolutely tragic. Mother Mac's hired them to perform on St Patrick's Day for a straight payment of £60. That worked out at exactly a £10 per Rat. Imagine trying to convince an uncontrollable, free-spirited bunch of cash-hungry Rats that they need to travel into Manchester - Rabcat from The Wirral travelled on a school night - and they lumped all their musical equipment over to Mother Mac's to interrupt an Irish Cèilidh on a cold, wet and windy Paddy's Night.

Somehow Gaz and Ray did. They soon wished that they hadn't bothered as, in a very funny way, the fervently partisan Irish crowd walked straight out pretty much as soon as they started to play. The pub went from a heaving mass of Celtic bonhomie to being empty in thirty seconds flat. *Wonderwall* went down like a lead fart as the band didn't know how to play *The Irish Rover*. *Ghost Town* by The Specials felt far more appropriate. The landlord came over and apologised for misjudging his decision and gave them £60 to fuck off. Garry shared out the tenners and a split of the day's busking takings and, over a drink, Ray helped Garry remind them all how fuckin' funny the situation was and how fuckin' cool they all were for being able to absorb the Phoenix Nights-ness of the experience.

Days later at The Nest a girl came up and handed Tommy a flyer for a talent competition. As Tommy didn't have any talent, he waited for an appropriate moment and passed it to Gaz, who wasted no time in chucking it on the rubbish pile ready for binning at the end of the day. The girl that handed over the flyer was clearly a fan as she'd stayed to watch the next performance and observed Garry ditching her leaflet. She came over and introduced herself, "Hi I'm Dawn, I'm the Entertainment Manager at The Bierkeller in the Printworks. You should enter the competition, you're actually really rather good and it's a £500 prize for the winner."

"Five Hundred Quid!"

Ray's eyes nearly popped out of his head and he instantly turned on the Manc charm reassuring Dawn from The Bierkeller, "We won't just enter, love, we will win this competition, easy. In fact, I could probably win it on my own but I wouldn't do that. These guys need me!"

Dawn, like so many others before her, loved the whole dynamic of the band and these mad old men. She was in.

The Bierkeller is a lively young person's venue that is busy seven days a week. Dawn's job was to keep it that way. The format of the competition was four heats with the winner from each heat going through to a semi-final. Dawn signed up The Rats and promised them £100 for their first performance in Heat Number One. Dawn had advertised "The Keller Factor Talent Competition" to the max and on a Monday night, the place was absolutely packed with students taking advantage of 'Messy Monday' discounted drinks and free entertainment.

The band watched on as a couple of seriously talented solo performers did their thing and were warmly received by the audience. Heath shared his thoughts, "Wow, the standard is really high - we've got no chance" before he was clinically corrected by Ray, "Don't be daft - these kids have never seen anything like us!"

When it came to the performance it was a toss-up who was more shocked; the audience or the band? The place went absolutely bonsai.

Ray was right.

The alcohol-fuelled young people were right in tune with The Rats' high frequency and The Bierkeller was fuckin' bouncing. The kids loved Ray and Dave, but they buzzed off Tommy the most who was absolutely ruling it. He nearly got dragged off the stage a couple of times as the adoring mob reached out and grabbed him. The poor fella was just trying to go about his normal wobbly police duties. Heath recalls, "It was hard to concentrate and stay in time because of the energy in the room. It took your breath away. None of us, bar Rabcat, had played for this many people before and they truly seemed to love us. It was quite overwhelming."

Everyone in the band that night got a taste of what could be and Ray was at his vibrational best, selling the band in a wired/vindicated ranting sort of way muttering away to anyone that would listen – "Going places us, best band in Manchester, never mind £500, we'll be on *Top Of The Pops* soon." Gaz was clever in different ways to Ray. For a start, he knew that *Top Of The Pops* stopped about ten years ago. Gaz was always thinking and, in the four weeks leading up to the semi-final, he discussed with Heath the different ways that they could take their performance up a level to make the final. Over a brew they dropped their big idea on Ray. "We've been thinking. In the semis it might be funny if Tommy comes out in a mankini! The kids will go mad for it."

Ray was outraged! "We are good enough to win this competition singing *Kum ba yah, Me Lord*. Don't even think about devaluing the band!"

Gaz and Heath giggled and asked Tommy what he thought. Tommy would agree to anything in return for a pie, a butty or a beer and he just laughed as if he knew what they were talking about. Later that week, Garry rang Dawn at The Bierkeller and asked if she thought dressing Tommy up was a good idea. She thought it was, but Garry was still unsure and kind of made a decision to let it drift.

Come the day of the gig and Gaz and Heath hadn't arranged any extra fancy (un)dress for Tommy but during a fag break after their initial sound-check and a pint at The Bierkeller, the Dastardly Duo got all devious and giggly again and pooled together a tenner for Gaz to walk round to Luvyababes Fancy Dress Shop and pick up a mankini. On his return, Gaz slipped it to Heath who took Tommy to the small changing room/ cupboard while Gaz went off chatting with Ray and his new found teenage entourage. Heath spent a very peculiar ten minutes explaining to Tommy what a mankini was and how to wear it. After ten minutes he was no closer to Tommy understanding so left it like this: - "Tommy, if you want to give it a go, just stick it on. You will suss it out once you've got your pants off."

How very wrong he was.

Tommy had agreed to wait in the cupboard until he heard the opening power chords of *Rave On* by Buddy Holly. Then he'd burst out Liam Gallagher/Big Daddy-style to delight the crowd. As the band were given a two-minute call Ray twigged that something was going on and started to question Gaz who managed to avoid eye contact. As the band walked to their stations all of them looked a little bit confused.

The audience cheered them on and then fell silent. Then the Rats lit it up. The crowd was even bigger than last time and just as wild and the energy was once again at fever pitch. Then before Gaz had even got his Buddy

Holly on Tommy came bursting out of the cupboard in more ways than one - wearing ankle boots, a Police hat and a mankini the wrong way round with the G string side of his garment pathetically attempting to cover his oversized super strength Hampton. His odd trick was flapping in the wind of exasperation from the crowd. The band remained tight and rocked hard if you'll excuse the expression. They were both visually and audibly magnificent. Both Heath and Rabcat watched the riotous scene from the inside of a rubber animal mask and they both agreed afterwards that it was the most surreal experience of their lives. Tommy's giant wrinkly penis display didn't stop the youngsters enjoying the performance. It's hard to shock students but everyone that was there will never forget that experience.

The Rats clearly got the loudest warmest reception of the night. They were hero-worshipped and cheered off by the adoring crowd but *The Politically Correct Do-Not Show Your Genitals Bierkeller Factor Trophy* and the £500 went to an okay five piece from Rochdale called The Potato Men.

Getting Tommy dressed again was a right mission. Ray said, "I've never seen balls like Tommy's and I grew up on a farm."

He was fuckin' fuming!

TOMMY 'TROUBLE' PIGGOT'S TALE

Soundtrack: *Steptoe and Son Theme*

On 12th January 1942 at 25 James Street in the shadow of one of the mighty cotton mills that defined the county of Lancashire at that time, war baby Tommy 'Trouble' Piggot was born in the insular northern enclave that he affectionately refers to as 'Monkey Town'. An extremely proud 77 year-old, Tommy explains that his birthplace of Heywood, Lancashire, hard by Rochdale, is still known (at least by him!) as 'Monkey Town'!

Legend has it that a travelling circus once came to town to entertain the good hard-working folk of Heywood. Locals legend has it that a performing showbiz monkey famously escaped the shackles of the circus and made its thirsty way to The Freemasons Arms Hotel in the Market Place. Seemingly house/pub-trained, the hairy chimp pulled up a stool at the bar. The legend doesn't stretch as far to say that the pub-savvy primate ordered a pint and a pickled egg but, according to Tommy, the town of Heywood got its pseudo name when a half-cut regular walked into the vault of The Freemasons Arms and muttered these immortal words: 'For fuck sake, it really is Monkey Land round here'.

Tommy's Mum, Doris, was a recognised free spirit in Monkey Land. She already had two daughters from another marriage before she gave Tommy Senior his baby boy. Doris soon split with Tommy Senior and gave Tommy Junior another stepbrother. Tommy doesn't seem sure if he had four or five step-siblings but, either way, he always loved his mother dearly and she was always there for him.

As previously stated, Tommy was a war baby but he has no other recollection of that time in history apart from playing 'hide and seek' in the local dilapidated air raid shelters long after the last Luftwaffe air raids had ended.

Unsurprisingly, Tommy can't remember being a baby but he only has happy memories of his childhood. He explains in a very coy and sheepish manner that he went to a Special School. He does this with supreme comic timing which is rather endearing. Tommy is kinda cute in that way. Less cute is the way he grabs my hand and squeezes it tight with Monkey Land super-strength to make sure that I laugh when he wants me to laugh. Less cute but still rather funny.

Tommy attended St Luke's Primary School on Bamford Road. Tommy's 'special' schooling and Mum's liberalism meant that he had a carefree, playful childhood inside and outside of school. He just ran free and spent his time doing stuff that kids should do. School games like Tick, Hopscotch and Pin the Tail on the Monkey.

Being naturally naughty, Tommy got his own desk and locker at the back of the classroom to stop him distracting everyone. That didn't work. Tommy is like a fly on a Wythenshawe wedding buffet in such scenarios. He just can't stay away from the action.

Tommy loved everything about school, especially the free hot school dinners. Yorkshire puddings and gravy were his favourite things ever. He looks very hungry as he tells me this. He's not very hungry as he's just had a free foot-long Subway sarnie. It was free issue because the staff at Subway love him. Famous people get free stuff you know!

When I think about Tommy's great Northern childhood, the works of the Salford's great L.S. Lowry spring to mind. His 1958 piece *Children Playing* could have starred Tommy as the chunky Matchstick Kid rolling round the floor, playing dead or pretending to be a sausage roll or something like that. Tommy was the kind of child that didn't have a care in the world. Tommy would have been the one that didn't even notice that he didn't have a pot to piss in. He had no idea that just by being born in Heywood meant that he was destined to one day walk out of the playground and into a mill.

Outside of school, his state of in-the-moment-ness enjoyment continued as Tommy was hardly ever home. He wandered the cobbled streets of Heywood making friends with every Tom, Dick and Fanny who would talk to him.

Tommy has minor celebrity status as he walks around Central Manchester today. He pretty much had the very same local status back in Monkey Land back in 1952. Aged just ten he was known to everyone that ever stepped out of their front door.

When messing around at Primary School, he says he was a loveable, scruffy little tearaway. Mischief, chaos and low level trouble have been his life flow. Being outgoing, kind, loving, over-strong and clumsy is the intricate mix of him as a man and he was exactly the same as a nipper.

Aged 11 Tommy was formally diagnosed as being on the autistic spectrum. Good going that for 1953. Fortunately, he avoided electric shock treatment and was sent to High Birch Special School in Rochdale. For a penny a time, he got to ride the Monkey Land Express Steam Train which was a real thrill. High School to

Tommy was just more of the same but he doesn't seem to want to tell me about this with the same enthusiasm that he did when talking about his Primary School experiences.

One thing that he did enjoy at this time was joining the Army Cadets with his mate. Instead of using their official regiment name which was The Lancashire Fusiliers, Tommy affectionately refers to them as 'The Lancashire Leg Feelers'. Unsurprisingly, Tommy loved the cadets because he got to play out a lot. Sometimes with guns.

Cadets was weekends but, in the week, Tommy loved Monkey Town that much he often wagged school in Rochdale and mooched around the neighbourhood checking in with friendly faces. He doesn't have much information on his high-schooling. I detect he's probably blocking out less fun memories. Tommy left school in 1958 with no qualifications.

Tommy's first job was as an adult paper boy. He delivered to houses and all the pubs. He sold *The Empire News* and *The Football Pink*. Tommy Piggot quickly went from knowing all the mums in Heywood to knowing all the mums in Heywood and all their piss-can husbands too.

Mr. Piggott reckons he's had over 100 different jobs in his lifetime. Unsurprisingly, he found himself working in six or seven different cotton mills but he soon realised he couldn't cope with the cotton dust on his chest and the restrictions placed on his free spirit by the rules and regulations in the mill. He was always getting told off.

Tommy is daft in many ways but he wasn't daft when it came to avoiding jobs that were not fun. His granddad lost an eye working in Snipe Colliery in Ashton and that memory stayed with him. Aged 19, he'd had enough of the mills and all that danger and structure so he set up his own business. A moment of destiny occurred on his way back from the chip shop one night when Tommy found a fairly sturdy discarded Silver Cross pram in the street and as soon as he established that nobody else owned it or wanted it, he decided that the pram was a big enough receptacle to justify trying his luck as a Rag and Bone Man. The business model was a simple one; he walked the streets of Monkey Land shouting, "Rag n Bone" at all the folk that he already had great relationships with. These were people that liked him and wanted to help him. He was relentless, often working dusk till dawn. He was a real character in the community and financially he did really well, regularly weighing in £10-£20 in a day which was a hell of a lot money in the sixties.

Most of his money came from Rag which is used clothing which got weighed in for cash. Woollens fetched the highest prices. He also collected furniture and bric-a-brac, which he also sold to the yard. Two years into the trade, Tommy's business literally fell to pieces when he collected a large wooden fireplace and loaded it onto his trusty pram. Like a scene from *Steptoe and Son*, as soon as Tommy transferred the weight of the fireplace to the pram it dropped like a stone and crushed like an empty coke can. Tommy's business career was over. By this time Tommy must have made a few quid but he never thought to buy a real cart. He just went with the flow and decided it was time to do other things again. His time on the Rag had given him the confidence to be able to take on 'real work' and that's what he did.

Tommy's CV expanded rapidly. He cleaned heavy good vehicles, worked in warehouses and on the line at Benson's Crisp Factory, although he isn't much of an advocate of the crisps. The job he really enjoyed though was making sausages at his local butchers in Monkey Land. He was given much more responsibility on this job as he got to work the pedal on the sausage-making machine that forced the minced pork through a tube into the casing. He then got to twist the sausages off and make them into a big chain that he then got to hang up on display. This made him feel amazingly proud. Tommy enjoyed life at the butchers and this took his confidence level up again. So much so he decided to apply to join the adult version of The Lancashire Leg Feelers and join the Territorial Army.

Tommy's mate from back in the day at cadets was joining up and he told our Tommy that he should join up with him as it would be just like old times. Tommy weighed it up and just saw it as an opportunity to get paid for messing around with his old mate. He had absolutely zero comprehension that if a war kicked off he might be asked to kill a man or two. Tommy is a strong man but he'd rather cuddle you than put a bayonet through your heart. Joining the military was never gonna be a good idea for him. Without realising it, he was just one shit-bag politician's decision away from becoming a casualty of war.

Even so, Tommy got paid to spend most weekends cleaning his kit, doing a bit of parade ground drill and firing off a few rounds down the range. It was all not very 'war-ready real'. Having seen him dance, I would have paid good money to watch him march around the barracks.

Left Right Left Right Left Right Aaaaaannd Right Turn. You guessed it, on occasion Tommy surely went the opposite way and maybe did a little 'get back in line' panic dance. He must have been beyond Frank Spencer value on the parade ground. To be fair to Tommy, I imagine that it was all a game to him and, when you weigh up everything, that's exactly what this life is. Tommy's consciousness just never considers the negatives and that is a pretty healthy way to exist in my book and the icing on the cake was that as long as there wasn't a war on, then he got paid rather well for just being part of the game.

After a couple of years of messing around at weekends, Tommy's regiment all had to spend a longer training period down on the ranges and practice battlefields of Wiltshire. Unfortunately, Tommy's beloved mum Doris was poorly at this time, very poorly in fact and Tommy received a telephone call to be informed that she only had days to live.

Tommy took the opportunity to formally request some leave to visit his mum knowing that he may never see her again. "No, Tommy. You're in the Army now" said some twat of a Sergeant who was clearly that indoctrinated by Army rules that he was unwilling to recognise the emotions of the real people in his care. Tommy showed real maturity and kept his cool seemingly accepting this piss-take response to his reasonable request. As soon as he strop-marched back to his barracks, he did exactly the right thing for him and his mum, he packed up his troubles in his old kit bag, buggered the consequences and did a runner. He legged it to the railway station and jumped the first rattler north.

Thankfully, he made it back in time and he thanked his Mum for the life that she'd given him before she passed away with her devoted son by her side. Tommy lost his mum to breast cancer.

In due course the MOD Plod – The Military Police – knocked on the family door and Tommy was taken into custody for being absent without leave. Tommy had a long time to think on that long trip back. On his return to Devizes in Wiltshire, he wasn't punished too severely for going to see his Mum. He copped for a short stint of 'Jankers', which was extra duties combined with getting shouted at a lot. The damage was done for Tommy though as The Lancashire Leg Feelers were no longer fun.

The TA played their trump card and sent Tommy on a promotion course to try and get him re-engaged but Tommy found a very dangerous way to raise the stakes and play his trump card. To buy his way out of the Army would have cost him a fortune that he clearly didn't have at that time. Tommy found a cheaper option down the firing range as he negligently discharged two rounds of ammunition just over the head of the latest Sergeant to bark orders at him. Tommy got locked up briefly before he was asked to leave the organisation completely free of charge! Thankfully, during his two-and-a-half-year service, he never had to hurt anyone properly.

Back in Monkey Land, Tommy got work as a dish pig washing pots in a hotel kitchen in Bamford near Rochdale and it was at this time that he met Shirley. He found her alone and friendly in Kings Park, Heywood, and they wasted no time in getting acquainted. Their courting consisted of Shirley walking all the way from Rochdale to meet Tommy – in their original meeting place where they liked to have relations in the Boathouse. It was a time of great of excitement for Tommy. Turns out Shirley had a tragic back story and a beyond dysfunctional family. Shirley was violated as a teenager and went on to give birth to a baby girl fathered by her own brother. Social services got involved and the baby was removed from her care at birth. Fifty years on, Shirley still pushes a pram around Manchester City Centre with a plastic baby in it. People think she's cuckoo, but everyone has a story and Shirley's is one that few people could ever comprehend. Unsurprisingly, as a missus she was a bit up and down. She had issues and, even though Tommy loved her, he couldn't cope with her mood swings, dramatics and violence. She was highly strung and would beat up Tommy when she threw a wobbler. Life was colourful but unsustainable and Tommy ended up binning her off because of the violence and he moved to Manchester in 2010. He never fell out with Shirley and they remain friends to this day and spend quite a lot of time together considering Tommy is now happily re-married.

Tommy became less employable in older age and had to learn to scrape by on a state pension. This gave him plenty of time to mooch around and mingle with the street-folk of Manchester. He's a people person and has never really been one for staying at home and gawping at the telly.

In town he gradually got to know everybody of note and he loved watching Garry, Ray and the other Rats busk. It became part of his daily ritual to watch them perform. First, he watched from a safe distance for everyone but, over a period of time, he gradually shuffled closer and closer to the band until he ultimately was in the band.

There was no formal invitation or conversation, Tommy just started wobbling and the smiles in the crowd got bigger. Gaz Stanley's core skill is acceptance and giving the public what they want. Gaz welcomed him in and, for the first time in a long time, Tommy had a real purpose in his life. He was now part of the most mental street performance band in the northern hemisphere.

"Tommy, did you ever think you'd be in a Rock 'n' Roll band?"

"'Nope, but I am a Legend and I am a Monkey."

Oh, Jesus! Tommy seems to think that he's the Monkey that escaped from the Circus all those years ago!

In The Rats Tommy became the scruffy, wobbly policeman and went on to become a more-recognised figure than the Scouse Lord Mayor of Manchester, often making it into the lighter-hearted columns of the *Manchester Evening News*. He's made a couple of TV appearances, had a film documentary made about him, as well as playing hundreds of gigs progressing from Market Street all the way to the Park Life and Kendal Calling Music Festivals.

On the romance front Tommy and Shirley were done but, unexpectedly, Tommy found a new love. His friend was Godfather to Mandy. Mandy had shit going on. When Tommy met Mandy she was on drugs, her life was a mess and she was at rock bottom. After a bust up with the Godfather, who by all accounts doesn't sound like a nice man, Mandy left the property she was sharing with him and went to The Apollo Music venue in Ardwick where she kipped rough for a couple of days. Tommy found her sleeping in a queue for a gig.

Tommy tended to her and took her home and cared for her. He offered her a new safe life with him and she accepted. The Godfather, who was supposedly Tommy's friend, went bat shit as he was also romantically linked to her but, as previously stated, he wasn't a nice individual and Tommy was happy to break away from him.

Mandy had serious issues and it sounds like she came off the drugs cold turkey style. Tommy isn't sure what she was on but says it was probably smack. After that initial intensive withdrawal she hit the booze hard to replace the drugs and when that didn't end well, Tommy says she went onto the wacky baccy, which she still uses now to medicate and calm herself. Cannabis soothes her and seems to be the best addiction to safely tick that box. Tommy says Mandy is 15 years younger than him – but sources close to the band say the gap is more like 25 years. I ask Tommy about this and he cracks a big smile.

Tommy speaks affectionately about Mandy and tells me about how happy he is that they have married. For five years he planned to walk her down the aisle but every time he made plans to do so it kept going wrong. Tommy doesn't go into details about this but chaos and craziness is his normal flow so it's hardly surprising.

During the five years that Tommy and Mandy lived together, Tommy and The Rats became his extended family so when the big day came Gaz, Ray, Heath, Dave the Rave and Rabcat all sat at the front of the opulent Manchester Town Hall waiting to see if Mandy would come to her senses.

Tommy was a nervous wreck and had to nip out for a pint to calm himself down. He was shaking like a leaf when she finally turned up twenty minutes late. Band mate and caring confident Ray Boddington stepped into the aisle to try and speak some sense into the odd couple. He tried to cancel the wedding in true slapstick theatre style as he announced to the people gathered there that day that, "this a joke wedding. It shouldn't be allowed to happen." Tommy told him to "Fuck Off" and Gaz had to step in to stop it going off. It was like the final scene in Dustin Hoffman's *The Graduate*.

Eventually they made it to the altar and Mandy made Tommy the happiest wobbly dancing copper ever to get married in that building and the union of the most unlikely couple was legally sanctioned. Tommy still carries around copies of his wedding photos to this day. Two fairly dysfunctional people have shared a happy home together now for over ten years.

People may say that Tommy isn't the most intelligent man but he knows about loving kindness and living in the moment, he's found his happiness, his own utopia. Monkeying around in Mancunia is it for Tommy.

5: DAVE THE GRAVE

Soundtrack: The Rolling Stones – *Honky Tonk Woman*

Even though Tommy's giant widge and dangleberries lost The Rats the talent competition, the boys had won the hearts of Dawn at The Bierkeller and in the late autumn of 2014 The Rats smashed another set for The Messy Monday Brigade. A hundred quid wasn't really a decent split between six men but a share of all that adulation was well worth another walk across town.

This time Tommy kept his tackle strapped down in his police fatigues, so Ray was a much happier Rat. The way the young people embraced and connected with the band was akin to the way a child feels freer and more nourished around nan and granddad than they do with their usually more authoritarian parents. Watching a Rats' performance for the young people in The Bierkeller flipped that dynamic again – as the granddads became the naughty ones and the kids just fuckin' loved it. Dawn was well happy with them and promised them more gigs at the venue.

For all of Garry's vision, he really should have recognised that this kind of adulation from young people should have been the trigger to get a businessman and manager involved to sign them and get them on a tour bus starting with all the universities around the country. He could see it but the doors to making it happen never opened. Gaz admits that he was a little bit lazy with it because the thought of sharing every minute of every day with The Rats on a bus in God knows where was as frightening as it was exciting.

Not that things weren't happening - the band was gaining momentum.

Out of the blue, Gaz received a call from Granada Studios. A female voice on the phone told Gaz that some of the crew on her show had been discussing the band's street performances and how cool and interesting the characters in the band were. She then went on to explain that she worked on *The Judge Rinder Show* and she wondered if the band currently had any kind of legal issues that they could highlight on the show. She sold it in a way that ticked all Garry's "all publicity is good publicity" boxes by adding, "If you can think of anything, we'd love to show the nation who The Piccadilly Rats are".

"Let me talk to the band, love."

Before he'd even hung up the phone, Gaz knew that the situation with exposing Tommy's tally-whacker at The Bierkeller was absolutely it. He rang Ray straight away whose response was strangely low key. Gaz put this down to him still having a shitty on. He then rang Granada back and the lady was very enthusiastic saying it sounds like a really interesting and funny situation. Gaz was buzzing. He came off the phone and told the lads – "You know what, if we get on the telly, we have fuckin' made it!"

Apart from Heath going on the downer missing list again, not a lot happened in the run up to Christmas 2014. The band kept doing their thing, making good vibrations, making people smile and most importantly bringing in the pocket money.

In late December, Gaz took the band to Wetherspoon's for Christmas Dinner. It wasn't the best office Christmas Party of the year. Ray and Tommy were on form but Rabcat had an anti-everything rant-head on. Heath was still missing and Dave the Rave was completely bolloxed with a cold but he didn't want to miss out on Christmas so he made the effort. They were all fussy fuckers when it came to the food which made them about as popular as herpes with the Wetherspoon's staff because it always took them ages to place an order. When a manager came to clear Dave's plate, he'd hardly touched it and was half asleep.

"Have you finished that, pal?" barked the manager and Dave came too in a very prehistoric, cave man, grunting way. Weighing up the state of Dave, the manager made his verdict – "He'll have to go!" and before they could pull a cracker, have a Christmas pud or a brandy, Christmas was cancelled.

Outside Dave admitted he was not feeling well at all and apologised for getting them chucked out. He'd acquired a big stash of rolling tobacco pouches for Christmas pressies for the lads and he gave these out and wished everyone all the best before getting off. Garry recalls that fittingly the first and last time he ever saw Dave was outside Wetherspoon's Piccadilly because the next morning he received a call from Lee Ferguson, the Giant Hot Dog Sausage Vendor at the bottom of Market Street.

"Have you heard, Gaz? Dave has passed away in the night. I've just fuckin' seen him on an advertisement board."

Gaz was lost for words but as his world stopped turning he managed to mutter, "Thanks for letting me know, Lee."

Gaz sat down, had a fag and mulled over the

catastrophic news and as soon as he was ready, he rang around the lads who were all just as devastated as he was. Gaz asked them all to turn up as usual for the following day's gigs but asked for them all to expect no cut of the takings as they would have to fund a good send off for Dave. Heath kindly put whatever was going on in his private life on hold and agreed to come back and play for his mate.

News of Dave The Rave's passing went viral and his death featured in an article in that afternoon's copy of the *Manchester Evening News*. Very fabulously and real, a life-size photo of Dave resplendent in his full Rolling Stones kit went live all around the city on the digital advertising boards used by the *Evening News*. Even in death, he looked cool as fuck.

Arthur Donnelly came on the phone to Garry.

"Garry, I'm sure you've heard the sad news about David?"

"Yes, Arthur - we are doing a few gigs to do a bit of fundraising for the funeral."

Arthur was pleased and arranged for some advertisement boards to be made and some leaflets to be printed to raise awareness of his friend's sad passing and the fundraising required to salute him.

The next day, the boards and leaflets turned up and The Rats played hard for their friend. Arthur somehow got a few members of the cast of *Shameless* to turn up and help pass around the hat for collections which made a massive difference to the size of the donations received. Jodie Latham, known as Lip in the series, did a great job with that and also chipped in a sizeable donation himself. By the end of the second day of Dave the Rave's Memorial Benefit Gig, the band had made £700 which was a cash mountain more than their usual take.

In a quiet appreciative moment between songs, Arthur told Garry how fit and strong Dave was back in the day. "We have a ten foot wall down the yard, you should a seen David go over it, two seconds flat. He was an athlete. I was always wary of him back in the day. He was a tough lad, David. I'll miss him.'

There was a huge turnout for David Copeland's funeral. It was a Bohemian kind of a bash and the numbers in attendance said everything really as did the diversity of the attendees. Dave must have had some input into the funeral service because even though it took place in a traditional church, the vicar didn't appear to be a vicar at all. Instead it was a fella dressed up all in white, like a doctor with a big multi-coloured scarf wrapped around his neck like a magnificent plume of feathers. His eulogy was a very entertaining and fitting tribute to Dave and it included many swear words. Dave would have liked those bits a lot. Ray suggested Arthur must have paid the real vicar to fuck off so Dave's mate could do it. They never asked. The best bit came at the end when Dave the Rave was laid to rest with favourite track playing him out – *Honky Tonk Woman* was the tune for one hell of a Honky Tonk Man.

As a special treat Gaz took The Rats back to town and bought them all a chippy by The Old Monkey on Portland Street. As they stood in the road eating their chips, Ray summed it all up when he said quietly, "Dave the Rave, he believed in us you know, the daft sod."

6: JUDGE RINDER

Soundtrack: The Clash – *I Fought The Law*

After the funeral, the next few weeks weren't much fun and the negative energy around the band seemed to seep into everything that they touched. Dawn invited them back to The Bierkeller but, unfortunately, she wasn't on duty for the gig. A younger Duty Manager, who clearly wasn't a fan of the band's work, put them on to play from seven 'til eight o'clock before most of the pissed up kids had even got out of bed for the day. After playing to an empty room, Gaz thought they must be doing two slots and went to check in with the young manager bloke. The Rats' rider requirements have always been ridiculously low key and reasonable. All they really want is a pint for Garry and Tommy and a glass of pop for the others - anything in excess of that like a bag o' crisps was always accepted gratefully as an unexpected treat. Dawn usually offered them a couple of rounds of such hospitality but when Garry asked if they were alright for a drink the Duty Wanker took the order then printed off a bill for payment. A few heated words were exchanged which led to the young man telling Garry and The Lads to do one! He had no intention of paying them for their crap set either. Garry was outraged but wise ole' Ray recognised that the idiot behind the bar was just showing off to his co-workers, who were probably very unimpressed in any case.

"We'll take it up with Dawn. Let's just go."

Lugging all the equipment out of the venue in

such belittling circumstances was the last thing Garry wanted for his pals. The last time that they walked out of this particular venue was on the crest of a wave of possible world domination. This time round, outside The Printworks, they dragged their feet through the puddles of post-Dave desolation.

Ray had been right to peace-make the night before, as the next morning Dawn was great and she arranged the payment of the band's missing set fee. Gaz was all set for setting Equity, the Actor's Union, on them but Dawn re-iterated her love for The Rats and agreed that the previous evening's Duty Wanker was exactly that.

Following on from this upturn in fortune, Judge Rinder's people rang to confirm that the band were all set to appear on the show. There would be no rehearsals or script as the show is an actual court of law. "Just turn up on the day and the crew will run you through the facts of the case again on the day."

Ray was still strangely distant every time Gaz brought it up. It was as if he still bore a grudge around it. Usually he would be the most passionate publicity-seeker in the band, but he refused to get excited about going on the telly and, after a while, this started to get on Gaz's tits because right from the genesis of the band Ray had always been on the same page in terms of wanting to take the project as far as it could possibly go. Garry wanted The Rats to have their own TV show like The Monkees did in the Sixties and he wasn't used to Ray not rubber-stamping his dreams.

On the day of the show the band had to be at Media City in Salford for 9am. Organising them all to be present was an almost impossible task. After returning to support Dave's funeral, Heath had checked out of the band's doings once again. Rabcat initially welcomed the TV experience but as the day drew closer he too showed plenty of signs that he wouldn't turn up at all. Ray was still in his temporary sulky zombie state but Garry knew that as soon as the cameras went on his side-kick would flick on the entertainer switch – he just had to get him there. Tommy was as good as gold as always and turned up at Garry's an hour early, before Garry had even had a brew and a piece of toast. After a fun start to the day with the wobbly bloke, Gaz's wife Diane, dropped Tommy and Gaz at Salford Quays. Ray lived close by and had agreed to meet them there as did Rabcat, who had to do an early morning commute in from outer-scouser-land. Gaz and Tommy stood on the steps waiting for the other two to rock up. First to show was Rabcat who got off the tram with his Rat Mask on and watching him walk up reminded Gaz how fuckin' cool the band's concept still was. Rabcat's opening greeting was predictably intense:"I ain't taking this mask off. We are The fuckin' Piccadilly Rats."

"Quite right" said Garry and with that Ray rang to say that he was already inside.

The sight of a Rat in the building's reception soon brought members of the show's crew over to make a fuss of them. They quickly and skilfully removed the mini-infestation from the reception area and whisked them away to the poshest dressing room imaginable. It had one of them giant lightbulb lit mirrors, a break-out area with brewing facilities and a shrink, yes, a shrink. Graham Stanier, the once acclaimed psychotherapist who is famous for being one of the main men in the toilet TV tragedy formally known as *The Jeremy Kyle Show*.

Graham and a team of helpers were rather cleverly and strategically already in place and waiting for the band to arrive. As soon as they did and they saw the scallywag state of Tommy a small team of stylists sat him in the mirror and started to comb his hair and dab him down with wet wipes because he had some egg stuck on his jumper. He had a very rebellious tuft of hair that just refused to settle down. This started off everyone laughing. Tommy got a bit pissed off thinking that everyone was laughing at him and when they suggested that they might need to wash his hair he started chuntering, he wasn't happy that he'd been singled out as the scruffy twat and he lasted about a minute in the chair before he jumped up and made a spirited run for the exit. The corridor down to the Courtroom/Studio was not the place for Tommy, it was a Death Trap as there were lots of cables and all sorts of technical TV obstacles scattered around. Thankfully Garry got to him before he electrocuted himself: "What's up pal, I thought you'd like the girls fussing over ya?"

"I'm not stupid Garry, they think I've got nits."

"Tommy you are stupid, they don't think you've got nits, they are tidying everyone up, I'm gonna get a bit of make up to make me look younger, come on for fuck sake." Tommy walked back in and sat in the chair. His bottom lip stuck out in a 'poor me' cartoon character protest.

All the crew were lovely and Graham also seemed to be a really nice fella. He chatted and had a brew with the three of them before he dropped a couple of bombshells that he put in place to explode.

First up, he told Rabcat who was still in character, that for legal reasons he wouldn't be able to appear in court with a Rat mask on. He could hold it in his hand. This information wasn't received in a gracious manner from Martin who gave it to Graham both barrels. The last line of his rant was – "I'm not fuckin' doing it!"

Before Garry got to start negotiating, Graham dropped in the next one. "The format of today's case is that Ray Boddington is bringing a case against you guys for making the decision to get Tommy to wear a mankini in a talent contest without his consent. Ray is suing you for £500 loss of earnings which is the value of the prize money that you had the chance of earning should you have won the talent competition."

"The sneaky bastard!"

Graham watched on as the news about Sneaky Ray took the edge off Martin's anger regarding him not wearing his Rat Mask. Gaz paused for thought... then he said, "Ray Boddington is one smart fucker. This is set up for us to make TV gold. If he had told us before, there is no fuckin' chance this would have ever happened, the sly old fox." Rabcat started ranting again but Gaz was in Alpha-Rat mode and told him straight that this wasn't an opportunity that they could afford to miss.

Five minutes later it was lights, camera, action and they walked out into a vibrantly full, bustling courtroom that must have been warmed up by Graham or somebody that had revealed a bit of the plot because, without much effort at all, everyone in the place was either smiling ear to ear or uncontrollably laughing. The Rats are a funny looking set of characters but the atmosphere was sensational. Gaz could feel that they were in for some fun. Ray was stood in the opposite box and had clearly been pampered by Rinder's team of charlatans - his hair was cut shorter than normal and they had bought him a new set of threads that were a sinister black, which may have been selected to make him the bad guy. Gaz would have preferred Ray to have been dressed in his usual offensive vest, shades and chunk chain but the TV crew clearly had their own agenda.

The show played out in legendary Piccadilly Rat slapstick fashion and Judge Rinder was brilliant at coaxing the funny lines out of The Rats. First up, they produced the mankini and showed a photo of a young stud wearing one in the correct manner. Then they asked Tommy to confirm which members of the band asked him to wear the mankini at the gig. The cameras then panned to Garry, who verified that Tommy's comments were true. Gaz did a very skilful, 'It was like this officer' straight man bit. Then the Judge asked poor old, cute and vulnerable Tommy Trouble, "Did you manage to wear the garment in the correct fashion, Tommy?"

"No, mi Lord. I had the part that should have been down there, up here, on my chest, but I didn't mean to. It was just I'd never wore a mankini before."

Tommy played it out as himself, loveable and innocently daft. It was all very believable, cute, daft and funny. The courtroom crowd absolutely lapped it up. When the punchline came and between them all, they confirmed that Tommy had exposed his tackle, there wasn't a dry eye in the place.

The Judge ruled that there was no evidence to suggest that had Tommy not shown his genitals to the talent show crowd that the band's performance would have elevated them from third to first place and Ray's dubious claim was thrown out of court.

Afterwards, Judge Rinder and all the crew came and congratulated The Rats, sharing his opinion that this episode would be their best and most popular ever.

Gaz embraced Ray and they both agreed that they'd just delivered the Golden Egg. Even Rabcat couldn't deny that he'd just had a lot of fun. Every housewife and sofa surfer in the United Kingdom was about to cop for their first spectacular sighting of The Piccadilly Rats.

Gaz was right. Ray was a complete genius of a publicist.

7: THE INDESTRUCTIBLE FLYING TOMMY PIGOTT

Soundtrack: The Pogues – *Fiesta*

Garry had got it into his head that the band should be involved in the city's St. Patrick's Day Parade. He'd been nudged by a few of the Irish lads in town to get The Rats on a float. Judge Rinder had just aired and the whole city was going mad for them. On the daily busk, kids were now coming up for autographs. The Rats had landed big time and Garry was keen to make sure that they stayed in the limelight and he hoped that by being part of Manchester's Paddy's Day would further embed them into the everyday consciousness of Mancunians. About thirty five percent of Mancs are of Irish decent so the band agreed with Gaz's thought processes and suffered a two week build up from him bigging up how spectacularly spectacular it was all going to be.

At The Irish Centre in Cheetham Hill, the Irish Community were limbering up with a long line of industrial vehicles lining up along Queens Road. Some were decorated, most were not. Troops of adorable little Irish dancing girls were practicing on the grass verges and every Irish navvy in Manchester who owned or leased a trailer was having a brew and chewing the fat at the side of their vehicles as the marching brass bands started to wind it up. The sun was shining and the atmosphere was really rather pleasant.

The organisation of the parade was tiered. The smarter floats had clearly had a lot of love and care put into their preparation and the people that were set to be transported on these premium floats were well-drilled and knew exactly what they were doing. Preparations were much more low-key bordering on manic when it came to finding a suitable Rat-Mobile. As the vehicles began to load people on board, Gaz made a beeline for an important looking fella with a clipboard and put it on him.

"We've been promised a float mate. We are The Piccadilly Rats… Blah! Blah! Blah!…'

The guy politely smiled, made brief eye contact then proceeded to sort out every person that was of obvious Irish decent with evidence for this coming in the form of red hair, green tops or a big smile. Frantic, unsmiley Gaz had to wait till last and struggled to get a word in as the Irish Event Co-ordinator talked really, really quickly, "Don't worry, Sir. I know all about you guys. Right, let's see what we can do for youz Boys."

"Noooo!"

A feckin' milk float was not exactly what Gaz had in mind and he couldn't get his words out quickly enough to butt in and defer that option. "Mate, we've got drums, dancers the lot, we need a proper wagon where we can stand up."

"Oh, let me see now - I did have you marked down for dat little beauty. What we got? What we got?"

As Gaz chased him down towards the end of the motorcade, onlookers Heath, Ray and Tommy had started lugging all the equipment along behind them. The very last wagon in the line had a crane on it.

"There you go lads, perfect. Brian will look after youz boys."

Brian was cool, he simply said, "Just do what youz want, lads. I'll drive slow, youz'll be fine. Sorry about da crane – it doesn't come off."

It took Ray, Gaz and Heath a full five minutes of slapstick gold action just to get Tommy the five foot from the ground onto the wagon base. Tommy is like a dog that doesn't want to be moved – he can double his weight just by taking up a defensive position. He did exactly that and Ray, in particular, was bolloxed by the time they had wrestled Tommy Lead Pants, all the gear and themselves onto the show wagon.

Thankfully there was about ten minutes for The Rats to sort their shit out prior to departure because Heath, who was playing drums in Rabcat's absence, had to find the best place on the wooden floor to try and fix his drum kit and stool in place to try and dodge the wear and tear holes that were all over the vehicle's well-dodgy base. Gaz put their iconic yellow Piccadilly Rats' sign up and reassured the lads that the procession was only going to be moving along at five miles per hour, "Trust me, we'll be fine".

The procession set off as slowly as promised through Cheetham Hill and into town down Oldham Road. There were little green pockets of Irish folk out all the way into Manchester. Gaz insisted that the band played to everyone that had made the effort to come out, so they played the start of *Honky Tonk Woman* at least a hundred times.

As the parade rolled into town, the pockets of green became streets of green and by the time that they arrived at the Town Hall Gaz likened it to Man United's Treble-Winning Parade. Heath, Ray and Gaz all agreed that this was one of the band's greatest moments – the joy and adulation coming off the crowd was unparalleled. The band had become part of the fabric of the city and they felt that their inclusion in the procession was a justified reflection of their hard-earned rise to citywide, if not nationwide, notoriety.

Playing for half an hour in front of a heaving Albert Square crowd outside Manchester Town Hall was a spiritual awakening for them. Everybody didn't just get them - they really fuckin' loved 'em and the boys could really feel it.

The crowd would have loved to suck up an all-day festival of Rat-Sounds but the organisers stuck to the script and the cavalcade rolled out having brought smiles to the whole city centre. The procession made its way down Cross Street, past The Printworks complex aka the scene of Tommy's mankini cock and balls show, and parked up on the swanky shopping parade known as Jackson's Row by Victoria Station. The Rat-Mobile slowly came to a gradual halt but just as the lads started to set themselves to dismount, the driver must have accidentally put the vehicle back in gear, so when he let the clutch out to park up - the whole wagon catapulted forward about a metre.

Catastrophically, this was far enough to catapult Tommy head first off the side of the trailer and The Flying Pigott landed five foot south, face first in the gutter. The three remaining Rats couldn't believe what they'd just seen. Garry kept his composure just enough to get a photograph of Tommy for the *Manchester Evening News* before anyone scraped him up. Tommy was out cold and when Garry bent over the side of the lorry to take the snapshot, he quietly murmured these sacred words, "Oh Jesus, I think he's fuckin' dead". Once the PR photo was out of the way, Gaz rang an ambulance.

Almost instantly Tommy was whisked away to

hospital and as he was being put in the ambulance the lads could see that all his face was badly smashed in. Heath and Ray were quite upset but Gaz went into funeral mode and insisted that Heath and Ray help him play an instantaneous fundraising gig for Tommy just in case but that didn't work out as they couldn't concentrate and stopped to call the hospital only to be told that "we can't give any information to non-family members" so Heath rang back as Uncle Pigott five minutes later to be told that Tommy had a broken nose, three broken ribs and concussion. He was stable. They all agreed that this was a great result as all three of them thought it was looking like a life-threatening situation for their friend.

When they visited the hospital the next morning Tommy was already causing havoc, literally chasing the nurses around the ward Benny-Hill-style. When Heath challenged him asking, "Why aren't you in bed resting, Tommy? You have three broken ribs, for God's sake."

"I'm not in bed because I'm Tommy Trouble."

Gaz, Ray and Heath looked at him stood there in his NHS gown, proud as punch, grinning ear to ear with his gorgeously smashed-in, ridiculous furry face.

"He's fuckin' indestructible!" said Heath admirably.

8: BRITAIN'S GOT TALENT

Soundtrack: Julius Fucik - *Entry Of The Gladiators*

One day on Rats' Nest Corner Sneak Ray informed the band that he'd arranged with his old mate, Simon Cowell, to make an appearance on everybody's favourite family friendly TV Selection Box – *Britain's Got Talent*. Ray had tried out for the show before and, in his own mind, he was already in Mr Cowell's Inner Circle. Rabcat, who was intermittently back in the picture, said "I won't be taking my fuckin' mask off." This middle of the road, less extreme reaction to being allegedly sold out led the lads to believe that he secretly liked the rarefied kudos that their relentless publicity drive brought them. Instead of embracing it all, he played out the part of the reluctant genius and, like everyone else in the band, he was very entertaining with it all. A week of audition-related tactical discussions followed and everyone agreed that if they were going to enter then they should do it full-on and give it absolutely everything.

A week later Gaz borrowed Lee the Sausage Man's six by four pushable trolley to lug all the gear from Back Piccadilly to the G-Mex on the south side of town. As previously discussed, organising The Rats to do anything logistically was always Garry's biggest challenge. Heath described Garry's role in trying to control them all as being akin to shepherding cats!

In true Rats-style, Gaz never checked the tyre pressure on the dubious-looking buggy and once they'd piled it high with gear, it became apparent that one of the four tyres clearly had a flat. So as they started rolling their rag 'n' bone buggy from Piccadilly down to Deansgate, it took four of them on one side and one on the other to try and keep the chariot upright. They looked like something off *It's A Knockout* where, if you can remember it, the teams dressed in silly clothes and had to transport silly things like brightly coloured gunk from one end of the course to the other. They gained extra points if they didn't spew the goo. The goo in this case was the only thing of any value that any of them owned – their beloved instruments, power sources and speakers. What makes The Rats so entertaining is the madcap energy that every onlooker sees in such situations is usually genuine panic-stricken mayhem and this mission was definitely one of those scenarios. Garry, Ray and Rabcat set new unofficial swearing world records for people commuting from Piccadilly to Deansgate. Luckily it was a pleasant day weather-wise and the "Not Right" Pageant arrived safe and sound with all of their equipment dry and in full working order.

On arrival the queue for the audition was mega, wiggly-worming all around the gigantic forecourt of the massive entertainment venue that used to be Manchester Central Railway Station. The rag 'n' bone wagon joined the end of the queue and while Rabcat minded the buggy, the rest of the lads went to find Tommy who had excitedly played it safe by arriving at the venue just the four hours early. They found him sat in the reception area being treated like a king. He admitted with a big furry smile that he was enjoying his third cup of tea. Heath had no regard for his pensioner privilege and told him to, "Get out and queue up like the rest of us. We nearly died pushing all that fuckin' gear here!"

"Bloody hell, I only came early so I wouldn't be late," said Tommy as he walked out blinded by the brilliant sunshine. If he was playing audition Snakes 'n' Ladders, he'd have just gone from two squares from the end, down the biggest snake and back to the start of the board game. Not that he was that bothered, Tommy wins every game that he plays because he finds fun in everything that he does, so walking through the crowd to the back of the queue was just another opportunity to buzz off people. That's why he came four hours early so that he most definitely wouldn't miss out on buzzing off all these people.

Heath's take on queuing with the creative, ambitious and fame-hungry mass of people was less admirable - "Look at all these cute, starry-eyed kids. I can't wait for us to destroy all their dreams."

Gaz followed Heath's lead and ordered The Rats to mask up and start making their presence felt. "When we walk in, let's make a fuckin' proper Piccadilly Rats entrance. Let's make the whole fuckin' place take notice." The Rats responded to Gaz's rallying call and when they finally made it to the entrance, Rat-masked Heath was pushed forward to take a place-in-the-audition-queue-ticket from the lady on the desk. She was that impressed with his rodent head that she didn't even look up and when they walked through the lobby into the main audition waiting room, their big entrance went down with all the razzmatazz of a silent fart in a library.

The giant waiting room was full of delightfully different hopesters. Just as in *The Greatest Showman*, they had every kind of entertainment freak lined up ready to make their dreams come true. The Rats took their place amongst the glitter-sprinkled masses who were caught between being nervously excited and bored with the long wait to perform. Looking around the room and discussing who might do well in the auditions was a light-hearted bit of fun. Ray chose a couple of rough-looking, underdressed female pensioners but he didn't share what he actually thought they might be good at. Tommy picked a clever-looking dog and Heath identified a very cute waddle of kids dressed as penguins. He really wanted to crush the little bastards' dreams.

After an hour and a half the band's number was called and they got set up and ready to rock. This first audition was clearly a straight forward culling mechanism to get rid of time-wasting super-loons. As soon as Gaz started singing they cut him off and the small panel of unknown TV execs gave a thumbs up and produced another waiting ticket. Rabcat kept his anonymity intact but couldn't help wondering what the fuck he was doing there.

Audition Two went well and was what the band would call a routine performance. Lots of funny shapes got made and Gaz brought a lively vocal performance that after a short discussion between the panel brought another thumbs up. As The Rats gathered their stuff to leave, one of the panel came over and said to Gaz, "We really liked you. Make sure you hang around for the next one, that's The Biggy."

Before they went in for The Biggy, Ray made one of his whispered speeches, "If Simon is in there, I'm telling ya, we are through and on the telly. If he's not, let's make sure we are that spectacular that they have to tell him about us."

Audition Three was filmed by a film crew but, sadly,

still had no celebrity judges or anyone claiming to be in Ray Boddington's inner circle. Regardless, The Rats brought plenty of high-octane action and Ray and Tommy went full throttle and showed off every trick in their Magic Box, skilfully nudging gradually closer and closer to the non-celebrity panel so when *Roll over Beethoven* wrapped up, Ray started chatting to them like they were long lost friends before the band had even stopped playing. Gaz de-guitared and came over to say, "Hello" but struggled to get a word in so he drifted away again and left Ray in place to seal the deal.

Three weeks later Ray got a rejection letter and Heath's worst fears became a reality - "Them fuckin' penguins, I knew it!"

9: BLACKPOOL

Soundtrack: America – *The Horse with No Name*

The aftermath of the recording of *The Judge Rinder Show* was a bit of a mixed bag. Rabcat had been totally exposed on the show. On the day he had been swept away with the fun of it all but, in the cold light of day, things felt very different for him. His secret hero status as the unknown face of The Piccadilly Rats was revealed. To the rest of the lads he was just a cool, clever guy and a great musician but Rabcat really lived out his own rebellious rat existence inside that mask and the day it was lifted part of him died.

On telly they made him use his real name instead of the fake title of Martin that he'd shared with the band. They were all shocked by this but none of them more than Rabcat himself, who now was outed as Simon. It was the beginning of the end of his attachment to the band. In his mind, he'd been sold out and his fear of people looking at him was about to hit record levels with up to 1.2 million people due to tune in to watch the real him on ITV.

Before Judge Rinder came on the telly, Gaz felt like a kid that knew exactly what he was going to get for Christmas. He rang Heath and told him how amazing *The Rinder Show* was and told him to come back and not miss out on the explosion of opportunity that was likely to present itself once the show was aired. Gaz was a good friend to Heath and always allowed him to return to band duties when he was well enough to do so, few questions asked. This worked both ways as Heath always added great value to the band both musically and as a person. Gaz missed him and was never going to fuck him off. As previously stated, "They all had shit going on."

Every time the sun shone on Rats' Corner in Manchester, Gaz would harp on all day that, "We should go and perform in Blackpool."

He had a vision in his head about having a quiet chat with the Chief Donkey Arranger on Blackpool Beach. Gaz thought that it would be a great idea to get Lancashire's Number One Cowboy Tommy Trouble saddled up on the craziest creature that they could find in the Blackpool Donkey Drove. Gaz thought that this would make for more TV Gold and ideal footage to capture in a promo-catalogue ahead of the band's imminent publicity explosion. Ray also liked the idea and was waxing lyrical about knowing everybody that there was to know in The Vegas of the North.

Manchester's weather is famously wet and a heatwave in the newspaper can often appear as nothing more than a sullen haze over the great city. On an absolutely scorching Monday of the week in question, The *Evening News* announced that the city was in for at least a week of pavement crackingly high temperatures.

Gaz had heard it all before but, by the end of a life-threatening Tuesday Inner City Sweat-Fest, he shouted over to Ray. "Fuck it - tomorrow we are bucket and spading in Blackpool."

Gaz rang National Rail enquiries and briefed the lads to be at Manchester Piccadilly for 09.20 as the train was going off Platform 14 at 09.31.

"Tommy bring ya trunks and a Cowboy Hat."

"Can I bring Shirley?" asked Tommy.

"Fuck sake, Tommy, who thinks to take their ex-wife to the beach? Course she can come." The next morning, Rabcat told them to fuck off and die by text so a phone call from Gaz led to Heath leaving his bass guitar at home and, at Back Piccadilly, he dutifully took on responsibility for a drum, a top hat cymbal and because Rabcat had ownership of the Rat Mask, he agreed to be a monkey for the day. Gaz had his trusty Fake Fender and his amp whilst Ray was fully prepared to get some use out of his famous sunglasses.

Despite the previous day's great weather, his skin was still white as fuck, like he had been bleached. As the train arrived at the platform there was no sign of Tommy but they all knew that once Shirley was involved anything could and would happen so they decided to get moving north - there were trains every half an hour so Tommy would catch 'em up - no probs.

On the train Heath had to stand up with the high-hat and watch on as Ray held court with all the not hot, not-really-interested ladies in the busy carriage.

"Played all the pubs and clubs in Blackpool, me... blah dee two hour blah..." ...as the train arrived forty minutes late.

In Blackpool the weather was great but due to the heavy nature of the band's equipment, Garry instructed them to head for The Tower which was just a short walk from Blackpool North. In truth it's not the nicest part of Sin City but, by the time Heath 'n' Gaz had gotten set up, Ray had been on a mission to use all the free Subway Vouchers that he'd been tearing out of the Metro Newspaper for a month. He returned with about nine feet of sarnies and a brew for everyone and that made the whole mission worthwhile before they had even started.

Just as they were about to start playing in the small square off the back of the world famous tower, Andy the Blind Guitarist Busking Artist from Manchester walks up and says, "What are you wankers doing here? You can fuck off this is my spot."

Heath replied, "Andy, we like you but why do keep insisting on following us around?"

With that, he put on his rubber monkey mask and the trio broke into a very colourful and fitting rendition of "Living next door to Andy, Andy. Who the Fuck is Andy?"

A very unimpressed blind man set up just around the corner and within ten minutes a Blackpool shopping precinct officiando came and informed them that –"The square isn't big enough for two bands, that'll be too noisy"

"We were here first," said Ray, who already had his milk bottle chest and rubber nipples out.

The man said, "Andy is our resident performer so can you please move on."

Reluctantly, they accepted the man's blind faith in Andy and headed down the seafront by the North Pier.

Even though it was red hot, there was a strong breeze and the music was getting lost in the summer day. They played for a few hours by which time they had expected Tommy to show up for some donkey fun but worryingly it just didn't happen.

Most of the public stayed on the beach, The Pleasure Beach or in the pub so there wasn't much passing trade and by 4pm Garry had had enough.

With just £45 quid in the pot, the day had turned

into a bit of a train-smash. They decided to jack it in and go for a pint and two glasses of pop before lugging everything back to the station.

Blackpool North station was a fuckin' joke. As you can imagine the place must have seen every kind of public disorder offense imaginable down the years, and this had clearly resulted in draconian crowd management policies being introduced to ensure there was no fuckin' around.

Garry doesn't like lots of people so when he set eyes on the never-ending conga of people snaking right out of the station he started to feel a bit queasy. By the time their part of the conga shuffled inside the building, Garry's claustrophobia was kicking right in and he started flapping like drowning duck. The more Ray told him to "calm down" - the more anxious he was getting. When the four carriages of the Manchester train arrived and the doors to the platforms were opened it was like a biblical scene as the huge crowd rushed the tiny exits.

"There is no way I'm getting on that fuckin' thing."

Ray had other ideas and started shouting, "Pensioner coming through," as he parted the ways of the common people. In no time at all, he'd Manc'd his way into a seat and he was good to go. As most of the station squeezed onto that train Heath agreed with Gaz that there was no way a monkey with a drum was getting on board that Sardine Tin and they waved Ray off and waited for the next one.

On the next one, which was thankfully a lot quieter, Garry got brave and said, "Fuck it, let's sit in First Class and see what happens". There were some middle-aged party girls in the coach who listened to a few Rats' Tales and shared what they had left of their Irn Brew flavoured

WKDs. The conductor never came through, so all in all it was just about the best part of the day.

In town the next morning Tommy turns up "You could of told me what train to get on. Me and Shirley spent the day in Warrington and her dog got sunburnt."

Ray asked, "Did you not realise it wasn't Blackpool?"

"Not till the end of the day - the people were really friendly."

Gaz just rolled his eyes – "I fuckin' give up."

10: CAPITAL GAINS

Soundtrack: The Clash – *London Calling*

Following their appearance on Judge Rinder, there was a notable spike in media interest in the band and the increased press coverage led to The Rats being approached by a Manchester-based film production company who presented plans to make a rockumentary about their crazy antics. Gaz and Ray never turned down publicity, so The Low Flying Geese Film Crew became part of the gang and started tracking the band's movements. The agreement was something like: We are fans, we think your mad vibe and representation of the Manchester street scene is perfect for our kind of film making. Director Nathan said, "Just do what you always do" and that was that - no contract, just a two-way business opportunity.

The Geese didn't plan to fund any of the band's shenanigans and this was proved when Gaz made the first real suggestion that got filmed that wasn't playing in city centre Manchester. Gaz had always wanted to go and play London. The Rats keep it real so he just meant he wanted them to play on a street corner in London. He wasn't thinking Wembley or The Royal Albert Hall at this point.

Heath spotted a great deal in the paper. Virgin Trains were offering tickets to London for ten quid each way. It was for a limited time only so he made the phone call to Gaz who said, "Go for it" and Heath spent his weekly budget on tickets for four. Gaz rang The Geese who agreed to come along but didn't offer any help with The Rats' expenses. They would have to recoup Heath's Universal Credit in the traditional buskers' way.

Gaz's usual train and bog phobias were eased by the extra company of the film crew. The four lads in the crew were really interested in hearing about The Rats' tales and keeping Gaz talking was the best way to make him forget about his fears. A couple of Stellas helped too.

Everyone agreed that Tommy should remain seated at all times for everybody's health 'n' safety and, for once, he was reasonably well behaved. Ray tried a bit of womanising on the train and as ever was not behind the door in explaining that he was a rockstar with a huge penis. "Nine by four inches I'm packing," he told a pair of interested middle aged ladies sat opposite. Heath skilfully brought him down a peg, "Nine down and four across, you're not a fuckin' crossword, Ray."

On arrival lugging the gear around was a busker's curse and this was more of a problem than normal in London. Rather than just get off the train and jam outside Euston Station, Gaz had plans to combine sightseeing with the band's busking with their first planned stop being Leicester Square.

Getting on and off tube trains and down and up crazily steep escalators on the underground was a massive gamble for this crazy gang of senior citizens but, as ever, they just went at it full throttle.

The Rats set up first outside a newsagent opposite the Odeon Cinema where they do all the glitzy red carpet film premieres. As soon as they started playing the resident shopkeeper came running out of his premises. Everyone thought, "Here we bleeding go," but he was cool as fuck and just popped out to say, "Thank God, we have some decent musicians out here for once. All we usually get here is shit Ed Sheeran after shit Ed Sheeran."

Garry was lording it up in London belting out his signature rock and roll favourites in fine style but it didn't take long for a fake Ed Sheeran to turn up and start ranting and raving about the band taking his spot. Garry suggested that, "You don't own Leicester Square, pal" but the guy was intent on spoiling their day. It was no wonder Ed wanted his spot back because the band had pretty much recouped Heath's train fare outlay inside the first hour which surpassed everybody's expectation of the day's graft. London folk seemed to think nothing of chucking a fiver in the hat and that worked just fine for everyone, or at least it did until the Manchester weather turned up and it started pissing down.

Shit Ed Sheeran got his wish as Garry announced a lunch break. The perks of having a young affluent film crew onboard paid out its first dividend as The Geese treated The Rats to sausage and mash out of their own pocket in a boozer called The Blue Post. Heath was flabbergasted that sausage and mash was a tenner a pop down South and he was also pleased that he didn't drink as a pint came in at over a fiver too.

As soon as it stopped pissing down, they made the short walk to Soho which turned out to be a very fuckin' long walk with all the gear. Gaz wanted a photo outside Ronnie Scott's and as they were capturing that moment a load of Man City fans, who were away at Spurs that day, turned up and started hero-worshipping Tommy and Ray. Garry, who is a blue himself, was made up to be recognised in the capital and hoovered up the fanfare and made the lads bang out a quick rendition of *Blue Moon* that made for a mental three minutes of Madchester in the West End of London. Ray and Tommy were masters of handling rowdy groups of pissed-up lads. They always went with that kind of energy and allowed the Piss Cans to jump all over them.

Next stop was Covent Garden, which is one of the world's premier street theatre venues but as soon as The Rats set up some kind of Street Entertainment Liaison Officer in a high-viz turned up and asked if The Lads were booked in to play and very quickly relocated them about three hundred yards away from where all the action and money was. He lingered like he wanted bribing to get a better spot, but The Rats weren't in a financial position to make that happen. Instead they were moved to a noisy street corner on top of the London traffic so Covent Garden didn't turn out to be the celebration of their craft that Gaz had hoped, so they jibbed it to Trafalgar Square.

Unexpectedly on Trafalgar Square, the band walked into a huge anti-austerity protest and as soon as they set up the gear it looked like the protesters and the police were going to go at it. This confused the shit out of Tommy who didn't know which side he wanted to bat for. Nathan, the lead Goose, had brought a giant Union Jack with him and he got the band to recreate The Who's famous album cover *The Kids Are Alright* with Heath, Ray, Tommy and Gaz all sat with their backs on the base of Nelson's Column with their bodies covered by the Union Jack. It created a really powerful image and in the quiet pre-lull of a cockney riot, for just a second, London was owned by The Piccadilly Rats.

11: SATURDAY MORNING ROCK GOD

Soundtrack: Pete Seeger – *If I had a Hammer*

Alan Jones is a lovely man. Salford born and bred he's the kind of fella that drives his wife into town on a Saturday morning and just has a good mooch around while the missus takes care of her shopping business. When top northern blokes like Alan have time to indulge themselves like this, a great time usually consists of a walk around the City, an investment in a great street-food snack, maybe a hot baked savoury product or possibly two, but what makes for a really top Saturday morning mission is walking into an unexpected situation of culture. Appreciating another human being creating something of interest is the kind of behaviour that sets us apart from our animal kingdom friends. Alan is an arty kind of guy, he makes things, writes poetry and appreciates great music so he often spent his Saturday mooch patrolling Market Street on the lookout for the latest good act. Market Street is a cultural hotspot for all sorts of performers anything from African Kora players to Beat Box Freestylers and Evangelical Preachers, you never know what you are going to walk into.

Alan is the silent Simon Cowell of Saturday morning moochers, he's seen a lot of singers, magicians and one man bands during his wife's illustrious shopping career but instead of putting them through to the next round, if they were any good, he'd tell them that they were great and that he connected with them and he'd give them a quid. He's that sort of a guy, an appreciator.

Like anyone that has never seen The Piccadilly Rats before, the first time Alan set eyes on them, he went into a state of WTF is this? This state of shock changed to a state of appreciation and wonderment in about three minutes and sixty-six year-old Alan, who wasn't looking for a new career or hobby, knew instantly that he wanted to be in the band. He loved the Rock 'n' Roll, the age demographic, the energy and the Rat-Artiness of it all. On this particular day he didn't have time to engage with the boys as his missus was just about done in Aldi, so he chucked two quid in their collection case and offered a big double thumbs up as he walked away but for the first time in years he was really moved by something. As soon as he got home and searched for the band on the internet he was blown away by the super-cool images and mad stories that filled his screen.

The following Saturday Mrs Jones got rolled out of bed an hour early as man on a mission Alan had plans to introduce himself to his new band mates. Infiltrating the Rats isn't that hard if you're a nice person. As long as you pass Gaz's initial character test then you're in and this is pretty much how it panned out. Alan walked the length of Market Street but this time walked right past all the other performers without stopping as he searched out the Rats. He found them on Rats Nest Corner and explained his situation that was basically "I fell in love with the band last Saturday and I'd like to contribute and support you guys, I wanna be a Rat." Gaz did his normal dead-pan, "Yeah mate we've got a load of gear to carry down three flights of stairs, that can be your audition." Alan passed his audition and that was that. Alan joined the band at the most exciting time, when they were at their six strong peak; Ray, Tommy, Dave the

Rave, Rabcat, Heath and Gaz.

If you make it through to the Life Stories of the band you'll note that those stories and life experiences power this side of the book, the band's madcap adventures. Alan doesn't fit in to that model as his life has been a success in the traditional 2.4 well-nourished children way. He played his career well and has retired just at the right time to enjoy his new baby granddaughter. He's not out busking to pay his electric bill, he's out there to be part of something great.

Alan always carries a magic bag and his first meaningful contribution to the band was responding to Garry's common moan of: "I wish we could put this sign up". Out of the magic bag came a hammer and some nails and up went the sign. Gaz was all over this: "Fuckin Hell Alan who carries a hammer and nails round town? Are you waiting for the second coming of Jesus or something?" Gaz was very impressed that the band finally had their very own set designer. Turns out Alan was the most chilled, helpful and humble guy. Heath describes him as unflappable, if the whole world was going up in flames Alan would have something in his magic bag to sort it out.

On Alan's first day in the band Ray asked the question that the rest of the gang had clumsily overlooked: "Do you play any instruments?"

"Not really, I played drums for a short time forty years ago but I feel like I'm gonna just be what you need me to be."

Gaz's phone went and Buster Rabcat was running late, "Alan we need you to be a drummer".

That made this nicest of men very happy and for the next fifteen minutes he was living out a dream that he didn't even dream. He did okay and that was more than enough for The Rats and as Rabcat reclaimed his drumsticks Ray and Tommy came over and congratulated him.

This is how things moved forward; if anyone didn't turn up Alan would step in and over time Alan developed himself musically as he went along. He added maracas, tambourine and most impressively a homemade lagerphone to enhance the rhythm section of the band. A lagerphone is a type of rattle also known as a monkey stick (back off Tommy). Back in less politically correct times English Buskers used to have Monkeys shaking their rattles alongside them as they played. Gaz has kind of kept this tradition going. Alan made his monkey stick by drilling through lots of beer bottle tops and attaching them to a stick along with bells, a kazoo, two rat figures and a Manchester Bee. It's the definitive Swiss army instrument and it's also his pride and joy.

Whenever Heath or Rabcat went on prolonged periods of AWOL due to ill health or protest, Alan really enjoyed his time in the drum seat. During these periods Alan would decorate the drums to his taste with garlands, soft toys and squeaky rats, he had that artistic touch with it all so the band let him crack on, he didn't stop there he also helped make The Rats Nest into a real celebration of the band and the city by making and adding signs and posters to the band's famous flags. It became a really popular temporary tourist attraction.

Alan always dresses in fairly distinctive hippy-esque colourful clothing, he customises his own jackets by making his own badges and patches and he likes an accessory too, be it a hat, scarf, beads or a monkey stick.

What is really cool about Alan is that he's pretty

much exclusively a Saturday performer and he's achieved all of the above mainly on his wife's shopping trips. He's stepped in and played many non-Saturday gigs over the years but always on his own terms and with his family always firmly put first. What is cool about The Rats is that they just let him do whatever he wants.

All he had to do was ask - Alan Jones Piccadilly Rat.

12: KENDAL CALLING

Soundtrack: David Bowie – *Fame*

Ray Boddington could talk and, if he wasn't the best Rock Star in the world over seventy, then maybe he would have talked a bit less or maybe talked about himself a bit less, or probably not. Truth is Ray made so many people's days by rocking up and spontaneously gibber-jabbering the shit out of them. Thing is when he didn't have a gig to rock he did what Rats do - he used his slight and pliable body to squeeze into the most secluded and interesting parts of town. One such place was Arthur Donnelly's scrapyard where he rocked up most mornings to update the workers on how good the band were. The thing with talking is if you talk to the right people for long enough without ever doubting yourself then opportunities will arise.

Since Dave the Rave had become Dave the Grave, Ray had kept Arthur up-to-date on The Rats' activities and he called in for a cup 'o' tea most weekdays. Arthur's very successful sons have become prominent festival organisers in the north and one day, out of the blue, Arthur says, "My lads saw you on Judge Rinder and they asked me to ask ya if you want to play Kendal Calling?" Ray had no idea what that was but accepted gratefully and headed back into town to tell The Rats. It turns out Kendal doesn't just do mint cake, it does a mint festival. Kendal Calling is the biggest event of the summer in The Lakes attracting up to twenty-five thousand revellers.

The Low Flying Geese were pretty pleased too and

Garry arranged for them all to get backstage passes in order to record all the action. The Rats have long had their own official photographer going by the name of AJ. He's a mysterious, dapper-looking gentleman. He's mysterious because even the band don't know much about him. He often wears a leather pork pie hat, a clear sign of mysteriousness. Like all of the band's supporters, he just walked up, offered some kind words of appreciation and offered his services to the band for free. The Rats are a photographer's dream and AJ has taken thousands of them. Hundreds of these iconic photos have been made available online and have helped build the profile of the band. Gaz got on the Rat-Phone and invited the mysterious one and AJ duly accepted and kept his covert side of the bargain.

Garry's missus, Diane, drove to The Lakes with their baby granddaughter strapped into the front seat next to her. Ray and Garry sat in the back like a pair of kids on their way to the school disco. Tommy went with the five-strong film crew in their van – they were just as giddy.

On arrival they parked up and signed in at the Artists' Reception then they jumped in a large Mercedes band Transporter down the backstage area of a giant Big Top tent. The Rats were very appropriately propping up the festival from the very bottom of the bill. That meant they were first on. This actually worked in the band's favour as later on in the day festival-goers had choices to make as there were different stages and marquees to suit musical tastes but at 1pm not that much was going on. To put on a decent show the band needed a bassist to replace Heath who was still off the scene so Gaz recruited Paul Sewell from up and coming Salford band,

Death to the Strange.

At 1.08pm The Rats came out to a smattering of applause from about one hundred programme savvy, expert fun seekers. It took them eight minutes to get Tommy up the steep steps at the back of what was a pretty impressive stage. As soon as the more than decent Rock 'n' Roll vibrations started to seep out of the sides of the giant tent, people swarmed the cocoon like ants all over a broken pot of honey. Watching the good noise enthusiasts storm the tent was like a scene from "War of the Worlds" and, by the end of the second song of the set, The Jam's *That's Entertainment*, Garry had to close his eyes so not to get caught up in the moment and forget how to play and sing the song. The marquee was now close to full and the atmosphere was fully charged with people intent on having a good time.

Ray and Tommy don't get stage fright - they are made to do what they do, so they were predictably phenomenal but Garry had to keep his eyes closed and concentrate for most of the rest of the set. The place went nuts, Buster Rabcat and guest Rat Sewell were sensational, and The Rats' media machine recorded all the extraordinary action and interaction with the band's new fan-base and, all in all, it was just a bazzin' experience for everybody involved.

As they came on late, the organisers tried to haul them off after 22 minutes in line with the designated running order for the day but the fervent crowd weren't having that and gave it the big, "One more, one more, one more" chant to trigger an encore. As Gaz had his eyes shut, he didn't see the officials calling them off – honest, he didn't.

Two thousand lovingly energised northerners

sang over Garry and The Rats version of *Wonderwall* that became the highlight of the band's career thus far. Rabcat fuckin' hates that song but as soon as his mask came off, he was grinning from ear to ear like the world was a nice place or something.

The Rats surprisingly descended the big stage steps and into a free bar for a couple of triumphant brews on the go before the film crew dragged The Rats round to the punters' side of the marquee where they filmed them getting mobbed, congratulated and hero-worshipped. Their new fans wanted photos, signatures and anything else they could get hold of. Gaz lost all the pin badges off his customised denim jacket. Tommy was relieved of his policeman's hat and Ray just about won a tug 'o' war to keep his shades and rubber nipples.

Back in the VIP area, the lads got into the complimentary butties and Garry was absolutely thrilled for his missus to have shared the memories of the day. Even though he really wanted to hang on and meet Noel Gallagher, who was playing the same marquee at 8pm, Gaz was on best granddad behaviour and the wife-taxi left at 5pm. Tommy was supposed to come back with the film crew but their youthful spirit drove them to get carried away as they seemingly combusted into a substance-induced haze of festival invisibility.

Luckily Rock Star Pensioner Tommy kept his wits about him and managed to turn on his Rat homing device faculties. This was confirmed the next morning as litter picker Garry Stanley went about his rubbish clearance duties on Piccadilly Gardens thinking "I knew I should have booked a day off". An incensed Tommy Trouble appeared to explain in a very angry fashion that he had been abandoned near Scotland. "I had to walk miles into Kendal, get on a bus to Preston, then a train to Manchester."

"Well done, Tommy! You're not as fuckin' daft as you look!"

13: PARKLIFE

Soundtrack: Blur – *Parklife*

Following on from the cashless jackpot that was Kendal Calling, Garry knew that he had a great product, a great band but without a great manager to sell such talented stock, he just had to continue winging it. So when he saw the advertising for Manchester's biggest festival go live, he took the opportunity to tweet The Parklife Festival announcing that The Piccadilly Rats would be playing the front gate. The cool-as-fuck Parklife powers-that-be, aka Sacha Lord, tweeted straight back – "correction: The Piccadilly Rats are playing the Main Stage."

Gaz looked down at his phone and thought, "Has that just fuckin' happened?"

The Twitter-ting blew up and went absolutely viral. The positive reaction of the 19-23 Party Generation clearly proved that most Mancs knew all about The Rats. Sacha Lord confirmed this in an interview going on to say that as soon as the Twitter storm kicked off, the people demanded that The Rats play the Main Stage so they made it happen. The *Manchester Evening News* jumped all over it too.

This Sacha John Edward Lord bloke is a big noise in Manchester. Apart from being the guy behind the grimy dance dungeon that was Sankey's Soap, he is the entrepreneur behind the hugely successful Warehouse Project Raves that are high-end in terms of the superstar DJs that play them but are very cleverly low-end on location, utilising underground car parks, disused breweries and Victorian warehouses. Gigs at those urban settings built towards establishing the world's joint biggest night club venue at the former Manchester Mayfield Railway Station. This former Railway Freight Container Base now packs in up to 10,000 ravers for Warehouse Project events and is on par with the biggest clubs in Ibiza. So Garry and Ray were rather chuffed to have entered this fella's consciousness.

Due to the increased media interest, the band now had three film crews vying for their attention. As the deal with The Geese was another cashless, you-scratch-my-back-and-I'll-scratch-yours agreement, Garry found it hard to stick to any exclusivity contract because there simply wasn't one. So when Pro-Manchester Digital Media and Marketing Company "MCR's Finest" approached the band to see if they could cover Parklife for them too, Gaz could hardly say, "No". The Donnelly Brothers were also interested in putting something together media-wise but when Gaz explained the double film crew situation, they laughingly reminded Gaz to remember that The Rats were not the fuckin' Beatles.

Garry and Ray bumped their publicist heads together ahead of the big day. They decided that it would cause a real stir to arrive in old school fashion by horse and cart. That on its own would have caused mayhem. Unfortunately, they got all Health 'n' Safety and ran it through Sacha Lord at Parklife first, who thought it was funny but didn't want the animal rights mob on his case for scaring the horses. In the end, The Rats went on The Donnelly's minibus. That was exchanged for golf buggies on arrival to get down to the uber-posh Artists' Village that serviced all the Diva needs of the top bands ready to play the Main Stage.

As they were in the top echelon of the festival, The Rats and all their entourage had Access All Areas all-inclusive passes for the day. They could not get their heads around the buffet set up as it was off the fuckin' scale. Complimentary fish 'n' chips, roast beef barm, puddings, cheeseboards and free beer. They really had to pinch themselves and be careful not to get too pissed too quickly. They didn't have to worry too much about that prior to going on, as their position in the Rock Pyramid was once again rock bottom. Unsurprisingly, they were on first.

The band line-up for the day had changed again as Buster Rabcat was having none of it. The O'Neill Brothers, from the supremely talented Manchester reggae band Ruff Trade, stepped in; Ryan on drums and his brother, Chris, on the bass. These two fellas are more chilled out than Cheech and Chong, so they were a very welcome calming influence on The Rats and had no problem with being asked to wear Rat and Monkey masks. They also don't drink, so the too-much-too-soon risk was low. Alan was also on Rat Duty - ready to give his monkey rattle a good public thrashing.

The stage was immense - approximately four times bigger than Kendal Calling - so the band set off early to get Tommy up the thirty steps to Rock Paradise. Liam Gallagher's band were headlining much later on and were just completing their soundcheck and exchanged niceties with the boys as they checked out.

Parklife attracts 70,000 people per day but at the time of The Rats' 12 o'clock lunchtime slot, 69,950 of them were still sleeping off Friday's party and the experience turned out to be the most surreal, hollow-sounding band practice.

Two film crews recorded the action and Tommy, Ray and Alan did their absolute utmost to make the film footage energised but the fun in the film was all about it being a fuckin' disaster.

The Rats dutifully rocked out for the full half an hour and fully justified the rousing reception that they received from a group of four interested volunteer litter pickers. Their surreal salute had a deeper meaning for Garry who had spent so much of his time in their shoes.

Leaving the stage feeling less than triumphant, the band set about the epic display of free food and drink in the Artist Village. This caused much more of a stir than their on stage performance, as all the other bands and crews wanted photos with the band. Gaz had a few beers then rather foolishly decided to take a puff of one of Chong's giant reefers. This totally fucked up his day and his mission to meet Manchester's second best Front Man, Liam Gallagher, 'cos Gaz didn't know where the fuck he was for the next two days.

Weed either agrees with you or it doesn't, as demonstrated by Gaz's one puff whitey.

Rotten.

14: A FRONT PAGE EPITAPH

Soundtrack: The Doors – *The End*

Imagine fancying a woman so much that by the time you get her naked, it's all over before it's even started. That was The Parklife Festival experience for The Piccadilly Rats. Only in this case, the sexy woman was in a field in the Orthodox Jewish bit of Manc-Land. Things like this can happen and the key to moving forward quickly without really feeling the impact of Post-Traumatic-Empty-Field-Disorder is to simply let the experience pass over.

Gaz and Ray are as resilient as a pair of armadillos in a nuclear bunker so they both took the positives from the experience and really valued adding The Parklife Festival to the band's increasingly impressive CV. Financially, the band never made enough dosh to justify days off.

They were pretty crap in that respect but the need to graft on an almost daily basis was also the key to their ongoing resonance in The City of Manchester. The engine room of Gaz, Ray and Tommy kept firing on a daily basis with Alan doing his stuff on a Saturday but, with the band now missing Dave the Rave, Buster Rabcat and Heath, the magical energy wasn't quite what it was.

The band's dip in fortune continued into the spring of 2019 when Garry was injured when a car clipped him as he was hurriedly making his way up to Piccadilly to catch his bus home. After a Rat-Jam, the speeding vehicle screeched out of the side street next to Sacha's

Nightclub and violently knocked him off his feet.

The fella in the car stopped very briefly to check that Gaz was okay. After confirming that he wasn't dead, he did one before the situation escalated. Garry had broken his foot, smashed up his hands and had badly shaken confidence.

News travels fast in the People's Republic of Central Manchester and Ray was on the phone shortly after to check on his friend. Gaz knew that he wouldn't be able to perform the next morning as he couldn't stand on his broken foot, so he told Ray not to come at 9am like he normally would.

"Come round at lunchtime."

When Ray turned up, he was all of a dither and Gaz asked him what was going wrong. He got all emotional and started to cry.

"What's wrong, Pal?" said Garry as his daughter went over to console him.

"I'd be fucked without you, Garry. I don't know what I do if you were gone."

It was an unexpected moment of vulnerability from Ray that highlighted how the friendships within the band and the responsibilities that came with being a Rat had become everything to him. The thought of losing Gaz made him consider all of this.

Seventeen cups of tea, beans on toast and a packet of pink wafer biscuits helped him get a grip on his vulnerabilities and Garry's daughter dropped him off nice and refreshed about 9pm.

He was back Monday morning to pick up some tobacco and on Wednesday for another catch up. Over a shared light lunch of Tommy's soup and bread, Ray agreed to take Gaz's sick-note to the MEN offices on his way to The Millstone.

"Don't forget the sick-note, Ray."

"Don't worry, You can always count on me, Garry."

The Millstone Pub in the trendy Northern Quarter of Manchester is always a Pandora's Box of interesting characters. There is nothing trendy about the pub or the clientele that frequent the venue. The Millstone is as old school as pubs come. It's dark and dingy in the main but it does have a couple of large windows at the front that open up rather smartly into the street, so passers-by can glimpse the best pensioners rave up in town. The pub is packed out every day with people coming in to grab tables from lunchtime to guarantee a good spot for when the massively fat resident DJ (Nice Man) goes live every day from 4pm. It's karaoke but it's a sing-a-long in the old-fashioned way and it really is a fantastic spectacle.

On this particular day, Ray's plan was to drop Gaz's sicknote off and get into The Millstone nice and early. Reports from the pub suggested that Ray was his usual self, having a great time singing a number of songs and he even gave his beloved harmonica a soulful going over. He went round every table in the place and entertained everyone that was out that particular day. Usual craic 'n' that.

Ray, who didn't drink alcohol, left the Millstone just before seven and started to make his way back towards Piccadilly. CCTV footage shown to Ray's family by Greater Manchester Police in the aftermath of his death shows him on High Street by Manchester Arndale. He seemed to follow a couple in stepping out behind a tram that was going away from the three of them but, tragically, the couple managed to step back in time before Ray was hit by a tram coming the opposite way.

When the tram came to a stop lots of people ran over to assist Ray in a scene that must have been deeply distressing for everyone involved. Some truly heroic people tended to Ray that night until the medical, fire and police services arrived. It brought some comfort to his family to know that Ray wasn't alone.

Garry saw a Newsflash on his *Manchester Evening News* App about an elderly man being hit by a tram, but didn't give it a second thought and rang Ray at 10pm to hear how he got on in The Millstone. A police officer answered his phone and his whole life fell apart. Ray's injuries were so bad that he was deemed untreatable and he was given less than twenty-four hours to live. It was a small mercy that his face had escaped the impact of the accident so visitors could recognise him. His family were constantly at his bedside. Garry was there the next morning and Alan the following day.

Tommy eventually gained access after being denied on numerous occasions. When he finally got into the ward, he blamed Garry for not letting him in – "You've told them not to let me in." Once he'd gathered himself and took in the scene, Tommy was completely overwhelmed and distraught at the sight of his friend on a ventilator. The family were quite rightly better informed than the band as to Ray's prognosis and the conversations and hopes of the band were completely misguided.

Garry visited three times and, on the first day, Ray seemed to really struggle breathing on the ventilator and Garry admitted that it was really hard to see him like that. The second time he was breathing more easily and, on the third visit, Ray seemed to be totally at ease which falsely led Garry to believe that there was some hope for him. Unfortunately his more relaxed state was the morphine taking effect. Ray was nil by mouth for almost a week before he passed, highlighting what a truly extraordinary spirit the man carried.

His eldest son, Daniel, clung to him when he finally slipped away expressing the great feeling of loss that all his family and Ray's friends felt. Tommy was a little boy lost and when he first heard the news that Ray had passed, he dropped like a stone, physically passing out with grief.

When people helped him up and he came to his senses he positioned himself on Rats' Nest Corner as a representative of the band and his friend. There was an outpouring of love on social media with Kendal Calling, Paul Arthur from Oasis and many others paying tribute. Posters, flags, flowers and toy rats decorated the pavement and the wall by Lever Street in celebration of Ray's Life. Tommy stood vigil all week - protecting the memories of his friend and giving well-wishers somebody to grieve with.

Among the devastation of Ray's passing, the irony of the situation was that, in death, Ray had finally fulfilled his ever-burning desire to be famous. He'd finally made the front page of the *Manchester Evening News* but in doing so the city had lost an icon. A man absolutely embedded in Mancunian culture.

RAY BODDINGTON'S TALE

1: WHO THE FUCK IS THAT?

Soundtrack: Prince Buster - *Enjoy Yourself*

This is the toughest chapter of the book to write by far because Ray Boddington died before I got to ask him about much of his extraordinary life. He never stopped his own infamous incessant chitter-chatter right up to the day of his death, but he mainly only ever spoke of future plans for himself and his beloved band.

It's important that I briefly re-explain my personal relationship with Ray and how I have come to gather what I consider to be a fair, if not factual, summary of the man's life.

As mentioned, I met Ray when I was an under-age drinker round town. I was intrigued by how open and engaging he was with me. He only spoke about himself and mainly about his ambitions going forward, but he did tell me about a song that he'd written in prison, long before Robbie Williams' *Angels* came out but it was in a similar vein. He sang it to me, one-on-one in an intimate-style, outside Sinclair's Oyster Bar before he put on his One Man Street Dance and Hip-Hop show for all the drinkers in Shambles Square. He almost whispered the song to me. It was remorseful and spiritual and he meant it.

I was young, daft and half-pissed but I sensed the depth of the story in the song - the vulnerability of a tortured soul that had come good. I had no idea what his story was or that thirty years later I'd be digging into that story for this book but, from that moment on, whenever I saw Ray he didn't know my name but he'd recognise me and talk to me like I was family. I think he was like that with everyone. I don't really know, as I only have my own experience to share. That first interaction with Ray was about 1989 and after that, just like everyone else that regularly passed through the city, I'd just see him doing his thing every now and then.

Roll the clock forward to 2013 when I started booking The Rats for gigs for the charity that I'm involved with and I got to know Ray a bit better. Not in terms of learning about his personal life or historic life story, I just got to experience how kind and engaging he was. For very little money I'd taxi the band to South Manchester and they'd play a small festival for me. Ray would find the time to seek me out and tell me to remember to stop and take the time to realise how lucky I was.

One summer I had a bit of boxing kit laid out for kids to play with in front of the small stage that The Rats were playing and Ray gloved up and had everyone in stitches messing around on the punch-bag with Tommy Trouble. Another time we held a posh Black Tie Ball at the opulent Masonic Hall on Bridge Street in town. I'd asked Garry if they could come and just play *Wonderwall* at midnight. Gaz was non-committal and didn't show on the night. Ray and Tommy showed up early and ready to perform instead. This put a little bit of pressure on me because we had a pianist, canapés, all the posh shit going down and in walk Ray and Tommy with their plastic bags; Tommy in police drag and Ray in a shell-suit. Ray explained that Gaz couldn't come but, "We didn't want to let you down so we will open up for ya". So I stopped the pianist and called everyone to a hush. Ray played his Harmonica to a silent room while Tommy wobbled a bit. Ray followed their performance with a short speech about the great work done by the charity and they wandered over to me and hugged me up. No fuss, no charge.

So that's my experience of the man. I didn't know him personally, but I loved him and valued the kindness and respect that he showed me and the organisation that I support.

The rest of this story is a mixture of facts and hearsay. I put it together from a starting place of love and respect but Ray's life not been a fairy-tale and I've just pieced together the jigsaw of his journey as best as I can.

Ray Boddington was born on 30 December 1941 in Levenshulme. At the age of five he was admitted to a children's hospital diagnosed with polio. The initial prognosis was catastrophic as he was given only 12 months to live. Wikipedia says that he defied the odds and made a full recovery after seven years, but anyone that knows Ray at all will recognise that he never got rid of his polio limp.

Details of Ray's childhood are vague to say the least but people close to him believe that he suffered sexual and physical abuse as a child and as a victim of the care system of the 1940's and 1950's. His polio was probably the main reason that he was in and out of these institutions.

Close to when the news about Jimmy Savile's career

in paedophilia broke in the press, I was in Ray's company and heard him open up a little about his experience. Savile was a regular visitor to Rose Hill Remand Home, one of the children's convalescent homes that Ray was supposed to be cared for in. Ray went on to explain that, "The dirty bastard made me sit on his knee and he put his hand up my nightdress."

"A nightdress, Ray? What fuckin' sort of place was that?"

Ray coldly informed the company that he was in that day that we didn't want to know. I've had a brief look to see what records are available about Rose Hill and, unsurprisingly, no early records of Rose Hill appear to have survived and all other archive content is restricted. The dark forces that run the show have it all sewn up.

The way Ray's early life played out leaves me in no doubt that he endured some very dark experiences in care as a child. He also told me that in Rose Hill he was once asked to go and make his bed. When he tried to discuss the terms of the request, the male member of staff repeated, "Boddington, go and make your bed." When Ray went to answer back again the bastard put everything that he had into punch that knocked him spark out. Ray told this story because when he went in for an unrelated scan fifty or so years later, the hospital informed him that he had a historical blood clot on the brain in exactly the same place that he'd been lamped all those years ago.

Experiences like that must have been a driver for Ray to train himself in the art of self-defence. So he trained as an amateur boxer at Proctor's Gym in Hulme. Unfortunately, I don't have any detail surrounding his bouts or boxing record. He must have been a confident fighter though because Ray claimed that he used to visit the travelling fairgrounds and fight for money with anyone that was game for a tear up. As previously discussed, I saw him glove up in his seventies and he definitely had his feet set right, he duffed Tommy up anyway.

From Wikipedia: "*At the age of 12, Ray went to Baguley Hall Secondary Modern and taught himself the harmonica. His father, Walter, played in the Phil Moss Showband for 20 years. They were the resident band at The Ritz Ballroom in Manchester. His mother was also a talented pianist. Ray signed for Ace Artists when he was 16 and played on the same bill as Dorothy Squires and Karl Denver. As a teenager, Ray played at the famous Band On The Wall venue in the late 1950s and also appeared at Bernard Manning's venue, The Embassy Club. He also played at The Domino Club, where he opened for acts such as Herman Hermits and the Everley Brothers. Ray also did a summer residence at Butlin's Holiday Camp in Rhyl. Around this time he met world-famous harmonica player Larry Adler who was said to have been very impressed with Ray's style of playing.*"

It's fair to say that Ray had endured and survived a turbulent childhood. As a reader – there is quite a gap between stories of his musical family and the care homes – I can see music may have been in his genes. Did he get to go back home at some point to get the musical influence? Was he in care until he came of age? Did his parents still visit him?

2: DIMINISHED RESPONSIBILITY

Soundtrack: Johnny Cash – *Hurt*

I will never know what exactly Ray Boddington experienced in the Care Home region of Hell in post-war Manchester but my prayers go out to him in relation to that. Likewise, I will never know exactly what happened in 1963 in a disused public toilet in Middleton when Ray Boddington killed a man by smashing him repeatedly over the head with a stone.

I have not investigated this in any detail or applied for the court records around the incident but I have read the newspaper archive relating to the court case that followed. It reads, "A sobbing Boddington cried out, 'I didn't know what I was doing.'"

I don't know the facts but I feel that Ray (21 at the time) was probably engaging in some sort of sexual practice with the 16 year-old and something triggered the violence that led to his victim losing his life and Ray losing his mind. To give this some historic perspective, homosexual acts between consenting males above the age of twenty-one only became legal in 1967.

My heart genuinely goes out to the boy that perished that day but it also goes out to Ray. I'll never know the truth surrounding this dark episode but my gut tells me that the action of manslaughter that he was charged with came from a very dark place relating to his past experiences.

He was sentenced to seven years for manslaughter on the grounds of diminished responsibility. He was sent to the notorious Broadmoor Hospital to serve his sentence.

3: JAIL HOUSE COCK

Soundtrack: The Specials – *Gangsters*

A conversation with a resident that spent time in Rosehill Remand Home after the time that Ray was sentenced shared details of a conversation that they overheard where a member of staff at the centre was said to have described Ray Boddington as a "ticking time bomb" in relation to the level of abuse that he had endured.

Hanging was still in play in the UK up until 1965 so had his court case gone the other way, there is every chance that Ray would not be part of this book at all. Instead, he went to pay his debt to society at Britain's highest security prison hospital, Broadmoor. This is where the United Kingdom Government house their highest risk, most dangerous prisoners so I suspect that within the sphere of much of Ray's life experience he must have carried tales of his experience that you and I would find hard to comprehend. The fact that he rarely ever spoke about his time in Broadmoor is not surprising considering the reasons why he ended up in there. I expect an account of his time-served experience would have been an absolutely fascinating story but that is a tale that Ray always chose to keep to himself.

There was one part-story from his time in Broadmoor that even Ray found too interesting to keep in. Ray is known to have periodically admitted to or discussed his connection to Ronnie Kray during his time spent in the facility. Ray, who had trained as a barber, somehow became Ronnie Kray's hairdresser inside. As Ray told the story he sets a scene where Mr Kray's inmate entourage are sat around while Ray is stood behind him shaving his neck with a cut-throat razor. Ronnie Kray addressed his cronies by quipping that Ray was the only person that he trusted to come behind him with a blade. At this time in his life, Ray had his signature Beatles-style straight-cut blonde fringe and was a bit of a pretty boy. Ronnie Kray eventually and famously admitted that he was of bi-sexual orientation. Only Ray and the other inmates will ever know if they shared that kind of connection but if Ray's story rings true, he may or may not have penetrated Ronnie's other inner circle (listen, I like to find humour in the darkest holes). If any of this reflective writing is on point then what a place and situation for Ray to have to navigate his way through! If he did catch the eye of one of Britain's most feared paranoid schizophrenic gangsters then that opens up so many questions. I could write another book on what might have happened but I have no idea. They might just have been friends or Ray might just have been a subservient barber. We'll never know.

I've never sat and counselled Ray around his childhood experiences. The only sex-related chats I've ever heard Ray indulge in is him boasting to some half-drunk, giggly girls on Market Street about him having an oversized wanger and, in that moment, nobody really took him seriously but then another time he told me that his new girlfriend was thirty-seven and she loved a bit of the Bod. The way he said it made me believe him. I wasn't creeped out, I just thought, "This guy writes his own fuckin' rules". He was about sixty-eight at the time.

The point I am trying to make is that I try to be

non-judgemental when it comes to what floats another person's boat sexually but obviously there are obvious exceptions with that chain of thought.

What went on in Ray's head and underpants as an adult is his business. How an adult comes to have their own sexual shopping list is not something I claim to be an expert on, but I'm sure that Ray's path to his adult sexual practice was unlike most of our own. What he was into and got off on, again is not something that I claim to be an expert on, but I am intrigued by this though; if he was involved in homosexual activity in Broadmoor, his sexual orientation, however it came about, could and probably would have determined his survival strategy and experience.

My ex-wife was a victim of sexual abuse inflicted by her step-father. In adult life she was a sex addict and seemed to enjoy her sexual practices but I'll never know what she was really thinking either during or after those interactions. She had mental stuff going on for sure. She ended up giving birth to eleven children by a variety of fathers. I know she would have been a loving mother because right in her heart she was a good soul and like Ray she was a beautiful person but her need to have lots of sex with lots of people always complicated her life and my gut feeling is that Ray had the same kind of coping strategy. It's less easy for men to get sex, unless you're in prison with other men in the same boat maybe. We'll never know!

One thing is for sure, we all have an in-built survival kit. Thankfully, most of us never have to use ours to anywhere near our full capability. People like Ray probably had to.

Ray served out his sentence, collected his belongings

and somehow thumbed a lift from Broadmoor to Salford. If you think watching Karl Pilkington get about is entertaining. Just imagine watching a recording of Ray's trip home. What the fuck did he talk about?

I imagine he acted like nothing had happened. That was how he played out the rest of his life.

4: THE REAL RAY BODDINGTON

Soundtrack: Gloria Gaynor – *I Am What I Am*

I didn't bump into Ray until almost twenty years after his release. What his mindset was as he was starting all over again, I just don't know. I know he came to have a wife and a divorce and six children. I saw his children sobbing at his funeral, so I know he played a part in all of their lives.

Whether he continued with a 'half rice, half chips' approach to his sexual practises is again all speculation. I've heard at least two accounts of this being the case, but the details of those accounts add nothing to the story, so I'll not expand on that - even though I think it's important to recognise how complex this man's existence was.

What blows my mind about Ray is that with this extraordinary life story behind him, the man I got to know was still giving off an enormous amount of good energy. He seemed to be humble, not in terms of not putting himself first (my God, he only ever talked about himself) but in his outlook, he'd spend ten minutes telling me all about himself and his performances with the band all delivered in a high frequency whirl, but then he'd lower his voice and deliver nuggets of wisdom.

"Keep helping people."

"Don't forget how lucky you are."

"If you ever need help, just ask for it."

As he did this, he tapped his head to suggest a connection to The Divine.

I believe in all those things, so I got him.

I believe that when he dropped his voice, that was the real Ray Boddington, the man that he had become. I had no idea about all the shit that he'd come through to be able to share that kind of wisdom but I once offered him a pint of beer and he shook his head in a way that suggested, "No fuckin' way. I've learnt those lessons long ago".

The Rats spent years busking with him on Piccadilly and they most certainly love and miss him. He was family to them. Ray was a major part of The Piccadilly Rats Love Machine and he made thousands of people's visits to Manchester memorable. The band has struggled to find a meaning for themselves without him.

15: UNFINISHED WORLD DOMINATION

Soundtrack: David Bowie – *Ashes to Ashes*

As mentioned, Tommy was stood on Rats' Nest Corner guarding Ray's Memorial from eight o'clock in the morning on the day of the funeral. It was a fittingly glorious, sunny day to honour the passing of Manchester's Vibe-Master Kingpin.

Tommy stood dutifully hugging it out with a steady trickle of well-wishers until the hearse came by just before lunchtime. The coffin had a striking portrait of Ray placed at the rear of it and, when it pulled up at Piccadilly Gardens, scores of people gathered around to touch Ray's image and Tommy stood by watching like a proud but broken father.

Ray was a proud Manc but he was also a proud Salfordian and his burial ceremony took place at Agecroft Cemetery in the Dirty Old Town itself.

Walking over from the church to the burial ground his son Stephen, who is autistic, excitedly spoke about horror films, graveyards and zombies and he spoke with such a speed and tone that it was as if it was Ray was lightening the mood for everyone himself.

Ray's eldest lad pulled out every stop to give his Dad the send-off that he deserved and, as he was lowered into the ground, all his children started to weep their goodbyes.

Back in the Church, the cruel and immediate impact of the dire way that Ray came to pass was evident as his family just weren't ready to let him go. His eldest son gave an intense and heartfelt tribute to his Dad.

There were few light moments and Garry and Tommy didn't take the opportunity to contribute even if they had been given the option to do so.

Back at The Millstone, the kindly landlord put on a bit of a spread to honour Ray. Buster Rabcat, Garry and Tommy all told a few Rats Tales about their friend.

One of Ray's street friends, Daniel, attended the funeral and the wake. He clearly had a drink problem but was nice enough in nature. At some point, he must have passed Garry's decent bloke test as he sat with The Lads to raise a glass to Ray for a good few hours. He was amiable enough but wore a pained expression on his face.

When Garry finally asked the question that everyone had been thinking – "Are you alright, Daniel? You keep grimacing?"

"Yes, Garry. I'm cool - the only shoes I could get my hands on this morning were size eights, I'm a fuckin' 10."

"That explains it then. I thought you were having a fuckin' stroke."

Rabcat was interesting and engaging but also depleted and dejected. Gaz seemed to be trying to portray a state of cool Manc acceptance but it was clear to see that he was hurting. Gaz and Ray had dreamed their massive dreams together for such a long time and the man that said he'd never let him down, never did but, in death, he'd left him alone and that was worse than anything.

After half a bitter, Tommy started trying to lighten the mood in the pub by putting his favourite super-strength squeeze holds onto the other guests' shoulder muscles but just like Ray's family at the funeral, everyone around the table just wasn't ready to move on.

"Fuck off Tommy".

16: SPINAL TAP

Soundtrack: Blink 182 – *Adam's Song*

Buster Rabcat's no-show at the Parklife Festival confirmed that he was no longer feeling the project. The buzz for him was being the hidden gem in the thorny crown of The Rats. His unveiling on *Judge Rinder* had dismantled the Harry Potter-style thrill that he had previously enjoyed under the invisibility cloak of his Rat Mask. For a deep-thinking individual like Martin, the revelation of his true identity on a nationwide scale was a complete violation and an absolute catastrophe.

Nobody in the band even knew that his real name was Simon before that fateful day as he'd been living a life of complete pseudo. He was a scouser in Manchester, going by a fake name, in a fake identity Rat Mask but now he'd been seriously outed. For a man that openly admits that he has a phobia of people, fame was the last item on his shopping list and when it started to come, it was all too much for him.

Bringing a level of notoriety to the band was part of the reason that Rabcat thrashed the drums with such verminous animosity. Unfortunately, all the punk energy that he had invested into that had become a regretful afterthought in the big thinker's mind. He wanted The Rat to be notorious, not himself. The pantomime of The Rats' publicity drive had really started to piss him off.

Losing Ray had temporarily put all those thoughts on the back-burner because, like everyone else, he was absolutely devastated by Ray's death. At Ray's wake he only had kind words for his creative and kind friend. They were kindred spirits with completely different outlooks and life skills, but they were friends all the same. Buster Rabcat loved Ray and his passing hit him hard.

Unfortunately, Rabcat had lost a lot of close friends over the eighteen month period that surrounded Ray's death and this combined with the UK and world political landscape lurching further to the right meant that his contempt wasn't just saved for the band and their publicity-driven antics.

I found out more about this after accepting a phone call from him to discuss the merits of Chapter Four of this book in which he features heavily. He told me that Chapter Four was brilliant, but it was "all fuckin' wrong". I explained that this version of how the band got together was Garry's version of events. I asked him to share his version with me and it might be possible to re-do it. His totally unoffended and genuine response lasted for over fifty minutes and was thoroughly entertaining and relevant but also bang in line with the whole dynamic of The Rats and I couldn't actually decide if he was being serious or not.

"Don't fuckin' bother as by the time your book is finished, we will all be dead, just like Spinal Tap, one by one, mark my words!"

"Fuckin' hell, Martin. That's a bit heavy."

"True story. I'm going to kill myself on New Year's Eve!"

There was no hint of sarcasm in his voice.

"Why?"

Then the punk spirit started to flow…

"Because the world is shit. Have you seen what

they have done to Manchester? It's becoming fuckin' Manchattan – bastard skyscrapers everywhere. The kids can't even live there. The whole place is becoming an Air B&B. It fuckin' stinks, I can't stand it. I've spoke about getting some Manchattan t-shirts made but nobody fuckin' cares anymore so I can't be fuckin' bothered. I've lost a lot of friends this year too, too many. It's hit me hard and I just don't want to go on. The council too where I live – I have been complaining to the fuckin' council for four fuckin' years, that's done me in too."

"Why is that?"

"Because the fuckin' lamppost outside my house hasn't worked for four fuckin' years. I fell down the kerb, did my leg in and rang the bastards up to complain. Do you know what the twats have just fuckin' done after four fuckin' years?"

"No. What have they done?"

"They have replaced the three lampposts on the street that were working perfectly well and left the one that was fucked. Somebody at the Town Hall is pissing themselves at my expense. Well, that's it for me. Not interested in the band, they've sold out playing, *Who the fuck is Alice?* all the time and bastard *Wonderwall*. That's not it. Fuckin' Rinder too. Do you know how hard I've tried to not get noticed down here? Fuck it – I'm done."

Again I wasn't sure if he was playing with me so I asked him this question: "If you do die on New Year's Eve, can I put this in the book as I've really enjoyed this conversation?"

"No problem."

I told him I loved his punk energy and let him know that I personally think that all the best people care about the shitty state of the world the most. I urged him to carry on making his own relevant rebellious ripple but he was adamant that he wasn't sticking around for *Auld Lang Syne*.

On the third of January the conversation came back to me and I admit that I had a slight pang of guilt for not remembering and said a brief prayer before I called him. It went straight to answerphone.

"Hi Martin. I'm just calling to check if you killed yourself on New Year's Eve. Hope you didn't. Please give me a call if you are still with us."

An hour later he called back fuckin' fuming that Boris and the Tories had defeated Labour and were marching us out of Europe. Getting back to the New Year's Eve plan, he explained that Brexit had refocused him and after visiting his beloved Amsterdam in the last week of a united Europe, he would top himself as discussed on January 31st ("Brexit Day") as he wasn't fuckin' avin' it.

"You'll miss out on the book royalties" I reminded him.

"They'll all be dead before you finish that book, not interested – Spinal Tap."

17: THE DOWNWARD SPIRAL

Soundtrack: Iggy Pop - *The Passenger*

Heath had been in a state of unexplained exile from the band for a prolonged period of time by now and it's important at this stage of the band's story to recognise how much Heath secretly revered his band leader and friend Garry. To Heath, Garry always seemed to have his shit together. He was everything that he aspired to be. Confident, kind and creative. He was a fuckin' someone.

Heath never mentioned it to anyone but he looked up to Garry on a daily basis, almost in a state of awe. Every day he'd watch Garry being someone while he consistently felt like an invisible nobody. Heath always wanted his easy way of being for himself. Unbeknown to Heath at that time, Gaz's own "He's-got-his-shit-together-radar" was not reading true for the following reasons: Garry has always been a drinker. He likes bottles, the physical look and feel of the glass. As a kid, he loved the McAlpine pop wagon and the thrill of purchasing the black syrupy Dandelion & Burdock that felt like Guinness for kids. Even better was the money-led game of chasing down all the empty bottles in the neighbourhood to claim 5p's back from the local bottle shops. Gaz revelled in that money out of nothing street business.

Gaz took this love of a good bottle into adolescence and, as soon as he'd grown a few pubs, he turned his attentions to the first beer-filled bottle that caught his eye. His first love was the blue star on an orange background of Newcastle Brown Ale and, from age fourteen onwards, he'd do in two or three a night. Star Beer. By the time he started to work he upped his bottle intake to six every night. Garry has always been a family man, someone that wanted to be at home of a night, so his drinking was usually done at home when his kids went to bed. He religiously got on it between 9-12 o'clock each week day night and 9-1am at weekend.

Gaz's worst idea of a drinking experience would be going to a pub for one pint. He was always a decent, well-behaved drinker but if he was having one then he was having six at least - that was his flow. For years, this model worked for Garry but when Ray passed away his life quickly started to spiral out of control. His anxiety intensified, and he started having regular panic attacks. He realised that a pint took those horrible feelings away so he started sticking 4 cans in his work bag to take the edge off things in the day time.

Garry has always worked extremely hard to give his family a holiday each year and even with his health beginning to slip he was still intent on treating his wife, children and grandkids like he always did. Due to his phobia of flying, Gaz made his mob hit the continent by train. Train travel is better for his nerves than flying but it still scares him to death and even before they'd hit London he had begun to vomit as his brain started to reject the travel experience and demand alcoholic fuel.

Benidorm seemed a world away as Garry's alcoholism started to go public. Garry was shaking like a leaf by the time they made the Channel Tunnel. Again that first pint seemed to take away all his problems temporarily, but all of his family could see that their rock was beginning to crumble right in front of them. The holiday was an absolute nightmare with Garry dismissing the mental health aspects of his drink problem as other unrelated illnesses. He'd experience panic attacks in the night, and he'd have his wife bringing in cold towels to treat him like he was a malaria sufferer, as if he had a contagious disease. Then he'd finally pass out and sleep it off. The next morning he'd act like nothing had happened and get back on the piss and the day would play out exactly the same as the day before. For the family it was like having another child along.

Garry's mental health was starting to slip to a disturbingly low level as demonstrated when on a shopping trip to buy his granddaughter a bracelet. He managed to buy and sup a can of beer at almost every shop along the seafront during the short walk down to Benidorm's old town shopping area. After funding the jewellery treat for his granddaughter he unexplainably got his knob out and started to piss up her back. He had no awareness of this as his family papered over the cracks of a very disturbing situation. Garry was starting to lose his mind. He was edging ever closer to rock bottom.

Back at home, gigs were Saturday mornings only now and all that everyone wanted to talk about was Ray and his death and this really started to fuck Garry's head up. Nobody had a good word to say and people started to tell him that he looked like shit. People did that out of concern but it just made Gaz feel as bad as he looked. He knew that people loved Ray, he did too, but to consistently go over and over it again and again was starting to seriously twist his melon. Garry the self-publicist was always the good news man but long gone was the good news that he and Ray always loved to create. His life had started to become a living hell, his customary six bottles a night at home had turned into ten on top of his daytime survival rations. Gaz had pretty much become an alcohol-dependent addict.

As the onset of a full breakdown became more and more likely, he had lost the ability to sleep, at one point he stayed awake for almost 14 days solid. He became engulfed by fear and suicidal thoughts. His thought processes became desperate and nonsensical and he kept thinking that going to London to become homeless was somehow a good option. His secret London escape route became his ultimate goal and, on the night when his world caved in, he had it all planned. He withdrew some cash to get him on a train to London, bought a bottle of whiskey and inexplicably donned a ridiculously oversized red overcoat to bring an element of maddened grandeur to the scene.

Thankfully Garry's daughter was aware of the immediate danger that her dad was in and started to track his every move. When he left the house unannounced and started running in the direction of Central Manchester, she followed him in her car. Her dad never ran anywhere. She knew that he had finally lost his mind.

As darkness fell and rain started to sweep into the cold wind of the night, Garry entered the gates of Boggart Hole Clough like a mad man in a horror film. The Clough is a woodland park in Blackley and, on this particular night, it was also a secluded, dark and lonely region of hell.

As his daughter bravely followed him into the parkland she pleaded for her dad to stop and come home. Garry was talking gibberish by now and told her to "go home now before the foxes and ghouls come for you".

Then he was off into the bracken of the wood like the Boggart himself - crashing through the undergrowth. His petrified daughter had no choice to but ring the emergency services.

In a state of madness Garry saw the lights of what he believed to be a police car and, as the torches of what were actually ambulance men came through the woods - the beast in the red overcoat smashed the whiskey bottle on a rock and cut deep into both of his wrists and then into his neck as he made a very serious attempt on his own life.

And with a tortured scream the lights went out.

18: THE REFUGE

Soundtrack: Gary Jules – *Mad World*

Garry drifted in and out of consciousness as the ambulance seemed to float its way to Manchester Royal Infirmary. On arrival, there was no time to rest as his wounds needed immediate attention.

The medical team stripped him of his outrageous sodden clothing and his neck was skilfully and tenderly stitched back together in a surreal interaction with an angel of a female doctor. A one-way conversation ensued, outlining how lucky and how stupid Garry was and reminding him how much he had to live for. Priceless human care that. In this country when you hit rock bottom, this is how we look after people. Garry had been very lucky in more ways than one.

Even so, there was every chance that he'd managed to end his music career as he'd managed to cut straight through the tendons in his wrists but, somehow, he had managed to avoid severing the veins that would have fully snuffed him out. That in itself was a miracle. He was made to plunge his wrists into a surgical bucket of disinfectant. He knew that he deserved every bit of pain in that bucket but, for the first time in a long time, he felt that he was in the right place at the right time.

In a completely dishevelled state of despair, Garry prayed thanks that it was all over. He was at the bottom, of his rock bottom, and he'd survived. He knew that much already. Before he was allowed to rest, they rolled his wheelchair in front of a panel of important looking doctors.

"What happened, Garry?"

Garry, who was still fairly manic, seized his chance to get it all out, and he told them about Ray's death and his fairly rapid downward spiral of alcohol abuse before he veered off wondering if he had a cancer of sorts or fatal insomnia in relation to his lack of sleep. The doctors politely listened to his lengthy manic rant before they were straight with him.

"Tonight's episode was the cry for help of a sick man, Garry. You have been lucky to survive, and you will have to come to terms with what you have done to yourself and your family. For your personal safety, we advise that you are sectioned under the Mental Health Act. We will arrange for you to have a sedative so you can get some rest."

Garry can't remember how he got to the loony bin but the effects of the Librium that they injected him were a God-send for a man whose mind had become a runaway train. The drug instantly stopped the maddening noise that had consumed and tormented him. The refuge of a mental health care facility in Salford was exactly what Garry needed. He wasn't locked in his room. He could move around the facility as he pleased. Pretty much everyone in the place passed his 'decent fella' test and Garry was surprisingly at ease among his new friends.

When someone gets a taste of the suffering that comes with depression and mental fatigue, it can open them up to a completely different level of understanding. This was indeed the case with Garry and his light-hearted view of the world began to resurface quickly as his newly enhanced understanding started to kick in.

Garry's dry humour and unassuming way made him very popular very quickly with his fellow patients. As you would imagine, there were a few characters in the place.

Like a scene from *The Green Mile*, the first time Gaz went in the TV room there was a giant black guy sat there with his top off. The six foot six man mountain turns to Gaz, looks him up and down and in the campest voice imaginable tells him, "Relax, you aren't quite my type, cock."

"Thank fuck for that," said Gaz as he shook his new friend's hand and pulled up a chair. The two of them clicked and spent a couple of hours sharing stories.

Another time, an excited kind of chap burst into the communal TV Lounge and looked like he wanted to make a speech. After a short evaluation Gaz said, "Go on then. What's up with you?"

The guy stared him right between the eyes and confessed, "I've just had eight wanks."

"I think I might need to try your medication, mate," Gaz sharply replied.

He spent a month there. He didn't seem to have major withdrawals from alcohol but he agreed with his missus that he couldn't go back to that way of living. He was embarrassed and gutted that he'd put his family through this, but like a lot of people that slip into alcohol-related depression, he didn't plan it. It just crept up on him.

Garry's brothers visited a couple of times a week and his fantastic wife visited him every single day. Garry owed his life to his daughter who followed him on that crazy night and he will be forever grateful to her, for looking out for him through the lowest point of his life so far.

The NHS and the good folk in that institution also helped save Garry's life and he walked out of that place a humbled grateful man.

The Piccadilly Rats was the brainchild of Garry and Ray and it was their chemistry and genius for self-promotion that took them to national fame but it all started with the two of them performing on Market Street as a duo.

The talents of Heath (monkey) and Buster Rabcat (rat) form the backbone of the band's sound but more remarkable has been their incredible journey that led them to The Rats.

The wider band has taken in many varied characters including the many faces of Dave the Rave (left), Tommy Trouble (with policeman's helmet) and Alan Jones (right). What they might lack in musical ability they made up for in dedication to the cause.

The Rats on their travels - opposite page (top) Kendal Calling; (middle) Park Life; (bottom) that there London; (this page) the Manchester Irish Festival and (below) the Printworks in Town.

One of the best publicity stunts pulled by Ray Boddington was suing the band on ITV's Judge Rinder Show *(above)* for lost earnings following Tommy Trouble's mankini malfunction. Sadly Ray's passing *(below)* left a huge void in the lives of the remaining band members.

HEATH DEAN'S TALE

1: THE LIFE OF NOT BRIAN

Soundtrack: The Beatles - *Love Me Do*

I met up with Heath Dean; the posh Rat, the humble Rat, but also the multi-talented musician Rat, in a dark and dingy café in Moston. I'm in attendance to start absorbing his life story. Heath is turned out immaculately. He's dressed in nicely tight trousers that are coloured somewhere between pink and purple. He's sporting a lemon yellow shirt under a Lyle and Scott-style golf jumper and a blue sports jacket. He has a full head of hair, that is immaculately cropped. He looks like a fresh-faced kind of guy who is successful and has always been successful.

Just to contextualise his creation, Heath was born on 14th January 1966 - five months before Eric Cantona joined us and seven months before England won the World Cup. Heath was born Brian to his mother, Anne, who was a Catholic Irish scouser, she was just thirteen years old. Because she was Catholic abortion was not an option, instead Brian was given the gift of life by her and put up for adoption immediately. A family from Manchester took him in in July 1966 and he became Heath Christian Dean.

Heath's new folks lived a decent life in the leafy Cheadle district of Manchester, but they were uprooted when his adopted father's work as a photo lithographer dried up and they had to move to Norwich.

Heath's earliest memories of moving south aren't that great as his Mancunian accent was fuel to those most cruel of beings known as Children. Somehow, they'd also caught wind that he had been adopted and didn't have "real" parents so the carrot-crunching little fuckers set about making his life hell.

Primary school was a debilitating experience which created an altered state of reality in his own mind. These viciously callous kids told him that many times that his parents didn't want him that eventually he took on this lack of self-worth as reality. At home, his mother was kind and giving. His father was less affectionate and more considered.

Heath passed the 11 plus very easily which seemed to make his folks happy. If he'd have thought it through, he wouldn't have fuckin' bothered because it meant that rather than go to a new High School close to home he shared a daily twenty-mile coach ride to the grammar school with exactly the same wankers who had tormented him at primary school. The long journey to school gave them the opportunity to torment him further, only this time they had a bigger window to add extras like relieving him of his dinner money.

Life wasn't fun.

Heath's coping strategy was to shoplift his way into a position where he could bribe the bullies into better behaviour. He found a rogue shopkeeper that would accept any stolen goods that he could provide at heavily-discounted prices. It was a good steady income but a completely flawed anti-bullying scheme. The twats just demanded and expected more and more of a cut of the cash. Heath was robbing the neighbourhood blind just to pay the fat cats. He made a decent criminal though and never came close to being caught.

School was lonely but, outside of that, Heath had a friend who lived close by that he would doss around with. He'll never forget the day that the boy produced a large bottle of cider from his school bag that he'd unexpectedly procured from somewhere or other. The alcohol hit was instant and, unexpectedly, all of Heath's many insecurities, worries and fears immediately left him. He was temporarily free from all the shite thoughts that consistently tormented him, he knew right there and then that he would have an ongoing need to replicate this kind of escapism technique. He also identified that the escape process would be a secret anti-social crusade. He'd do his drinking alone.

From then on, most of the funds from his shoplifting business were redirected into getting twatted. At home his parents either didn't notice or chose not to show that they had noticed that he kept coming home wrecked. It was so easy to be a teenage wreck-head in the seventies as parents often sent their children to the Off License to buy them cigs 'n' booze. So Heath started wagging school and getting annihilated in the park. He would drink to oblivion, cider or vodka mainly. He'd drink until he blacked out and sleep off the effects until it was the equivalent of school home-time when he'd bumble on home like everything was normal. His parents must have noticed but they never said anything and therefore he never faced any consequences or punishment for his actions.

Two solid years of these intermittent one-man self-hurt park parties followed. Heath was clever enough to wag it just often enough not to trigger any investigations around this from the school authorities and he was also brilliant at keeping the details of his alcohol binge habits to himself. He was a one-man self-hurt team. A Soul Trader.

Tragically for Heath, a sexual predator had noted his exclusion from school and from any sort of friendship group. Heath jokes that other people got Jimmy Savile and "I just got a sad bastard in a Mini". He was groomed in the traditional paedophiliac way; compliments, affection and a "Nobody will ever know" verbal contract – "This is our little secret".

Heath doesn't tell me what the bastard did to him but I can see that it is still raw. He tells me with great passion that if a child ever tells a parent that they have been abused, then those parents are duty fuckin' bound to act and sort the bastard out. Heath's parents chose not to believe his story and that was an act of betrayal from which he their relationship never recovered.

Unsurprisingly, Heath failed all but one of his O-Levels and, to rub salt in the wounds of his surprisingly astonished parents, his one success was a B+ in English. This was achieved the year before. He passed that exam aged fourteen. It was a candle in the 'look what I could have done' cake. Truth was, besides the alcoholism and the perverted attention that destroyed him, when it came to schoolwork Heath found the whole curriculum pointless and tedious. He states that if he had attained or was given some idea about how different subjects related to different job roles then he might have had a completely different attitude to it all. Later in life he acknowledged the importance of mathematics in his chosen field of Electronic Engineering but, aged fifteen and a half, he didn't give a fuck about any of it. It was all bollocks and he was thrilled to be leaving the shit school experience behind.

After the traditional period of doing fuck all in the first few months of leaving school, Heath started to hang around with a local lad he knew from the area. His mate had a chick who was older than them. She was everything a teenage boy wanted: older, more experienced, fit as fuck and she had a car. For some reason, Heath's pal kept inviting him along.

At school Heath had developed a phobia of people. He would walk into a room full of people and feel completely isolated and alone but, strangely, talking to and engaging the hot chick came much more naturally. Unbeknown to his oppo, Heath had obviously fallen head over heels for the fit girl. His mate didn't register this as Heath was never seen as a threat to anybody.

His pal wanted to join the RAF so the three of them set off to Norwich Town Centre in the lady's hot wheels. Heath's inner voice was telling him, "Right we can pack off Numb Nuts to the RAF and I am in like Errol Flynn". Heath's Norfolk Trouser Snake was coiled and ready to strike. Unfortunately, reality didn't play out even close to his best fit vision. His friend went in and failed the test while Heath exchanged more pleasant small talk with his dream girl. A surprising twist of fate then ensued.

The Flight Sergeant, who had just rejected Heath's enthusiastic mate at the recruitment event, came out to the car with his disappointed comrade and revealed that Heath had been dobbed in as being a Grammar School Bod. "Your mate says that you would easily pass the test as you're a bit of an electronics boffin. Why don't you give it a whirl?"

Without any due consideration Heath saw this as an opportunity to impress the girl and, in just ten life changing minutes, he'd passed the aptitude test and had signed up for a nine-year stint as a serviceman starting off as a trainee Avionics Electrician. Any chance that he had of shagging the beautiful girl disappeared like a turd up a U-Bend.

When Heath got home he reflected on the day's events:

"How the fuck did that just happen?"

"Why am I such a people-pleaser?"

He was in a very temporary state of despair regarding the girl, but he did have an interest in electronics and an aching ambition to get the fuck out of 'Worzelville'.

Norfolk was shit.

His life there had been shit.

His subconscious possibly recognised this would explain why he chose to sign a nine-year service contract over the six-year option.

An alternative view on that was maybe he just didn't know what the fuck he was doing. Who does at sixteen?

2: FRESH AIR MAN

Soundtrack: Tom Petty – *Learning To Fly*

The aftermath of Heath's unexpected militarisation meant that he finally had something to get excited about. A path laid out in front of him that was just about him rather than something that his folks had chosen. He felt that he had to give this a genuine go and he took the decision to cut down on his binge-drinking and on the smoking habit that he'd also added to his addiction collection. He recognised that to get through the basic training he would have to kerb the one-man self-hurt club for the time-being or at least streamline it so that he could progress.

He'd finally stumbled across something that might just be a way to prove to himself and his parents that he had his own mind and that he could be someone so he took the decision to hurt himself less.

I asked Heath if it was this an easy decision. "No, not at all – it killed me not to escape into drink, really killed me."

That's a serious statement said by a middle-aged man about how he felt thirty-seven years ago and one that Heath delivers in a tone that makes me think that he almost still regrets that he had to temporarily break his cycle of self-hurt. That's a real insight into the mind of an addict and an addict's everlasting need to never give themselves a break. An addict's life is a relentless regime of self-torture, non-forgiveness and fortitude.

Opened in 1940, RAF Swinderby in Lincolnshire was so much more appealing to Heath than HMP Norfolk. Heath's first impressions of the County of Lincolnshire were positive – it felt slightly less backward. They had a bigger cathedral than Norwich, people dressed better and it just felt like children and carrots would be safer if they were left unattended in the county of Lincs.

Of course, being on MOD Land, Heath's view of the local community was muddled as most of the people on the base were misfits from all over the UK trying to escape their own shite existences in their own specifically shite towns. Outside the gates, who knows what went on? Lincolnshire has long been the Veg

Basket of England. Farming and 80's animal porn were probably just as rife there as they were in Norfolk but inside the gates of the base Heath felt renewed. This shit was different.

For a start, his new classmates were misfits just like him, which was brilliant. Everyone was a little bit apprehensive and a little bit more open than the average twat on the school bus. For the first time in his life, nobody had a preconceived view of him. He wasn't introduced as the boy that his family didn't want.

Heath liked the routine of it all. It was like prison. You were told when to wake up, when to shower, when to eat, when to exercise, when to eat more, when to sit in a classroom, when to clean your boots, when to march, when to eat more and finally when to sleep. The Military Training itinerary was a perfect fit for a young functional addict; just enough ritual to cling to and not enough free time to be focus on the self-hurt side of things.

Heath was mildly amused by the discipline side of things. His Flight Sergeant consistently got his name the wrong way round. He had Heath Dean down as Dean Heath - so every time he ranted in his face, he would scream his Christian name at him and this personalised and lightened situations that were designed to break down and intimidate a young man. It was child's play to Heath and he cruised through Basic Training. His Parents attended his Basic Graduation and Passing-Out Parade. Like it or not, he'd done something to please them. This was a best fit for all parties.

Looking back, he celebrates the joy of that experience. Nobody had any other agenda apart from simply getting by. He had actually been in a group where the goal was to have fun and support each other without judgment. It's a shame that war can sometimes get in the way of people having a good time in the services. Luckily for Heath, he'd just missed The Falklands Conflict. Northern Ireland and The Cold War were on, but Heath was unconcerned – after a successful seven weeks basic training, he was ready to get on with learning about Avionic Electronic Engineering.

Heath carried a pre-knowledge on the subject as he had a genuine interest in the field prior to joining up so he'd been down the library and also stolen a couple of hardbacks from shops in Norfolk on the subject of Electronics.

His pragmatism was instantly rewarded as his new classroom peer group revered his knowledge base. Being a valued member of a team was a massive shift from his usual bottom-feeding place in the hierarchy and Heath temporarily broke from his usual insular existence. He experienced genuine friendship and camaraderie. It's a time he holds dear. Heath completed his twenty-four-week trade course and passed out as an Avionics Mechanic.

He carried one friend over from Basic Training to his Trade Training experience. He was a Scotsman and for the record we'll call him "Jock". When the pair were granted their first period of leave together, Heath chose to dodge a return to Worzelville and travelled up to Glasgow. He received a warm welcome from Jock's family although he didn't understand a fuckin' word of what they were saying. Jock was married to an English rose, who we will call "Rose". Heath had a much better understanding of Rose's dialect and, unsurprisingly, he fell right in love with her.

They talked for hours. He felt relaxed in her company and Jock felt completely relaxed to have her in Heath's company. This 'no threat' gift is a double-edged sword. It always gets him access to his associate's partners and he always falls head over heels for the girl. Over time this can work its way out in many different ways but, in most cases, Heath eventually ends up getting a bite of the cherry or at least a nibble. This kind of bad behaviour (manipulation, deceit and total betrayal of trust) leads to an instant high followed by crashing, overwhelming feelings of guilt and self-hate, which is an absolutely perfect cycle of self-destruction for an addict. It creates lots of shit to help drive a man to self-harm.

Perfect.

Unnoticed, Heath managed to skilfully plant a seed in the Rose Garden despite being surrounded by a room full of kind but potential very abrasive thistles. That's a rascal's skill set right there.

Back on Base, Heath filled out his draft forms to request his new air station. He wasn't enthused by fighter jets. He had already established that a career on the Military Transport side of the operation was safer – more suited to his skill set and, if he's honest, it was also the lazier option; there was less to learn and more opportunity to just get by unnoticed, to almost appear to have a civilian-style role and lifestyle. He was drafted to Brize Norton, which is the big 'un near Oxford. This place sent airmen all over the globe.

His first draft job role was fixing headsets and other low level bits of kit. Heath was really interested in fixing stuff and took it upon himself to keep studying off his own back in the evenings, which earned him a reputation as a newbie that really did have something about him.

He'd been teaching himself easy-fix troubleshooting for the kit he was maintaining. So he became an expert in recognising the exact faults that always cropped up. It was common sense to Heath but to the untrained eye, he looked like a miracle fixer of things and, all of a sudden, he had the respect of his whole division.

Senior ranks worked the night shifts and got things a lot easier because they only got called out in the night if a flight crew discovered a fault that could potentially delay or cancel a night flight. They weren't required to maintain stuff, just fix things so as the stand out 'Fix It Man' Heath got the call to step up. He didn't need asking twice, as he immediately recognised what a cushty number this was. There was one job a night if he was unlucky and nobody could begrudged him the role because he had proved himself to be the best fixer in the business and nobody else wanted the nights.

Heath enjoyed this sheltered lazy life very much. He spent his days listening to music and developing himself through the medium of book study. Mainly he'd learn more about electronics but he also self-taught himself the guitar. He loved, above all things, The Beatles.

Things were chilled for the majority of his time in Oxfordshire before his friend, Jock, got unexpectedly drafted back alongside him at Brize. Jock had been doing what most young service men do at his tender age – pissing up and shagging around – and his relationship subsequently imploded leaving Rose rather conveniently unattended to but before Heath had time to cherry pick the situation, he got drafted to Belize and took a head full of Rose infatuation with him all the way to Central America.

3: RICH IN PARADISE

Soundtrack: FPI Project – *Rich In Paradise*

The Army Dude experience in Belize was a very different experience to one enjoyed by Heath on his arrival in Central America. The RAF shuttled Army Lads (Pongos) to and from the jungle for hard, hot, insect-ridden 'Hell and Back' training experiences. Heath skilfully fixed a few headsets by day and lapped up the sea, sand and sounds down at the beach bars of San Pedro on the Caribbean. He also discovered rum which he abused in private.

Down at the beach Heath struck up a relationship with a couple. The chick was older so there was no cherry-picking action risk. They were musicians and Heath was impressed by the tight fresh sounds of their band. Funnily enough, they had an alcoholic drummer who was reliably unreliable. They had a drum machine in place for the days the he went missing. So from this point on Heath started stepping in and tapping away in time with the Drum Machine until, eventually, he didn't need it any more.

The band leaders were more than impressed when Heath started to step in on both bass and lead guitar whenever the opportunity arose. In no time at all, he was the band lynch-pin and that's when a life-changing offer came his way. Unbelievably, the lady in the couple owned the country's largest fleet of aircraft. She suggested that her company buy Heath out of the RAF and give him the job of managing the maintenance of the electronics on-board her fleet of aeroplanes and, more importantly, he would get to join the band full time.

Heath agreed and shook hands on the deal. They paid his flights home, financed his buy-out from the RAF and his flight back. This was a very exciting opportunity and Heath was that overwhelmed that he had his first ever panic attack on the flight back over. This was soon forgotten as life was suddenly epic.

His new workload was messing about with planes on the same base with all the same flight crew as before, so even though he was back as a civilian contractor, he maintained all the perks of being in the RAF and was treated like he was still part of the Mob and still received invites to all the Jolly Boy Socials.

Everything had fallen into place and it couldn't have happened to a nicer man, not that Heath would ever recognise that.

Heath got the opportunity to trust in local engineers to do the maintenance work. It was his role to check the work and sign it off. He just signed it off and drank the guilt away down the beach, then in private at home.

It was at this point that he decided that he'd like some focus and a more structured life. A life that could possibly give him shit to maybe encourage him to start acting more responsibly. By letter and by phone Heath contacted the still supposedly single mother Rose, who carried a child into her break-up with Jock. At one point Heath had convinced her to consider bringing her now two-year-old daughter over to Belize to start a new life with him. Surprisingly she agreed.

That very same night, rather inconveniently, Heath fell in love with a local girl by the name of Jacqueline. Jackie was down at the bar with friends. As soon as he looked into her huge, honest brown eyes, he could see the purity of her soul. They came together easily and instantly the two of them became inseparable. She accepted him as he was and for the first time he experienced inconceivable reality of unconditional love. The impending English Rose Importation Project became a lazy afterthought.

For the next four to five months, Heath felt like the King of San Pedro. He was living a high life. He was welcomed into Jackie's family and wider friendship group and the local community. Life had become a never-ending celebration.

Tragically, Heath didn't have the skill set to be able to accept this or maybe any level of consistent loving happiness at a time when he really did have it all. On top of the dream job in the dream location, he now had a caring, intelligent, beautiful, funny, fiery, shit-hot Latin life partner. Unquestionably, he was in the midst of a once in a lifetime love job. He'd met a lady that genuinely fuckin' loved and liked him. Unfortunately for everyone involved, Heath's hidden shopping list didn't have 'happy ever after' on it. His shopping lists always need to include pain, suffering and driving away all risks to not achieving these self-hurt goals. So, bit by bit, his demons got to work and he started to resent Jackie's loving relationships with her family. Heath's low level demonic thought processes started to despise the kindest mother in law imaginable and the most fuckin' perfect father in law of all time. He even managed to find fault and alienate himself from Jackie's siblings who had done everything possible to make him feel welcome.

Heath became jealous of Jackie's relationships with every single one of them and he started slowly pushing them all away. He started picking fault in everything and gradually chipping away at the best relationship of his life so far. He was escaping more and more into alcohol. Eventually, his angel vanished ten regretful steps behind her folks as, back on point, Heath struggled to see her leave through the haze of his own alcohol-fuelled self-pity.

Up until the beginning of the end of the relationship and across his military service in general, Heath had kept his drinking at a controlled and generally reasonable level but now he had every reason to really start punishing his ridiculously pathetic self.

Now he had more than enough funds to do so as he was now earning $3000 a month which was big bucks back in the 80's. From this point on drugs became his new friends and he started hoovering up large amounts of super-deluxe standard cocaine. This top notch powder from Brazil was the perfect mood lifter and Heath left no nostril closed as his addiction catalogue and his nostrils quickly started to expand. The locals had good weed too. Consuming plenty of this really helped to take the edge off his multi binges.

In no time at all Heath went from being the popular 'nice guy' King of San Pedro to becoming a reclusive toxic bum. He was back where the fuck up in him wanted to be. The place an addict calls home.

His toxic tastes were getting more and more expensive but his income just kept increasing in line with or even in front of his spend. His self-esteem may have been shot but his apparent business acumen was intact, at least from the outside looking in.

Unfortunately for Heath and the mother figure and part-owner of the airline that had treated him so well, her whole aeronautical operation started to quickly fall to pieces. Luckily for Heath, it wasn't his flawed business practice that was the root cause. His conscience was hardly clear but the outcome was positive for him in more ways than one.

Government regulations changed like the wind on the Caribbean coast and this combined with a traditional smattering of Central American bribery and corruption brought her company's Belize airspace franchise to a prompt and non-negotiable end. She sold up rapidly.

Heath struck gold because there was no record of his flakily managed maintenance practice. On paper it looked like his time in Belize was a job very well done and his CV actually looked amazing. He had somehow successfully managed the maintenance contract of a country's whole fleet of aircraft without incident over a two-year period. He could name his price to the new operators of the franchise and he did. He agreed to carry on but this time as a stand-alone business offering quarterly avionic electronics MOTs to a whole new fleet of aircraft. He charged them $500 a pop and the pops kept popping.

From the inside looking out, Heath was now manipulating as much money as he could from these companies in return for providing a chocolate fireguard of a maintenance service. He was completely taking the piss out of the system by literally charging $500 just for his signature. Heath may have been cutting safety corners but when it came to making business decisions he had ingeniously made his services 100% indispensable. Before the new operator came in, he stashed all the maintenance manuals and all the spare fix-it bits for all the aircraft safely away so it would be a very big ask for any external agency to come in and pick up the contract. He had the keys to the safe. He hired the cheapest local tradesmen to do the maintenance and if they said an MOT was good then he never checked over a single job. Now and then the maintenance crews would call the beach bar for advice on troubleshooting obvious faults that needing attention and, on the odd occasion, Heath would have to attend. He recalls having to do so one night after playing a set with the band on three grams of the Brazilian Marching Powder. He can't remember if he resolved the issue.

His income for booze, drugs and general pain relief was secure but, by carrying on in the same vein and not really fulfilling his work obligations to any sort of standard, he was bringing layers and layers of guilt and paranoia to his already suffocating seedy situation. Heath's cocaine consumption increased in line with his sky-rocketing income stream. His paranoia also hit new heights.

Being a white, rich, business-owning musician in 80s Belize was a very privileged position to be in and even though Heath tortured himself on a daily basis regarding his inability to maintain his relationship with Jackie, it didn't stop him getting friendly with more world-class local talent. Cocaine is a confidence boosting drug so Heath had no problems hooking chicks whilst he was off his tits. He tended to implode and melt down later on in the middle of the night when the high started becoming a low. During one such ill-fated situation, he informed his current party girl that she'd have to leave, "I'm sorry everything has gone wrong here. Please leave as I've got to go." And as simple as that, Heath's time in San Pedro was done.

Addicts often relocate once they feel that they have exhausted all their positive connections in one place or just because they have become too known and need some solitude. For Heath on this occasion, it was a case of both of those scenarios were under the surface drivers but, in the main, his decision was mainly driven by good old traditional cocaine-encrusted paranoia. He was losing his shit.

Heath relocated to the capital, Belize City. The next morning as soon as he rationalised the situation, he acted quickly and contacted the airline authorities to inform them that to improve the quality of his maintenance service his company had relocated to Belize City where the avionic maintenance facilities were better suited to guaranteeing a more robust safety focused service. So he simply instructed all the airlines to send their aircraft to Belize City for their inspections. At this point in his career, he had become one hell of a cheeky, crafty, paranoid fucker. He was just about getting away with it. In Belize cocaine became crack cocaine and Heath started paying up to $500 for world class rocks. He started doing escapism on a grand scale.

The new routine in Belize City was Rock 'n' Roll' - two rocks and bottle of rum, sleep it off, then go and sign off an aircraft. The new routine didn't last very long at all as his disfunctionality and crack consumption hit gross new heights very quickly. He scored another huge $500 dollar rock and a chick to go with it. After failing to sexualise the situation Heath threw another paranoid wobbler and told the girl that he had to get out of Belize. He scraped together his passport and the $5,000 in cash that he'd hidden in various plant pots around his flat and then he jumped in his clapped out 1973 pale yellow, three cylinder Chevrolet and, rather ambitiously, set out on an insanely long drive towards America which was two thousand, three hundred and sixty five miles just to the border.

The shit Chevy had other ideas and just over the Mexican border it completely expired. As he had no baggage and a pocket full of dollars, this didn't stop him in his tracks for long and he made his way to the local bus terminal and jumped the first bus heading north.

Unfortunately for Heath, at the first service station stop at Vera Cruz, three Amigos took the opportunity to jump the fuckin' stupid white tourist with $5000 in his pocket and, at knife-point he reluctantly handed over his fortune. He stood outside the service station and watched his bus disappear along with his ticket into America. His shit had turned upside down.

Optionless, he set out hitch-hiking north on the baked gravel covered main road to Mexico City. He saw few cars on his initial four-and-a-half-day trek. A combination of a lack of any available life-sustaining liquid such as water and a void of any real hope of meaningful human contact caused Heath to do something very out of character. For the first time ever he made contact with the divine and sent up a prayer that went something like, "Please God, don't let me die here." God's reaction was instantaneous and generous. As the first car on the road in over an hour raced past Heath's desperate hitch-hiker's thumb, it came to a gradual divine halt in the distance. Heath's eyes struggled to focus on the mirage of the vehicle in the afternoon haze. The vehicle and its driver were sat stationary, clearly mulling over whether to investigate the hitch-hiker's situation or not. Heath reaffirmed his heavenly request for help and the miracle happened. The car started slowly reversing backwards the wrong way down the motorway until the car was level with Heath's desperate situation. The driver's window slowly came down to reveal a beautiful Mexican girl, exactly the type of beautiful twenty-year-old Mexican girl who should never stop and offer a desperate stranger a lift. Unsurprisingly, Heath fell for her in an instant. God moves in mysterious ways and, in no time at all, Heath was back at the family ranch, desperate charming English Cherry Picking equipment at the ready.

4: UNCONDITIONAL MEXICAN KINDNESS

Soundtrack: Christian Nodal - *Adios Amor*

The welcome that Heath received back at the family condo in the middle of what we would call a Mexican Council Estate was ridiculously warm. Complete strangers provided water, washing facilities and a delicious traditional meal with cornbread. Sadly for Heath they didn't include their daughter in the rescue package. In broken English, the family established Heath's need to get to the USA and duly got an understanding that he was destitute.

Even though Heath was still in the midst of a shocking comedown, he had clearly managed to appear genuine and trustworthy. He has one of those faces that people just want to help. His face inspired the mother and father of the house to go down to the local village to share his hard luck story with their community. Unbelievably, they returned to the home with the local equivalent of a month's salary which they duly presented to the now truly astonished Englishman to fund his bus trip to the States. The family explained the terms of the donation. It was exactly that "a no strings attached" donation. This kindness really did knock a lonely, lost and desperate addict into a state of humbled overwhelmed wonderment. He could not fuckin' believe how kind these strangers had been to him. Heath was packed off and waved off by his new adoptive family. He'd been hit by an unexpected love bomb launched from the dusty depths of a Mexican ghetto. Twenty hours later the love bomb landed in the form of a bus at the U.S border. Heath stepped out into the blinding sunlight and took in the awe-inspiring view - the border crossing was set just in front of a bridge over the mighty Rio Grande.

Heath apologised to all the local vendors who had gathered at the border to sell their wares to all the rich travellers waiting to be processed into the US of A.

Unfortunately, he didn't have a solitary Peso to spend on water, tortilla crisps, sombreros, toy donkeys and various other tat so he just waited patiently in line and kept smiling and apologising for his poverty-stricken existence until it was his turn to go into the hut with the men with the red tape and the guns.

The guards were impressed by Heath's imperially impressive British passport and nodded with good intention as they perused his papers. Then they dropped the whoopsie bomb. Welcome to the United States of America that will just be $10 for your entry visa. The Mexican collection had been a ticket fund only situation. Heath didn't have a Mexican mole pot to piss in.

Seemingly unflustered, Heath delivered in his quintessential English tongue, "Oh, thank you. I don't seem to have any cash on me. I will just have to pop back into town and use the ATM. I'll be back very soon."

Back outside the hut Heath looked over to the vendors hopefully and innovatively and, because of his impeccable manners on the way in, it didn't take him that long on his way out to convince a female, middle-aged, sun-dried tacky bracelet vendor to hand over $10 for his own cheap gold tacky bracelet. Heath has a face people can't resist helping. His bond with the Mexican race intensified as he walked back in, paid up and walked over the hugely impressive bridge into the States.

Heath was still in a hugely compromising hole of a situation but, right there and then, he made a promise to himself that he would come back and repay the unbelievable kindness that had been shown to him in Mexico. That for me registers him as a good man... regardless of whether he would ever get the opportunity or the means to ever do so. His addictions have never taken his heart. Maybe his childhood and his coping strategies may have temporarily taken away his ability to love himself but he clearly has the ability to appreciate and love people in general. That said, he had become a complex individual. His infatuation demon at this point in his life always made things a bit layered for him so rather than just have an intention to eventually go back and repay the beautiful people that had come to his aid, he just had to set his mind on capturing the heart of the young maiden that had helped to rescue him back in Vera Cruz.

That pipe-dream would hopefully come later but, crossing the border into the US, he had layers and layers of reality to unravel before he could even consider a return to the Mexican lowlands.

5 – UNEXPECTED KINDNESS EVERYWHERE

Soundtrack: Razorlight – *America*

Heath had no cash, only the clothes that he stood up in and by now he was on about day five wearing the same undies but fortunately for him quite a few things were still stacked in his favour. Most importantly, in this still deeply divided country, he had white skin. He also had a posh accent and 18 months left on the travel visa that was connected to his British passport. His golden ticket though was the airline ID card that was still in his possession from Belize. This card gave him free travel to his place of work as long as there was space on the flight and as long as he passed the Reasonable Human Being visual evaluation and smell test by the staff at the check-in desk.

He had lots of airline contacts based in Miami but he had already implemented the addict's trick of starting a new life free from all the regret of the past one. He was adamant that he was leaving the airline industry and all those memory-filled associates behind and this left him with only one discernible contact in the whole of America.

Rose was a friend and fellow wreck-head from Belize. Rose was a middle-aged lady who was into her music. She spent her days in Belize partying hard and generally rocking out to the sound of Heath's rather smashing band. Rose was terminally ill with some form of cancer, so she'd come to the Caribbean to burn out rather than fade away. Rose was Bohemian and enjoyed the local Rum, weed and company that were all readily available on Heath's Belizean paradise patch.

Heath had a friendship connection with her that could have been lost on one boozy night back in Belize. A situation developed on an after-gig drinking and smoking session at Heath's place. After a brief moment of booze-tiddly contemplation, the pair discussed the possibility of a pants-off dance-off but they both agreed that it was far too much of a mission to go shopping for the contraception to make the transaction safe so they just carried on the chat, the weed and the music-focused small talk. The fact that they respected each other in this way cemented their friendship and made future contact and gigs at the bar completely unawkward.

It was fortunate for Heath that it panned out that way because it meant that he still had one person on the continent that just might help him. To get to her he needed to get to the nearest town to do some research because the only information that he had was her name and her City. The last bit of information that Heath remembered about Rose was that her illness had progressed and she had moved back to her hometown in Idaho. It was a long shot but it was all that he had. Ringing Mum and Dad for help just wasn't an option that he wanted to explore.

Heath was bright and innovative so he used his British accent and his true story about being relieved of all his currency at knife point by a trio of Mexican Bandits to his advantage. He shared his story with anyone that would listen and had little trouble finding his way onto a shuttle bus where he used his Airline Privilege Card to catch a ride to Valley International Airport, a thirty-five minute drive from Brownsville.

Here he blagged his way onto a flight to Houston Texas International Airport which was his gateway to the information that he needed.

On arrival Heath spent two days in the Airport Terminal 'Tom Hanks Style'. He shared his story and people were kind. It was a case of needs must as Heath hadn't really had any food since leaving Mexico so he kept an eye on the eateries that were servicing families waiting for people on incoming flights. He openly approached diners that seemed to have left parts of their meals unattended on their plates. He'd politely ask if he could finish their remaining food and, if they didn't run off, he'd then share his hard luck story and absorb the sympathy that these tactics seemed to generate. These desperate acts soon earned him a full belly and eventually a kind-hearted cowboy lined his palm with four green paper portraits of Alexander Hamilton - out of nothing he'd conjured from kindness forty bucks. Yanks were indisputably cool.

With a pocket full of collateral leverage, he decided it was time to try his luck in the departure terminal and see if he could blag his way on a flight to Idaho or somewhere half way there. At the check-in desk, he was informed that he no longer met the "Reasonable Human Being Test" Criteria and, unfortunately, he wouldn't be able to travel north to carry out any fictional maintenance on any imaginary aircrafts. Clearly, he was looking and smelling a bit dishevelled. He took this on the chin and didn't make a fuss. His manners and reasonableness gained him access to the free shuttle bus into town and kept him in possession of his Airline Privilege Card.

For the first time in a long time, he was in a

narcotic and alcohol free state. Survival tasks had kept his mind focused on exactly that and his journey into town was a positive one. On arrival in Houston, he noticed a shop buying and selling mobile phones. He didn't have a cell phone but minding its own business on the belt of his work pants was the ultimate eighties telecommunications gadget he was still in possession of; his Airline Issue Pager. He tried his luck in the kiosk and received an unexpected bonus of four more Alexander Hamiltons - somehow, he'd accumulated $80 dollars. That was equivalent to a decent weekly wage at the bottom of the American food chain.

Heath's next stop was Houston Central Public Library. This place is a wonderful treasure trove of free information; there were books on everything from what to do from a legal perspective when stranded in Houston, how to get a Green Card and geeky electronic manuals. Heath spent the whole day absorbing it all. Most importantly though, Heath got to use the internet for the first time in his life. At the push of a few buttons, he was amazed to find the contact details for three Rose Sanchezs in Idaho. He called the first one and was amazed to hear his friend's voice on the line. She listened to Heath's sob story like a mother would and Rose offered to pay for his hotel for the night and a flight to Idaho in the morning. Bohemian Rose explained that she needed an excuse to ask the non-rent paying inhabitant of her spare room to leave. Heath was doing her a favour. Hanging up the phone, Heath felt blessed. Rose had given him the most extraordinary gift.

At the hotel, guests were encouraged to enjoy free live music entertainment and a four pint pitcher of beer for as little as 75 cents and he gladly took the cut price opportunity to damage himself.

Luckily, he woke in time to make the flight and had suitably recovered by the time Rose's neighbour and part-time lover picked him up in Idaho. Snow and ice were all around but Rose's welcome was warm and generous. Her health was clearly deteriorating but her spirit still shone as brightly as her smile. Outwardly and genuinely, Heath was overjoyed to receive Rose's red carpeted welcome but inside Heath was terrified that she might alert the Belize Crew to his whereabouts. It wouldn't stop him fretting about it but his gut told him Rose was cool. She was running too. Their connection was kindred.

Bohemian Rose was friends with all the best musicians in town and all her connections led to the non-stop jam that was The Blue Bouquet. Playing bass guitar in America can be mind-numbing because every cowboy tune has the same set up. The ability to maintain a bottom-end bass line in a steady beat was the only challenge in Ole Time Country Bass-land. The chromatic run to the next chord was as fancy as it ever got. This tedium meant that country bands often struggled to retain the services of a regular bassist.

To encourage bass player engagement, The Blue Bouquet had a free beer policy for bands in jam and, just like in Belize, the opportunity to play all day was always available. No brainer. Step forward, Heath.

Life passed by coolly and quickly at The Blue Bouquet and Heath slotted in because everyone's focus was on escapism. The music and the beer and the great weed all helped to turn his life into an ongoing funky haze. Rose knew everyone that was someone on the local music scene and she put out a "musician in need" request to equip Heath with a bass guitar. A few phone calls later and a top of the range Fender P Bass came to him on loan from another bassist who was sick of strumming along to the same ole same ole. The same ole, same ole was exactly what Heath needed and it brought structure to his day and actually stopped him from having too much time to think. His drinking was semi-regulated by this focus and the weed also helped to keep his self-abuse under control.

The whole scene was free and easy and non-judgmental but, as a posh Brit, Heath got more attention than he would normally choose to receive. After a few beers, Americans all thought he'd walked straight off the set of Fawlty Towers or Monty Python. As the beer was free for musicians in The Blue Bouquet, Heath chose to spend his days on the bass rather than spend his time explaining that he wasn't off the telly in exchange for beer. Time whizzed by on the bass in the Blue Bouquet and the clock on his visa kept ticking down.

Away from the club Rose owned and maintained a decent patch of land and a country smallholding. Her health situation meant that she relied on friends to look after the maintenance and upkeep of the property. Money wasn't free-flowing so Heath was encouraged to take up some part-time work with Rose's main love interest who conveniently lived next door. This gentleman was devoted to Rose and did most of the tasks around the place but like most of Rose's associates he had 'shit going on' so Heath was employed on a cash-in-hand basis to drive the handyman to jobs and, more importantly, to drive him back from jobs when he was really pissed. The man was a skilled driveway/paving layer and he took great care and pride in his work but, by lunchtime every day, he was rotten drunk and Heath would decide when it was time to break off and go back to the ranch for his boss to sleep it off. As ever, Heath had found easy work and he was happy to do it for Rose. Nobody really knew how Rose came to own her estate but she was very resourceful when it came to opening enough income streams to sustain her matriarchal prominence for the communal good of the group.

Rose got Heath sporadic paid bass guitar work in bands and he was also encouraged to make donations to the local blood bank. At $20 a visit, he could earn up to $60 in a week. Rose also knew her way around the food banks and was skilled in cutting through the red tape required to implement a steady supply of tinned goods coming into the dwelling. As Rose's health deteriorated, Heath was tasked and armed with the dodgy paperwork to con the local authorities into not stopping this happening in Rose's absence. Heath was happy to contribute and took pride in helping to ensure Rose stayed afloat and fucked the system at the same time.

6:DIFFERENT GRAVY

Soundtrack: Garcia, Crosby, Slick & Kantner - *Mountain Song*

Before Heath came to stay, Rose had been forced to evict a less than savoury group of characters to make way for him. These hangers-on had serious narcotic habits and were becoming troublesome, they went peacefully but drifted back intermittently. Heath came to know them but formed an instant mistrust for them as his gut feeling was that they only ever came to take advantage of Rose's kindness. This didn't stop Heath smoking their weed or becoming interested in their tales of drug-fuelled adventures in the Rocky Mountain Range but he didn't let his distaste for these people stand in the way of getting fucked up with them.

The tales of the mountains became reality when Heath accepted a place in their vehicle for a weekend trip to the middle of nowhere. He'd signed up for a once in a lifetime (twice actually) unforgettable drug tourism experience. The journey up to the snowy mountains alone was unbelievable and Heath didn't overlook this. He had already developed a love of America and its people. His eyes were wide open.

The snow fell heavily but the mood among the party group was appreciative and playful. They smoked a little meth through a modified broken bulb in the car which helped lift the spirits of the group before they stepped out into the winter wonderland scene that was Idaho. The drugs took away the cold and most of the mistrust that Heath felt for the bandits in his company. The magic of the chemistry put everyone at ease and the majesty of the landscape waiting outside for them was awe-inspiring.

Out in the snow, Heath eagerly shared the group's poison – painfully snorting crystal meth powder like he was eating his last meal through his nose. He liked the pain of the transaction as it intensely burned his nose and throat. It was the least that he deserved. The hit took slightly longer than crack cocaine to hit but it was the opposite of Heath's usual drug bag shopping list. This wasn't self-hurt, pain relief and obliteration.

He felt a oneness and, not just with the group, but

with everything in the universe. He felt a connection and a love for others that was completely unexpected. Everyone felt the same and, as one, the group stripped down and waded into the geothermal hot springs that overlooked the most beautiful winter vista imaginable. It was the equivalent to the Garden of Eden with the crystal meth standing in for the forbidden fruit. It was a truly incredible experience and the drug squad came loaded with enough powder to keep topping up all weekend long - they maintained a 72-hour high. The thrill of the buzz in the hot springs was matched by the breathtaking sensation of the cold when they came up for air. The star-spangled sky was phenomenal and they chatted a whole lotta shit. Even though these lost souls weren't Heath's kind of people, they certainly had facilitated an unforgettable meth-powered mountain safari.

Heath has been categorical in not wanting to glamorise any of his drug career in this book. He's not proud of any of it but this happened and it happened over a short period of time. This group of sinister addicts pulled out all the stops to get their evil claws into Heath. Rose warned him about the powder and the danger of it but Heath wanted to try it and he played them. His come down wasn't harsh - he felt fairly magnificent on the Monday after the trip and it took the rest of the working week for him to want another go at it..

God only knows what crimes the meth squad committed in the five days leading up to their next mountain trip but, whatever they did must have been successful because Heath accepted their invitation to repeat the experience and once again they were fully equipped to get nutted all weekend long.

Trip two was just as spectacular. The clarity of the buzz was sensational. The beauty of the surroundings, nature and the opulent bohemian unity on offer buried the dark vibe that lurked in the underbelly of the group. These guys weren't just party people – they were hard-edged ruthless business people in the drugs business. Rose had explained that they were the kind of people who had introduced their own daughters to the lifestyle to share the financial burden of financing their activities. They were soul-sellers of the worst kind. They had no moral compass to speak of. On these two safaris, Heath wasn't asked for any money but it was clearly a business strategy to bring him on-board. They wanted his soul for future gain.

Unfortunately for the meth squad, two trips to the crystal meth Garden of Eden wasn't enough to trap Heath. Epically bubbling away in a mountain top cauldron was one thing but it simply didn't fit Heath's long term needs. Heath preferred escape and obliteration over epic-ness. His long-term need was to hurt himself and bury any trace of love and empathy for himself. In Belize he'd done plenty of crack cocaine but, like his serious drinking career, it was always best facilitated in a solitary confinement. Meth was a group activity. The dark forces in the group invested heavily in his experience to gain a manipulative control over him. Worse still, Heath sensed they were trying to come through him to get their hands on Rose's property wealth.

On the last day in the mountains they took him deep into a giant underground cavern and, on the tricky descent for the first time in their company, Heath was hit by fear. There was every chance that they'd kill or rape him right down in the depths of nowhere. He was grateful that they knew that he had no money as that might have led to a robbery that may have led to his end or him feeling someone's end right in his ass before they chopped him up. Luckily for Lucky Boy Heath, he dodged a dry bum gang rape and a murder and they simply sat him down and passed him a pre-rolled spliff which took the edge off but even then he couldn't relax until they were safely back on the road to Rose's.

Heath would never really have to mix with the rogue bunch again. His visa was close to expiry and his unplanned exit plan that was always subconsciously planned was just about to come to fruition. Rose and friends had put forward a half-hearted scheme or two to gain him a Green Card to enable him to take up official residency in the States but the plan never really got off the ground. Most of the Idaho Music Scene Wrecking Crew lived day-to-day and grand plans rarely got past the hot air stage so Heath's failure to sort his papers out was no great surprise to anyone. The real reason that he didn't have the drive to sort it out was that all the roads of opportunity to do so clearly led straight back to the aircraft industry and he was hell-bent on leaving that part of his life behind… so he just chose to drift.

In the interim period between coming back from the Mountain meth experiences and checking out of the US, Heath felt the pressure that hoovering up all those complimentary chemicals brought. The undesirables and their subliminally bad intentions were never far from his thoughts.

Ridiculously, Heath managed to get another meth session in. On an innocent enough post-gig midnight-jaunt to the petrol station to get some supplies in, he noticed a group of youths loitering in a way that hinted that they were obviously up to something good. Heath scored something good in the form of a gram or two of crystal meth and spent a couple of days messing around with broken light bulbs and chatting shit with Rose. She was in the last stages of her life now and it was a wrong-right privilege to be around her in such a heightened state. Meth wasn't Heath's chosen poison but wrong poison was always better than no poison at all and it created a memory that summed up his time in Idaho. It was a trip.

It seemed inevitable that the meth gang would gobble up Rose's wealth when she came to pass but Heath was comforted by the fact that she didn't really seem to have noticed. She had no children to pass her property onto so, as her consciousness gradually started to slip away, it really didn't matter.

With just a few weeks left on his visa and with the Meth Vultures subconsciously circling, Heath had to bite the bullet and call his folks back in Norwich. He swallowed his pride and asked his Dad to finance his flight home. In order to save face, he retold the Mexican knife-point story and this brought back a hint of regret at his inability to have revisited the kind Mexican family that came to his aid back in Vera Cruz.

Unfortunately, he was far too disorganised to ever fulfil his promise to go and pay them back and claim their daughter's affections. That fairy-tale was long gone and he'd soon have to face the nightmare of living back with his parents.

Thankfully, Rose was well enough to bid him a very fond farewell. It was hard to question what their most unlikely friendship was meant to be. Fate decreed that they shared this time and their connection grew into a deep one. Heath will always take a smidge of her kind, open spirit with him. Respectfully, he returned his other real friend – his adopted bass guitar – to its rightful owner. He did consider taking it back to the UK as the guy simply wouldn't miss it but, out of respect to Rose, he did the right thing.

Rose's parting gift was a Greyhound Bus ticket to New York. Heath had no money for drinks or food but he wasn't going to ask his friend who had done more than enough for him. Three long stinky days followed on the silver tin can on wheels and it was minging. The bus stopped in all of the shittiest poverty-stricken areas and a wide selection of characters joined the bus along the route. Heath woke from one nap to find the empty seat next to him inhabited by a fit young bird. He woke up to smiles and chat and much needed refreshments in the form of coffee and sandwiches. Obviously Heath was invested from the get-go but he didn't even get to finish his coffee before the young hottie had extinguished any sparks of his interest. She nonchalantly explained that the bus had just picked her up from the State Penitentiary where she had just served nine years for murdering all her family. This soiree was over before it started. It was definitely time to leave the US!

On arrival at the New York bus terminal Heath discovered it was a ridiculous twenty miles from the airport but Heath was now a skilled operator in this field. The old hard luck story came out and the good people in the bus terminal provided food, drinks and his onward bus fare in no time at all. Heath loved the people of America – they had never let him down.

7: BACK TO NORMALDOM

Soundtrack: Amy Winehouse - *Back to Black*

In the airport Heath's dad had saved himself $60 on the plane ticket that Heath thought he was picking up at the check-in desk. Unfortunately, a $60 saving meant another $48 in an airport lounge which made Heath's foreboding return-to-parent feelings intensify. He was dreading going home. Of course, he blagged himself refreshments in the airport and on the flight but when he landed back in Blighty stark cold realism set in.

Rather than admit that he was completely broke, he compromised by making a reverse charge telephone call to his folks, he briefly considered prostituting himself. He never came close to going through with it but to even consider this was clear evidence of how much his adopted father's view of him still affected him.

Again he bit the bullet, rang and begged. He sold another portion of self respect in return for a train ticket from London to Manchester and onto Altrincham. His folks had moved back north and relocated in Winsford to live out their retirement. Dad picked him up from Altrincham in the same boring car that he'd always had. Mum came. She was really pleased to see him. She always was.

Living with his folks was suffocating. He just had too many bad memories that could never just be buried. Three hours into day one back at home, Heath was in the Job Centre looking for a way out. He found a job card outlining the role of an electronic engineer fixing computer monitors. Working hours 0830-1600. One short phone call later and Heath was employed. The job was a doddle. He'd come in half an hour early and cherry pick the easiest six monitors to fix and then he'd spend his day smoking or fixing the machines. Heath was now pre-loaded with a plethora of fun-time stories from his travelogue and he found it easy to befriend and impress his supervisor in the workplace.

His supervisor lapped up Heath's Belize and band stories and this led to him fixing up a meeting with a friend of his that coincidently needed a bass player in his band, unbelievably their previous bass player was again happy to lend him his guitar. Seems he was simply meant to keep on gigging.

With his new band he had just twenty songs to learn in comparison to the eight hundred that his band in Belize used to rock out to. His new band mates were impressed. In the Americas, Heath had also learned how to sing harmony backing vocals to a decent level and it took the new band's offering to another level. By British standards, they were good but very rigid. Their set was the same twenty songs in the same order every night.

Heath always joined bands to fill his time doing something that he enjoyed and to not have to talk to people. Unfortunately, gig structure was different in the UK. Instead of the usual six hour American Rock Bar Set with free beer and brief toilet breaks only, Britain's pubs and working men's clubs just wanted a thirty minute set followed by a thirty minute break followed by a thirty minute set with no free drinks. Heath dreaded having to speak to people in the breaks so he quickly got into the routine of spending that break time finding the nearest off-licence where he'd get a quarter bottle of vodka to neck on the way back to finish the gig.

The pressure of being home and the monotony of the band routine accelerated his drinking and this impacted Heath's health rapidly. For the first time in his drinking career, he started to have trouble with his pancreas. He was starting to poison himself to a decent standard.

Heath lasted eight weeks with the band and, in this time, his father actually supported him by attending a gig. What should have been a rare moment of recognition was spoiled somewhat by the sight of a pissed-up woman trying to get off with his dad. Rather than push her advances away, he just sat and stared at Heath while the lady licked his ear. He was too polite to tell her to "fuck off".

Heath's time to shine was forever tarnished by his adopted father's inability to ever put him first. The next day fate posted an advertisement in Martin's Newsagents and the small white card was to be his ticket out of the family home. "Working man seeks other working man to share the bills."

Dad was more than happy to provide a £160 deposit to help him move out. His new flat mate and saviour worked in Kwik Save and went by the name of Phil. Phil was impressed to have a musician in the house but, on the same weekend that he moved in, Heath played his last gig with the band. At this gig he met a groupie kind of chick called Jane. She was complimentary about the band. She told Heath that she had some weed and he could come back to hers for a spliff if he liked.

Jane was married but clearly open to a flirty kind of friendship of some sort or another. Heath went back for the smoke. Hubby was out but nothing happened.

She passed him a stay-in-touch baton in the form of her phone number and a promise to score him some weed in the not too distant future.

The weed deal went down and when Heath came to pick up the goods he was introduced to Jane's six foot two, runner bean of a husband, before sharing a spliff. He was thin and wiry and wily and Heath sensed that the Runner Bean sensed that Heath would like to be the runner bean. He was right.

Heath had a way of being accepted into these sort of relationships and he became a regular visitor to their home. It was clear that Jane and The Bean had a volatile relationship as they were always arguing. Without setting out a clear plan to help break up the couple, it was clear that Heath could become part of a spectacular car crash situation.

To make a car crash, you need a car and Heath picked up a 26-year-old Mini, again off the back of a white card in Martin's Newsagents window. He paid £80 for the motor that had three just months MOT on it. Having never worked on cars, he bought a Haynes Mini Manual and taught himself how to get the vehicle road safe.

A call came from Jane that The Bean was working and Heath took her out for dinner and drinks; five pints of Stella for the lady and three pints for Heath. Bizarrely, Jane asked if she could drive them home. At this point she could have asked him to set himself on fire and he would have obliged. She was in charge of wherever this was going. She drove the short drive home without too much trouble but, on arrival at her matrimonial residence, she got it all wrong and crashed the Mini straight through the brick wall at the front of her house.

Next door's curtains twitched as the unharmed pair

fled the scene and went indoors for a spliff. Five minutes later there was a blue light outside as the apparently not pissed or stoned next door neighbours had clearly dobbed them in. They recognised inebriated parking when they saw it. It was a fair cop and the attending policeman in charge of the investigation was just that. Heath and Jane were both breathalysed and Heath registered 37ml with the alcohol limit being 35ml. Jane registered much higher up the Stella-o-meter and, unfortunately for her, her next door neighbour had pinned her as the guilty driver. Heath tried to play the gallant submissive hero and claim the blame but the fair cop went something like this – "You are just over the limit but we are going to let you off because you clearly weren't the driver of the vehicle so best you call a taxi."

Jane got nicked and The Runner Bean was less than impressed. He absorbed the situation and came to the conclusion that Heath and Jane were on the slippery slope to finishing his marriage. Surprisingly, his proposed antidote wasn't a kicking for Heath, instead he lined up some employment for him and filled Heath's daytime diary so he would no longer have the opportunity to pop round and build on his relationship with Jane.

Heath couldn't believe his luck. He managed to sneak through the drink-driving situation unscathed and land a job as a road-bound field engineer fixing point-of-sale units around the north-west, all on a Belizean Driver's Licence. He'd never actually passed a test but was issued a brand new Ford Mondeo by his new firm.

Heath and The Runner Bean now shared the same boss but worked for different companies. The boss's name was Duncan and he owned both firms. He was clearly the man who had responded to the call from

The Runner Bean to make this happen. Even though Heath felt massively under-skilled; he could fix stuff but this was way out of his comfort zone, Heath correctly identified this as the right time to start over and The Bean, Jane and his time with the band all became his past incarnation.

On his first call out Heath spent the whole job on the phone to Duncan talking himself through the fix and by the end of the first week he knew that the job was a bad fit for him. He felt he'd eventually pick up the fix task side of the job but the interaction with the shop staff was completely terrifying. Communicating with strangers while sober was a whole crap new ball game. Trying to be normal was overwhelming.

Week two felt worse. Heath had to facilitate a point-of-sale fix in a swanky branch of top of the range HiFi equipment shops called Richer Sounds. The staff looked down on Heath from minute one and he felt like a fraud. Luckily for Heath, his new boss was cool as fuck and, after a brief tragic review of his first eight days in the job, Duncan drove back to Richer Sounds and gave it them both barrels: "Just because somebody is polite and unassuming doesn't mean they are weak! Heath knows his shit so I'd appreciate it if you showed him the respect that he deserves!"

Heath's mind was blown by this endorsement and in a mini-business and life epiphany, he decided never to be somebody that appeared weak and unprepared. That day he invested in three smart shirts and a crispy business suit. From his next appointment onwards he was smiley and professional and, even if he had no idea about what he was fixing from now on, the shop staff would never know. Most shop managers were women - and women were always the half of our species that Heath felt most comfortable around.

At this time he moved to Northwich for business reasons. As a North West Field Engineer, it was advantageous to be as close to as many motorways as possible so he could be anywhere by 9 am if need be. Again, Heath had made himself the best in his field quickly as no other field engineer had anything close to this capability. It was smart thinking as all of a sudden he was indispensable and his Mondeo wasn't going anywhere but it was more than that, it was a "thank you" to Duncan for believing in him. The job and Heath's worth started to fly as his experience and customer service confidence soared. His drinking was regulated and under control for the first time since teenage-ism. Work was his driver at this time.

Six months later, he made himself even more indispensable and moved to Warrington which is the north-west gateway to everywhere. Unfortunately, he accepted an offer to move in with a rather dull friend of Duncan's and the pressure of this lady having an awareness of his controlled drinking quickly led to him escalating his alcoholism back up to a dangerous level.

He had become his job, he was totally invested. Unfortunately hidden beneath Heath's recent supreme temporary focus, all the insecurities and self-harm intent was still there haunting him like a snake slithering through long grass looking for its prey. He just couldn't get away from having a very low opinion of himself.

8: GETTING A REAL ENGLISH BIRD

Soundtrack: Christine and The Queens - *Girlfriend*

Things were not cool. Being cooped up with a work spy was the pits, so Heath came to the conclusion that at thirty-one years of age, it was about time he had his first real British girlfriend. In 1997 the equivalent of Tinder and Plenty of Fish was the *Warrington Guardian*. Heath bravely place an ad in the singles section. To do this he had to record a voice-mail message for ladies that were interested enough to make the call to dial into it. They would listen to the recording and leave their details if they were still game. They also incurred a 25p cost. Heath had become a low-level male hooker. His advert went like this, "Male, 31, seeking long term relationship. Good sense of humour more important than looks."

Heath still had a trace of a North American accent at the time - he sounded somewhere in the middle of Alan Partridge and Magnum PI. After a week, he dialled in like a Cornish fisherman collecting lobsters from his pots and, to his great surprise, there were quite a few women with better personalities than looks in the north-west. Three of them had left interesting recordings to follow up.

The first lady sounded exactly like somebody that he could spend the rest of his life with. Yes, you guessed it, she sounded female. No, but more than that she was witty and funny. She was everything his current flat mate wasn't. Honourable chap that Heath was and is, there was no real need to check out the other interested parties and on the back of a cup of Earl Grey, milk, two sugars and a lobster mayo butty, Heath sat down and nervously made the call.

On the line she was less humorous than in her message, but they agreed to meet at hers for a meal and drinks. On the date her cooking was dreadful, but the beer and wine laid on was exquisite. She had a daughter from a previous relationship and Heath struggled to connect from the off.

Only someone that has lived through being made to feel like an outcast as a child who then goes on to make the same mistakes can explain that. You'd think that somebody who was adopted as a child and somebody who faced alienation in their own house as a child and somebody who has ruined their health living as an addict because of this must be able to reach out to that child. Unfortunately, at this stage of his life, Heath just wasn't that wise. He preferred to bring selfish pain to himself and here was another opportunity to bring more guilt. I'm sure Mum was lonely at this time but, in my opinion, all single mums should fuck off any new fella not buying into the whole package of their family.

This fail-safe wasn't put in place at this early stage, neither was the, "you're not as funny as I thought you were" downgrading the potential of the relationship by Heath. Fate had brought them together and they were destined to do something. When the opportunity to do something came, fate kicked in again. Heath has always carried condoms since missing out on relations with Rose back in Belize, so even though he had the option to protect the transaction, he chose not to and very soon after he learned that he was going to be a real dad. Looking back, Heath takes responsibility for drifting into this relationship. Both parties were lost and needed and wanted the situation that they were about to create. They were both guilty of not finding the right person to do it with. Instead they both did first come, first served but unfortunately neither were prepared to serve the other.

Things moved fast. In Belize, Heath mixed his spirits with lots of coke and Fanta and over time his teeth had paid the price. He decided to get them done and received a whopping dose of Novacaine at the dentists that altered his state of consciousness to such an extent that it led to a proposal of marriage. A £500 higher purchase agreement in H. Samuel's and he was done.

Fuckin' dentists!

One £500 loan led to another worthy one; Heath enjoyed kitting out the nursery with this money and was totally invested in becoming a dad. His new wife had obviously came to the conclusion that he was a piss-can and she wisely restricted his piss-cannery down to two cans a night to safeguard his job and their future. Heath upgraded his can strength from piss-water to Special Brew, the Great British Alcoholic's signature aperitif.

A month later, baby time got real. At 1.30am, the Wife started having contractions in the house and his step-daughter started sobbing. She screamed, "everything will be different when you come back from the hospital". Heath silently agreed.

At the hospital it was real. He kindly stroked her hair and shared her gas and air. She was nil by mouth, Heath wasn't and addictively binged through the whole contents of the vending machine.

Shit started happening fast.

The epidural injection went a bit wrong and blood

started spurting everywhere, then at 06.30am the baby's heart rate flat-lined and the whole medical team sprang into action. Heath called off the vaginal inspection before it had started as he'd already diagnosed that the monitor was at fault and, sure enough, plugging in a replacement monitor brought the baby back to life.

Phew..!

9: THE GREATEST MOMENT

Soundtrack: Johnny Mathis – *When a Child is Born*

By 08.30am, the Wife was in extreme pain and the hair-stroking intensified and, at 08.50, she informed Heath: "If you don't stop stroking my hair, I will fuckin' kill you!" She was exhausted and confused as the epidural made everything in the birth process make less sense. She was pushing but couldn't feel the result and, just at the point of exasperation, "Pop" and out came the most amazing, perfect little baby's head and right there in that moment everything changed for Heath. He was awestruck and, seconds later, a baby boy was born and wrapped and delivered straight into his arms. It was the best moment of Heath's life. He wanted everything in the world for that baby. Sadly, he didn't give the mother of his new-born son the respect that the magic trick she had just facilitated deserved.

His whole life experience so far now had meaning and, at that point in time, he solemnly swore to give up all the self-hurt and coping habits that had come before. The unconditional love that he felt for his son was overwhelming. He would have passed a lie-detector 100%.

No more chaos. Let it go.

Heath wanted to stay in the hospital all day and all night long just to look at his beautiful boy but this wasn't the accepted protocol. After he had called both sides of the family with the big news, the nurses expertly dispatched him back into the wild.

All the silent, golden, good behaviour promises that he'd made to himself and his boy in the hospital went straight out of the window because seconds after leaving the hospital, he spotted an off licence and the inner beast took back control.

Before he went home to get wrecked, he hit Mothercare and spent a fortune on the most expensive newborn baby shit in the shop in preparation for bringing his boy home the following day.

Twelve hours later with a prolifically mashed head of a hangover, he was driven by the outlaws to scoop up his step-daughter. She was loving and doting towards his boy and even towards Heath but even at this massive opportunistic moment to make them into a real family, Heath just couldn't do it. His demons just wouldn't allow it. Even though he was the cuckoo in her nest and even though he was once in her position as a child, he just couldn't and didn't really want to break the cycle.

It's said by clever shrink-like professionals that, "Give me the child for the first seven years and I will give you the man" and he just couldn't break this truth. Until he could, everything he ever got into would almost certainly be doomed. He wasn't evil, he just never grew up emotionally. This made him selfish, resentful and hell-bent on self-destruction.

The antidote of forgiveness was nowhere in sight.

All the desolation in his private life and thoughts

were masked by his smart Greenwood's shirt, tie and business-suit combo. That mask made him a success at work and it also was the key to maintaining the status quo of the family unit that both Heath and Wife wanted – even if they didn't really want each other; stability in the Capitalist Matrix. That's the dream we are all spoon-fed to keep us keeping on.

Heath genuinely wanted to earn and provide for the family, but it wouldn't take long until he came to the realisation that his work/life balance was all wrong. Before he got to that point, he just cracked on with being a good dad – at least to his natural born son.

Breastfeeding was tough on The Wife; she found it very, very uncomfortable and her midwife must have been on some kind of Nipple Wrenching Commission because she kept on and on and on and frickin' on with the scare stories of what would happen if she turned her nipples away from her son. It was a tough time for a new mum. Her body was still in a state of post-birth ruin and she was sleep deprived. Thankfully, after two weeks of low level bullying, the Nipple Nazi in the Blue Tunic conceded and agreed that The Wife could start to express her milk.

Heath enthusiastically stepped up to night feed bottle duties and he shrewdly stepped his booze intake back up to five cans a night. On his own secret terms, it was a controlled, responsible and magical time. It was the best time of his life so far. He'd spend hours starring into his boy's eyes, coochy-cooing and just pumping out the bottomless reservoir of unconditional love that he had stored up for his lad.

Drinking more cans never put his son at risk – he'd often nod off holding him but, as soon as he made a peep,

Heath was back in the room. It was a special time that created special memories for Heath and he's always keep those memories filed safely away in his mind. When his boy was big enough for mum to demand that he sleep in his cot, it was a bit of a downer. Their Overnight Boys' Club days were temporarily done.

Wife 'n' Heath both drank pretty much every night. Wife wasn't an addict as such but she probably needed a drink to cope with Heath having a drink and all her own grim relationship realisations. Their marriage wasn't nasty or bitter but it was fractious. Heath told her he loved her at all the right moments, but the only unconditional love he really felt was for his son, so he lied.

Heath valued the idea of a perfect family unit and, even though he didn't have the tools for the job in the form of the ability to love and respect all four people in the perfect family set up, he still tried the best in the best way he could – he threw money at it. He gave all his time away and worked like a demon, with the end result being less opportunity to engage in bringing the family together and more opportunity for the demons to start adding resentment to the growing list of negatives within the marriage.

His Baby Boy was still his go to for love and for a social. When Baby was about two years old, Heath loved it when he cried, he'd scoop him up and take him downstairs for Boys' Club. Wife got rest, Baby Boy was content and Heath had a beer. Heath was a very, very proud dad. On one Overnight Boys' Club during his feed just before going off to work, his lad puked on the shoulder of his business suit. Heath cleaned it up just enough so he could showcase the stain to whichever shop-staff he was about to work alongside that day. He beamed: "My boy was sick on me this morning". They must have thought, "Get away from me, you demented minger!"

Wife was just the same on the daytime shift as they both showered their unconditional love over their son but, when it came to having any other shared interest, they were never on the same bus. Wife had friends; Heath had work associates but they had no shared friendship group or social life outside a few beers for Heath and a bottle of white wine for Wife.

Heath concentrated on work and believed that if he created a set up where he was indispensable to his employer then everything else would just about be okay. It wasn't. He just created a gigantic workload and responsibility that would eventually start to crush him. Temporarily, it was still a relatively helpful guard to protect him against actually having to take full responsibility for being a well-rounded loving family man - which is exactly what he wasn't quite capable of ever being.

It all made sense to a scared and still very vulnerable boy in a man's body. His health was also slipping, his drinking was increasing, and his body was starting to crack. He began experiencing stomach pains and vomiting and he couldn't fathom if it was alcoholism or stress or both so he just buried it.

Stress and guilt came from the various layers of his life that weren't quite right. As a step-father he was crap; selfish and crap. To his step-daughter, he was just the man that took her mother away so to ease that situation, Heath would take his son away for Daytime Boy's Club as often as possible to let the girls hang out together.

This line of thinking did actually work. He was a great childcare outlet for mum and he definitely helped Mother and Daughter maintain their healthy relationship. Unfortunately, he wasn't as skilled at maintaining his own matrimonial relationship in the same vein. Wife and Heath drifted towards becoming something akin to unfriendly flat-mates with a child-share. The relationship also lacked his usual infatuation buy in.

The signs were not good. His drinking and mental health followed the same trajectory as the relationship. Heath started to quickly spiral towards disaster. He kept losing his breath. Wife noticed that he was on the slide and referred him to his GP. He did the stiff upper lip thing and shared next to none of his worries or symptoms with The Quack.

10: GAME OVER BREAKDOWN

Soundtrack: Dave Mathews Band – *Too Much*

It took just two more weeks for his downer to escalate into a show-stopper. Lots and lots of hard work had financed a first foreign family holiday to Spain but come the day of the flight Heath went right under – "Sorry, I just can't go!". Wife's patience output was exasperated, she was fuming and desperate. She knew that he'd lost the plot but she couldn't stop herself freaking out as she screamed, "You are ruining my life!"

In an almost cabbage-like state, Heath drove to the airport where he dropped off Wife and Kids before somehow auto-piloting his way back home. He spent the next two weeks in the family home strangely frozen in a state of purgatory in his garage as if he wasn't fit to be in the house. His brain had stalled - he was in a completely dishevelled state. Somehow two weeks later, he managed to pick up the sun-kissed trio from the airport. His boy ran and jumped into his arms and it hurt him that he'd missed out on the shared memories that should have been. If he could have thought straight, he would have detested himself but as it was he just felt completely numb.

Wife let him sleep on the couch with his boy and, in the morning, she recognised that he had hit the wall. She took the decision to book him off sick with work and arranged a home visit from Heath's GP. The doctor confirmed Heath had experienced a nervous breakdown and he prescribed him some antidepressants. Wife rang work who were very supportive. Take as long as you need. Keep the car. Just get well. Heath rode the storm and slowly regained some of his marbles and admirably Wife stuck by him.

Nine months later, he resumed classed fit for work.

During this long period at home, the marriage didn't really reach any higher ground and feeling low Wife understandably started to match Heath's drinking. It wasn't a healthy environment and arguments started to erupt almost every evening. Wife always said Heath started the arguments but Heath always felt that he was forced into the argument in the first place.

Heath wasn't a pleasant drunk, at this point. When it came to heated exchanges with his Wife, alcohol armed him with an ugly, cutting arrogance. When he drank, his opinion of himself was wildly disproportionate to his real opinion of himself. He looked down on his life partner with shocking disregard. His ability to play with the words of the English language gave him the dark, mean weaponry that he used to deliver cruellest of caustic jibes. He had become everything that his inner evil tormentors wanted him to be. He'd become someone that was really worth hurting.

Unfortunately, the children started to become aware of the arguments. They were never directly involved but children just know. Children see and hear everything and this only added to the pressure of the situation. Wife kept telling Heath not to drink but he was well past that. He needed to drink now. Not drinking made him fell more poorly than drinking did. He was about halfway down the Highway to Hell.

Both parties kept on drinking until one night a barney of massive proportions erupted that was never ever winnable from either side of the fence. It resulted in Heath leaving the family home to go and stay in a hotel. He had his mind set on an all-night sesh in a residents' bar. Unfortunately, he ended up with an all-night sesh in a police cell as, once again, he was detained on drink-driving charges.

There were positives; he saved £100 on a hotel room and down at the police station at midnight, he triggered the administration of a heavy dose of Librium to himself every six hours just by admitting that he was an alcoholic. The sedative was exactly the reality-stripping escape that he needed. Unfortunately, it didn't last for the rest of his life. Come the morning, the stark reality of the situation was staring him in the face.

His decision to admit alcohol dependency and claim the complimentary Librium on offer on the night of his detention had a significant knock on effect. Declaring his illness and hiring a decent solicitor at the cost of

£1,000 probably saved him from receiving a custodial sentence for the drink-driving offence. He was proved to be three and a half times over the limit and should have been looking at jail time and a two to three year ban. Money talks though – and he was fortunate enough to be able to pay his way out of the really deep water but his declaration of alcoholism meant that his career in the field and on the road was over.

His boss and friend Duncan was amazing and tried to prolong his tenure within the company by temporarily swapping his job in the field for one in the office but it very quickly became apparent that his value to the organisation was severely compromised. His great ability to get everywhere and fix everything before any of the other engineers had even got out of bed was gone meant he had become a grossly overpaid desk monkey.

For a period of time he participated in the corporate 9 to 5 Rat Race and commuted into the office by train but it was all very dull. His newly found chocolate fireguard role offered a troubleshooting phone service to tech-confused store managers and field engineers but overall it was a load of bollocks.

Heath didn't have to wait too long before the opportunity came to escape this period of enforced office purgatory. The company was bought out. Everybody's role got evaluated and Heath's Chocolate Fireguard Role quickly melted into the murky pool of uselessness that it was. This was quickly monetised into a £3,400 redundancy package and Heath took the opportunity to jump before he got pushed. He was grateful to Duncan who had really looked after him.

The drink-driving debacle should have really led to a charge of Gross Misconduct and the termination of his contract but his boss and friend had supported him right through to the pay-out and Heath really appreciated that kindness. He'll never forget him. Back in the family home things were never quite the same. The argument, the arrest, and the loss of good job were all cherries on top of the 'This marriage is a pile of shit' cake. Things with the Wife had never been particularly spectacular but 'the pile of shit cake' was now well and truly over baked.

Heath's coping strategy was a bit warped as his intellect concluded that the end was near, but if he became a super nice model husband then he couldn't be blamed for breaking the marriage. So he spent the next six months being super nice and polite and helpful. His horrible strategy worked a treat and Wife was quickly repulsed into an exit strategy.

One day she came home from work and announced that she'd got a flat and she was taking the kids. Heath freely admits that had he not won that absurd moral victory and if it had been he who had been forced to leave the family home, he would have become acutely disputatious and war-like and he would definitely have fought for half of the house.

Thankfully the pathetic little boxes in his mind got ticked so he was more than happy to sell up and give his soon-to-be ex-Wife, his boy and his step-daughter everything. He wanted to give them a future. Wife deserved it. Heath has been a shit husband. He summarises this by stating, "It's fair to say that as a husband I failed to reach my potential."

11: DISASTROUS SHORT TERM PLANNING

Soundtrack: James - *Getting away with it (All Messed Up)*

Heath's addict thought process was doing the old kid on Christmas Eve thing as even though his conscience was clear as he'd done the right thing with the house and the money in regards to the family, he was still sitting on £3,400 of redundancy money and in 2004 that felt like an exciting amount of Beer Tokens to get through. Addicts tend to set short term goals and Heath's mind was set right up for a gigantic wrecking sesh. His demons had it all planned out.

When the house was sold, he rightfully handed over the proceeds to his family and took up a six month residency agreement for a one bedroom flat at The YMCA in Birchwood. Two days into his new single life, Heath attracted the attention of a lady that he describes as 'a right nutter'. She was manically frantic both in speech and in action. She bumped into Heath while he was out walking the dog that had become his unwanted half of the divorce settlement. Heath's new high-energy friend instantly fell in love with the pooch and even showed an appetite to get to know Heath a bit more exclusively. Inside sixty seconds of a very one sided intro-chat, she invited Heath back to hers to smoke some dope. No brainer.

Walking to her flat Heath already knew that she wasn't going to be his next wife as she was waffling shite, making no sense at all and acting completely erratically. As men and addicts often do, he concentrated on the positives. He didn't know what he was going to get out of the situation but he did know that something was definitely going to occur.

Over a beer and a reefer, Heath signed over custody of the dog. Result. Next, she confessed that she smoked Brown (Heroin) and wondered if Heath would like to partake? Most normal folk would have given this a bit more consideration than Heath did but, two days into going solo, this was exactly the kind of hurtful escapism he was craving. Heath pretended it was the norm and watched on as she did what she did with the brown powder and the foil. He watched her intently and saw her whole erratic demeanour change as the effects of the chemically-charged smoke took effect. Her eyes went from scared to orgasm-happy and content and, as she laid back to feel the effects of the drug in a more relaxed position, Heath took over use of the equipment and wasted no time in following her down the escape route.

As soon as he sucked in the smoke the hit was instant and undeniably comforting and for the first time since he was a baby he felt completely safe. As he lay back beside the Angel-Being nested beside him, he felt like he was levitating inside a cocoon of deliciously warm candy floss. He felt a oneness that had always been missing in his life.

When the anaesthetic subsided and reality seeped back into his consciousness, he puked on his new friend which confirmed again that she definitely wasn't going to be his next wife. He made his excuses said, "Goodbye" to her and the dog and left the scene.

He couldn't remember giving her his phone number but the next day the girl's mother rang to ask Heath to come and pick his dog up. Heath just said "I think you'll find the dog now belongs to your daughter" and that was that. The pooch had gone to a better place.

The ex-Wife moved on in much less dramatic fashion. She was free to be free and she wasted no time at all. She was focused and resourceful. She opened income streams through employment and better relationship options on the Dial-a-Date scene and Heath was happy to help her through this re-building period. He relished Daddy Daycare Duties that included the school run.

Ex-Wife would drop her daughter off at school by car and Heath would walk it with his boy. It was special because previously he'd always missed out on such duties by loading himself up with break-of-dawn Field Engineering appointments. The pressure and chaos of the fake marriage was passed. Boys' Club was back on and Heath regulated his drinking to match his responsibilities. He'd pick his lad up in the morning and walk him to school, have a few cans and then pick him back up. They'd watch the Simpsons back at the YMCA digs and it was just pleasant. One day, in school hours, Mum called – "You'll have to go into school now. He's in trouble for swearing." Heath prepared for war. Out of the wardrobe came his Field Engineer Protective Suit of Armour.

Resplendent in his bestest suit, shirt and tie, he marched into that primary school with the sole purpose of winning an argument for his son. His angelic little boy was summoned to the Headmaster's office where the Headmaster spoke first.

"Thanks for coming in. The problem that we've got is that your son said the 'F' word.' Then the Headmaster turned and faced the child – 'Say it.'"

"Fuck!"

Heath wasn't completely sober so he was braver than he could have been.

"You've given him a way of getting attention, that's all. It's just words."

Then he took his boy's hand and marched him out without bothering to offer an apology. He'd fought his corner. On the way home, Heath read his son The Riot Act and the Little Fella absorbed it without complaint.

Five years later his son put him right, "I never swore in class that day you know, it was my mate. The teacher was a bully and I didn't want him to get in trouble." Heath beams as he explains that his son has always been that kind of kind guy. Someone willing to take a hit to protect somebody more vulnerable than himself. Heath loves that. He's a very proud dad.

Flip back five years to primary school… Boys' Club time and it didn't take long before his son had another very proud Dad in his life. One day on drop-off, Heath was introduced to his son's new guardian. Part of him was jealous but it wasn't justified. She deserved a better relationship than the one she'd just escaped from. It wasn't long until the new flame moved them all to Crewe.

Back at the YMCA it turned out that the majority of The Village People all had drug dependency issues, which suited Heath's needs at the time. Amphetamine was the House Poison and it was his dirty block paste version of the drug that was on offer at this time. It was cheap and long lasting. Alcohol appeals to Heath because when it kicks in, the mind races and takes away a large portion of reality. Amphetamine or Speed as it's universally known, unsurprisingly, gets the mind racing much faster. Just like alcohol, it takes away the stark reality of life but, instead of an up then downward path to black out and shut down, it concentrates the mind and brings extreme focus and energy. It also blocks out the cold.

Heath put all the positives around his new speed habit quickly into play. In the two month period since his family went to Crewe, his £3,400 redundancy nest-egg disintegrated so his new routine was learning to survive on basic benefits while twisted off his nut on speed.

Unsurprisingly, Heath's chemically-sharpened business mind soon came up with new revenue generation streams. He was never one for straight begging so he was grateful that on one occasion an opportunity caught his eye. At 1.30am, just before club chucking-out time, he spotted a crumpled twenty pound note on floor. He gratefully scooped it up and wondered how many of these get dropped outside Warrington night clubs every night. Clubbers are usually out of their minds so Heath decided it was worth investigating.

Each night for the next six months his routine was; dinner with The Village People with a gram of speed up his hooter for dessert, then he'd trawl the road surface at the Drive Thrus at KFC and McDonald's where people were that rich that they couldn't be bothered picking up their change that dropped on the floor during transactions. From there, he'd collect all the one pound coins from the discarded shopping trolleys at Tesco before searching out the big bucks among the pissheads and ravers queuing to get into Mr Smith's, which was the best known night club in Warrington at the time.

He strategically planned out a circular money-picking route so he would never appear offensively in anyone's face. He was always inoffensively just passing by. The clever trick he tagged on his circuit was to check the phone box near to Mr Smith's. Ravers were always ringing someone and they usually left some credit on the unit. Heath would regularly find 40p credit on the public phone. He'd add 60p and hang up, then a pound coin would pop out generating more money for nothing. Begging wasn't his preferred strategy but, on occasion, Heath could sense that people wanted to help him. In such cases, he simply had to ask for help to open the conversation piece.

In Heath's mind, asking someone for a pound was a clear as saying, "Would you like to buy me some beer and drugs?" so he'd say, "Sorry to ask, but could you spare me 87p to get a place in the night shelter?" That felt much more genuine and it worked.

Heath revolutionised the art of begging in Warrington. One old lady in particular heard this and connected with the absurdity of Heath's request. She reached out to him gave him some money and eventually explained that she owned a caravan by the Thelwall Viaduct overlooking the M6 Motorway. She'd be happy for him to stay in her van.

Heath took the opportunity to check out of the YMCA and spend some really hurtful time in isolation. The bonus was after his nightly money scooping speed walks, he could now get back to the van and come down off the amphetamine by smashing in as much White Lightning mock cider as possible. This most distasteful liquid has nothing to do with apples and is a go-to staple for alcoholics. His escapism boxes were getting well and truly ticked. He also tried British weed but it just made him paranoid which took away his ability to engage with the public that funded his existence so, in the main, he stuck to Speed for supper and booze for breakfast.

After nine months of this mashed-up vibration and on a particularly messy come down, he decided it was time to relocate back to the city that had always been his spiritual home.

12: AN UNEASY RETURN TO THE PEOPLE'S REPUBLIK OF MANCHESTER

Soundtrack: The Jam - *In The City*

Without any possessions and just a small amount of loose change, he jumped on the 100 bus service to Manchester and his latest geographical new start shift was in play. On arrival, Heath had no idea that he looked like an absolute bag of shit. He stepped off the bus into the big city just as the speed was wearing off and extreme thirst and mild hunger pangs started to torment him. He trudged around the city in a lonely state of what-the-fuck-now-ism. He was back in geographical terms to the place he considered closest to home but reconnecting to the place where he grew up would take a little time.

First, he just had to get a drink down him so he walked into the Co-op and loaded a basket with groceries including a bottle of Fanta that he discretely supped on his way around the store. Then he attempted to ditch the basket and the goods and walk out of the store refreshed and ready to decide what to do next.

Unfortunately, the mirror in the shop was a Harry Potter anti-shoplifting one-way viewing device and

Heath's little crime was a big deal to the onlooker behind the screen, who probably spent most of his working life bored out of his brain. Heath was an easy low-risk catch so the man came out of the side door just as he was leaving the scene and lynched him. Heath got his photo taken and was informed that the photo would be put through the Co-op's Facial Recognition technology and he would be banned for life from all Co-Op Stores. He could take getting nicked and the public shame of his capture but he simply could not abide people taking him for a fool.

"Bullshit that, I've worked in retail. You are talking shit."

Clearly taken aback, the security guard fixed his stare and Heath could almost hear the man's brain ticking as he was being evaluated. Heath's comments clearly stimulated him into seeing more than the bedraggled excuse of a man that stood in front of him. Rather than be an arsehole, the guard took the time to step outside the store and explain to Heath that he could get fed and watered close by at the soup kitchen on Store Street.

Even though the guard's kindness had connected with Heath's out of place intelligence, it was still a bitter-sweet tonic to taste because it was also confirmation that he had been identified as a homeless tramp.

Heath didn't take offence and followed his directions to the soup kitchen. The kitchen was a mobile one that was run by two of the nicest God-Bothering Do-Gooders to ever grace the earth. Heath accepted their kindness and truly appreciated it. His new street-folk friend-sct were also warm and welcoming and - without signing any sort of tenancy agreement - he took his place on the Street. Heath had no fixed abode for the next two years. That's one day at a time for 730 days.

Night one: Heath asked, "Where do people sleep that have nowhere to sleep?"

After lots of complimentary shared alcohol, he found out that people with nowhere to sleep, huddle together like penguins in city centre car parks to shut out the cold. His first experience of this was a humbling communal episode. At 6.30am, the Penguins were up and mobile.

Their day seemed to be planned out with military precision. By 7am, they were all on the tram to Victoria Station where a philanthropist restaurant owner laid on a bespoke beggars' breakfast for them. Heath seemed to have passed the 'One of Us' interview for his new post and quickly recognised that his new, small family had a remarkably honourable way about them.

If you got given anything by the great Mancunian public, then you had to share it. Monetary donations got invested in the necessities - cigs and booze - and then these were shared. It was an experience of considerable worth. Homeless people can sometimes be invisible to people with jobs but Heath's heart-warming initial experience was that, in Manchester, the Homeless Community look after each other and that was a most welcome and unexpected comfort in his life at this time.

Obviously, life on the streets can be desperate so it's not going to be an ongoing fairytale of kindness. Over the next two years, Heath experienced most of the ups and downs that come with this kind of basic existence. On the street, folk need to graft. You can't expect a share of the bounty of your circle of friends if you haven't added to the communal Treasure Chest.

Heath was a silent beggar. Passive. Some homeless

folk let the side down by refusing free food or coffee offered by kind strangers. Heath was never about that. He'd gratefully accept anything - not just because he's always had impeccable manners but because it was always the key to opening a conversation. People that are aware and kind enough to stop and communicate with someone less fortunate usually want to help in some way.

One such fella opened up with, "If there was anything I could do for you what would it be?"

"Well sir, I've seen an acoustic guitar in Argos for £25 that could really help me get by."

The chap didn't have time to go shopping but he was more than happy to pass £25 over to the stranger on the pavement. Heath was skilled but also genuine in offering appreciative thanks to such kind people. The obvious brief addicts' conundrum followed. Do I spend the £25 on a guitar or do I spend it on getting fucked up and get the guitar next time? He did the right thing and honoured the kind man's investment in him.

The £25 Argos nylon-stringed acoustic guitar was undoubtedly a bargain and a great tool to help Heath get back on the strum. He loves music but to this day he is still shy and scared to perform alone.

Unfortunately, in busking business terms, the £25 wasn't a sound investment as it was barely audible from pavement to a passer-by without an amplifier. Heath was also shit-scared of singing publicly even though he had been a celebrated backing vocalist in all the decent bands that he'd performed in.

After a couple of days sat in doorways tinkering and mumbling away to himself, a police officer stopped to question Heath's musical credentials.

"You're only holding that guitar so I can't fuckin' move you on." Suddenly offended and stimulated into action, Heath said, "Do you know *Blackbird* by The Beatles, officer?" Before delivering a pretty complex and impressive version of a great protest song, the message in the performance was "Fuck Off, Wanker" and he did.

Quiet busking in the daytime was shit and Heath soon moved to a night-time routine. He set up camp on a step in what is now known as the trendy Northern Quarter. Late Wednesday, Thursday, Friday and Saturdays, he'd passively finger-pick away from memory. Interested passers-by would have to really come in close to engage and that was an amazing way to hook people in to connect and, after a song, people would gladly listen to his shit tale of homelessness and give him a donation.

Underneath his need to play music, Heath's entrepreneurial mind knew that he was on the first rung of the business ladder towards sustainability of some kind. Unfortunately, sustainability to an addict usually includes the continual opportunity to self-harm to a higher standard and this definitely played out as Heath became more and more skilled at getting by.

As previously stated, life on the streets was all peaks and troughs so he'd have the high of a successful night playing music connecting with people and making a few quid and he'd have nights that were harsh, cold and life-threatening.

On one particularly dark, discontented night, Heath tasted the desperation of a pair of addicts on a lower vibration. A chap came to him shaking and shivering in the cold night air. He seemed genuine and asked if Heath wanted to put together and share a room in a hostel. The man produced £18 and Heath had the rest of the funds to take up the offer of a £35 room share for the night. They walked round the corner together where they were met by the man's underling partner in crime. He produced a nasty-looking flick-knife and relieved Heath of his rucksack, cash & basic mobile phone. Heath told them he'd die for his guitar and he managed to keep his only significant possession without having to physically fight for it.

That guitar led a charmed life. On another occasion Heath hit the bottle too hard and woke up somewhere random and unpleasant to the horrific realisation that someone had half-inched his beloved instrument in the night. Later that day, the beautiful God-bothering duo that ran the Soup Kitchen reunited Heath with his guitar explaining that it was taken from him to safeguard it because he was so pissed. The kind person that facilitated this good deed had asked for anonymity and the soup-dispensing team realised the Do-gooders right to do something special without any need for recognition. Accepting free food and drink from these amazingly enriched folk and hearing the tale of his guitar's righteous journey was a moment of humility. Even in the midst of an ear-splitting hangover, Heath felt the privilege of being among people that cared.

Over two years on the streets, Heath learned all the best ways to stay alive. Kind businesses and security guards were a key part of swerving the worst of the bad weather. At places like the Polish Embassy, Heath and his cohort were allowed to huddle together and sleep in the doorway - as long as they cleaned up and left before the public got up. Maintaining these respectful relationships was so important but not always easy. Sometimes people got ill or wrecked and against their best wishes they would jeopardise relationships and established safe havens for everyone but, in the main, Heath's Crew were very respectful.

Interestingly, a path to getting off the street was always available. Council officials walked the streets every morning at 5am; waking people up to check that they were alive and recording the numbers of homeless refugees for their records. Their dawn raid technique of waking someone up who was just into their only decent sleep in a 24-hour cycle didn't often lead to the street-folk taking their business cards and making the contact required to start an improved life off the street. Truth is, once you are immersed in a social scene where people seem to care about you, even if it's only sporadically, the decision to give that up is an easy one to put off but during one particularly cold dawn raid Heath took a Homeless Services Card from the officials and later that morning took the decision to move his life on.

Heath contacted the homeless charity Cornerstones and was amazed to be offered a room at The Salvation Army set up on Oxford Road. It was absolutely luxurious – there was no lock on his room but the sight of a bed with clean sheets was sensational. Heath timed taking up his new tenancy perfectly because, not only did he swerve a freezing cold winter snap spent on the street, he actually qualified for free meals every day the temperature dipped below zero. So, for the first frost-laden two weeks of his stay, he lived like a king. The food was exquisite as they knocked out all the great British classics; Full English, Cottage Pie and Fish 'n' Chips on a Friday. It was a magical place but, like all Great British Institutions, it had many rules and regulations to abide by. Heath still needed his addiction boxes ticking so he collected up his busking kit to go out and do a bit.

On his way out he was stopped in his tracks in the foyer where the staff quizzed him on his intentions before arranging for him to obtain an official busking license. He was amazed to have been given the opportunity to make his business legal. As far as he knew, he was just about the only busker in town with a permit and he felt that this was the first and only useful qualification that he'd ever obtained. He could now perform wherever he fuckin' wanted.

He wasted no time at all in playing pavement busking chess with the authorities. Heath took great enjoyment in waving away Jobsworth Coppers and he started to choose more and more antagonistic spots from which to perform. In his mind, he was playing "Rock, Paper, Scissors" with the Police but his paper always won. Heath loved the smugness of it all. His new ability to rock up and play anywhere didn't just annoy the authorities - grafting beggars weren't best pleased to have a mini-Paul McCartney turning up in all the prime spots stealing their thunder or more accurately their grafting revenue. Heath became very unpopular very quickly and was often verbally and physically threatened. He even received knife threats. Heath enjoyed the game and realised it was mainly hot air and business manoeuvring.

He chose to become a bit of a snob with it by looking down on the aggressive, unskilled begging folk from his own lofty place in the gutter. This was just another light-hearted survival mechanism and a decent way of maintaining a reasonable level of sanity. His new set-up at The Salvation Army on Wilmot Street had alienated him from his usual street contacts in the more central Piccadilly area.

Over on this side of town, the begging game was less genuine with more beggars actually having acceptable accommodation arrangements and welfare benefit income. In the main, they were just begging for drug money. Again, Heath was a snob about this as his addictions were funded by playing a guitar and that was much more acceptable - at least in his mind. His musicianship was steadily improving and he was even starting to sing a bit.

At the time, everybody who was staying with The Sally Army was cool. They were all communal sharers and the "What's mine is yours" philosophy was the norm. It was here among this sort of kindness that Heath had his second taste of heroin. Surprisingly, it was a pretty low-key experience. The naughty gang in the dorm put a sock over the smoke alarm and shared their poison. They took out a piece of foil and sanitised it by heating it all over with a lighter then added some heroin in the form of a brown powder - then they heated the foil from below and inhaled the heady toxins produced in the chemical reaction. This is the process known as, "chasing the dragon". Everyone else in the dorm was injecting too.

Heath watched and pitied them but was still astonishingly open to having a dabble. They would intermittently share the smoking side of the habit as a communal treat - almost like a "this is us'" recognition club. The truth of the matter is a lot more sinister as all heroin users tend to look for opportunities to lure new users in to open new revenue and gear streams, with the intention of feeding their own habit on the back of this shared energy.

Heath thought he was too clever for this lot; he'd done his research and it apparently takes a lot of effort to get hooked on smack. He wasn't going be around these kind, sharing manipulators for long. He could handle it…

In the short term, his evaluation of the situation was fairly accurate and, without too much fuss, he politely exited the scene into shared accommodation in Beswick but addicts don't try stuff once, the clue is in the name…

13 - TRYING HARD

Soundtrack: The Velvet Underground - *Heroin*

Even though his ego-demon was telling him that he was too intellectually superior to get hooked on smack, circumstances had led to his demon meeting with The Dragon and those two evils are the perfect formula for addicts hell-bent on self-hurt. Heath thought he was too clever for that but, at basement-level, the dark forces of this world were holding planning meetings to map out more and more opportunities for Heath to make all the wrong choices.

His new shared abode in Beswick was pretty rough. His new residential circle were all Phet-Heads and Heath just went with it and got strung out on speed every night for two months and drank off the come-down every morning using the liver-smashing White Lightning Cider as his poison.

The Council visited and assessed him as a good potential tenant as his room was meticulously clean. Of course it was, he cleaned the place from top to bottom six times a night, wired off his fuckin' tits on speed!

Unsurprisingly, that two-month period passed very quickly.

Out of the blue, the Council offered him a flat of his own and without bothering to view it first, Heath rang and accepted. He received a £200 grant from a charitable organisation to spend on decor. Obviously, he tried to sell his £200 B&Q voucher but nobody living at 200mph was remotely interested in decorating so Heath reluctantly purchased some nice wallpaper and paint and, as soon as he walked into his flat, he made it his own.

Predictably and unpredictably, the first new neighbour that he came across was Fat Karl upstairs. Karl was a drug dealer and Heath had a handy outlet to give away all his income from minute one of his tenancy. The unpredictable and unusual thing about Karl was that not only did he use as much gear as he sold (not that unusual), but he somehow managed to stay mega-fat even though he had raging phet, crack and smack habits going on. Karl was the first person to share a Methadone Script with Heath and 25ml in a tea cup was enough to take away his pain all day. He drifted in and out of consciousness and just loved the escape mechanism of this particular medicine.

Karl was dangerous and fortunately for his health but unfortunately in addiction terms, Heath didn't have much cash to waste relieving Karl of his eclectic contraband cache so he got back into the busking and re-established his music business flow around the Piccadilly, Oldham Road and Ancoats side of town. His new not-homeless status gave him an extra incentive to earn cash, pay bills and get by on his own steam. He put the hours in and managed to earn enough to finally make the investment to upgrade his guitar and grow his income stream by getting louder. Argos came up trumps again and his new best friend was a steel-stringed acoustic. He still couldn't afford an amp but that was the next item on his shopping list.

Heath shared a few treat nights in with Fat Karl. No sign of pizza, kebabs or Chinese but they did chew the fat over smack smoke, cider and a disappointing go on his crack pipe. UK cocaine-based products were shite compared to the Belize experience so Heath never wasted his money on that. Fat Karl was scary and psychotic so Heath only visited him in times of great need. A relationship that was the polar opposite of this seller/buyer need-based relationship came into fruition at around about the same time as Heath decided to try to avoid Fat Karl as much as he could.

Sunday mornings without seeing his son were always poignant so Heath would often go to the library which was free and very good for filling his mind with useless information to stop all the other stuff going on. At the library Heath met Alan, who was an absolute whizz on cryptic crosswords that appeared in the free newspapers there. Alan did all the crosswords and, every now and then, he'd fire a question across the table. Heath was shite at the cryptic clues but decent on the general knowledge and, after a few weeks of flirting in this way, Alan popped the question and asked Heath back to his flat.

"I have crossword books. I could teach you how to do the cryptic ones."

Obviously even Heath had received better offers in his time and he had to quickly evaluate if this guy was a sexual predator. He listened to his gut on this and his gut told him that, "No. This guy's a genuine Gentleman Geek like me" and happily that proved to be the case.

Like a Star Wars Jedi in training camp, Heath was shown the way of the Cryptic Crossworders and soon became a whiz. It turned out Heath and Alan had much in common. They were kindred spirits. Surprisingly or unsurprisingly, again they shared an interest in opioids. Alan had a Methadone Script which he supplemented with heroin.

The pair of them spent Sundays stretching their minds like the great thinkers of the past. Unlike Homer, Franklin, Napoleon and Hitler, their opium-fuelled thought-processes were much more crossword focused. It was a beautiful time and Heath was quickly invested in a genuine friendship. Their relationship wasn't just about the drugs. Their conversations swung between high-brow discussions around literature and politics to witty self-depreciating anecdotes about their life experiences.

Alan lived a simple life investing his DLA Benefits on books and three bags of smack a day in addition to his Methadone Script. When Heath came, Alan would always lay on complimentary tea, biscuits and one of his three smack bags for Heath to smoke on his behalf. At the time, heroin cost £10 a bag or three for £25.

So… Alan was doing approximately £600 a month on gear as a fairly responsible controlled user. He must have had a pension or something going on income-wise because he just wasn't the kind of fella that you could ever imagine begging, stealing or blagging his way through his addiction. He always seemed in control and he was generous.

Apart from his traditional Sunday foil roast with Alan, Heath's main poison was still alcohol and he still liked to do his drinking mainly in private so having his own place was the perfect set up. His relationship with the bottle was a treasured, straight forward one. Drugs went up and down in quality but on a bottle 40% meant 40% and he could always escape and do a number on himself. This constant and private campaign of self-abuse was slowly starting to shut down his body.

Smoking heroin on top was another layer of escapism. Heath never injected but when the smack was good, he was sometimes able to achieve a high close to the one he experienced the first time he used – where for a short period of time he would be free from reality.

He'd inhale the harsh acrid smoke and lay down and feel completely and utterly comfortably numb, like he was lying on a warm cotton wool cloud back in his mother's womb – a home from home.

Chasing that level of escapism was always Heath's game and, without recognising it, he did end up trying really hard to get hooked on smack. It took him a couple of years of sniffly little colds before Heath even started to consider that these little colds just might be the morning rattle of the heroin addict.

Truth was he wasn't that far behind Alan in terms of consumption. He'd just taken the moral high ground because he didn't inject but he was conning himself. On top of keeping the NHS busy by wrecking his digestive system with the drink, he could really do with a detoxification program for the smack.

Heath wasn't close to admitting any of this even to himself. He certainly wasn't quitting a lifestyle that fitted his hurt plan. He just had to take steps to increase his income stream to match his lifestyle. He did this by stepping up his efforts on the busking front.

Heath got organised and stuck religiously to his set times. Even though his health wasn't the best, he still played well and engaged with people easily. Heath freely admits he was a fuck-up, but he was always a humble, talented one with good manners so, as long as he put the graft in, he could always make decent money.

It was at this time that the Government got on his case and started to put pressure on him to be signed off as fit for work. Even though he was clearly capable of organising himself to be in a shop doorway to play a Beatles classic set five nights out of seven, he was also clearly not capable of doing forty hours manual labour in a warehouse.

Heath continued to make good use of his Golden Ticket. His Busking License enabled him to play in all the prime locations and, in line with his enlarged habit costs, he started coming out earlier and playing longer even though he had to balance this with pretending to try and get a job.

The council had a scheme to get formerly homeless people back into work. Heath had to attend workshops and seminars with potential employers and was even issued his very own back-to-work coach. Heath's coach was a pretty cool fella and the two of them put a CV together and week-by-week the coach was slowly building trust and edging Heath towards a possible career on the railway as his contact was a somebody at First Trans Pennine Trains.

Ridiculously, just before Heath was due to attend an interview with the Train Operating Company, the DWP called to inform him that he must call an end to attending the coaching sessions so he could find a job. This was just the excuse Heath needed to raise his middle finger to The System. He was never going to pass the drugs and alcohol screening anyway, so he decided to go down the honesty path with the DWP and shock them by admitting that he was unable to work regarding his addictions. This took a long time to manifest but eventually, after many meetings, tests and evaluations, someone ticked a box to say "Yes, Heath. you're a fuck up."

Heath's relationship with Alan was a constant and they spent more and more time together. For a good period of time, Heath would walk off the morning rattle by traipsing seven miles to pick up a copy of the *Manchester Evening News* for 40p. On good days, he'd also pick up some smack to share while they completed the MEN's Cryptic Crossword. The two of them often shared a day-saver bus or tram ticket which gave unlimited travel around Greater Manchester. They both had a set of keys to enable them to access each other's flat to ensure that their daily movements and ticket-swap offers were seamless and cost effective.

Nothing ever lasts forever.

One morning Heath was waiting for Alan to drop by with their shared day-saver bus ticket to travel into Manchester to enable him to go on his daily busking mission. Alan was half an hour later than usual which was quite unusual but he was a cyclist and he might have had a flat tyre or something. Heath's mobile rang - Alan's name flashed up but it wasn't his beloved friend on the end of the phone, it was a Police Constable.

"Hello, this is Police Constable So & So. May I ask if you're Alan's next of kin?"

Heath just knew, "No, I'm not, I'm his friend. Is he dead?"

The policeman told Heath that he couldn't say.

"He's got my fuckin' bus ticket."

Those words were the stark bleak words of despair. Half of a bus ticket was one way of describing their friendship but it ran much, much deeper than that. In a state of numb loss, Heath explained to the Police Officer who was who in Alan's phone so that the authorities could contact Alan's family down south. Heath still went into Manchester and played and sang for his friend. Heath cried himself to sleep that night.

The next morning the policeman came to visit Heath. Alan had suffered a massive heart attack and died aged 47. Heath explained details of their relationship and admitted that he had access to Alan's flat and all of his belongings. They went to Alan's flat together and the policeman accepted Heath's story when he saw that Alan had the keys to Heath's place too.

Alan's family made contact and they were really lovely people. They totally understood how much Heath meant to Alan and gave him the pick of Alan's belongings from the flat. Heath didn't want anything but he did the right thing and put his suit on and took up their invitation to help carry the coffin into his friend's funeral. Heath didn't last long at the wake as he just wasn't ready to celebrate Alan like his family were. He just felt completely robbed.

The nice people gave him £30 for a taxi home. Normally he would have driven around the corner handed over a fiver and got the bus before spending £20 on getting fucked up - but he let the taxi driver drive and when the meter hit £30 Heath said, "I'll walk from here"

The taxi-man said, "No mate, I'll drop you all the

way – it's not every day you lose your best friend."

The next morning Heath felt unexpectedly energised as if Alan was urging him to go out and make something of his day. He had a brew and a cigarette and decided to go into town early, arriving around lunchtime which was six hours earlier than normal. Heath still had his Busking License in hand so he headed for a prime spot on Manchester's busiest thoroughfare, Market Street.

It was too early to sit in a doorway like he usually did, so he just put down his man-bag outside Jessop's Camera Shop and started strumming his guitar. It didn't take long before he attracted the attention of a man who he'd often seen holding up a "Pizza Hut £7.95 - Lunch This Way" sign.

As soon as Heath stopped playing the man said, "Let's have a go of your guitar." Heath realised the man was unlikely to run off because he clearly worked for Pizza Hut so he handed over his prized possession. He tinkered with the guitar and told Heath that he should buy an amp as there's no point standing here playing in silence. "In fact, if you buy an amp, you can use my Fender copy to perform here. Then if you make some money, you can buy the guitar."

Garry Stanley has a way of doing this. Without even introducing himself, he'd given a stranger a life plan and a purpose. He invested in Heath from the very first moment that he met him. Heath took Garry's advice and started playing in close proximity to him every day. In less than a week, he had managed to make enough dough to buy an amplifier from Cash Converters.

Garry was true to his word and the next morning he presented Heath with a rather smart Fender copy. Heath got excitedly noisy and paid off Garry's hire purchase agreement within three weeks. Garry had the air of a proud dad and his overall general demeanour made Heath feel safe. Garry seemed to know and have the respect of everyone that worked the area. Garry could be seen chuckling to himself when Heath attracted some of the city's more colourful characters.

Garry was often amused by one particular character on the scene and he watched on with great interest as Heath endured his first Ray Boddington experience. Ray had the appearance of a walking corpse; whiter than white and bony as fuck. He may have looked dead but his character was warm and engaging. Heath let Mr Skeli-bones have a quiet impressive dabble on the guitar before Ray passed it back to him before leaning in to whisper, "I can make you a lot of money you know, I'm a dancer."

Heath started to play and Ray started to move. Heath had never seen anything like it. The Old Boy, who must have been about seventy but just let it all hang out. His moves were structured and eye-catching but his money-making prophecy didn't manifest at all as he seemed to scare off the passers-by. After a twenty minute performance, they had collected one solitary English Pound in the begging bucket.

He walked back over to Heath and said, in all seriousness, "I can teach you to dance like me if you like."

Ray spoke softly, kindly and warmly and was clearly self-worshippingly full on barking mad.

Interestingly, Heath felt just as safe with Ray as he did with Garry and from that moment on he knew that he would always be connected and associated with the guy with the Pizza Sign and his delusional friend. They were on his frequency.

He was home.

14: WHY PUT OFF TIL' TOMORROW THAT WHICH YOU CAN PUT OFF TIL' NEXT WEEK?

Soundtrack: The Strokes - *Someday*

This chapter is written by Heath himself to summarize his rebirth from addiction and share his gratitude for the great people and services that helped him ultimately beat himself.

The dystopian nightmare of consistently putting off facing my truth reached its tipping point in early 2019. Imagine reading a book about your would be inner hero, imagine reading it a thousand times over and always rooting for the protagonist in the tale, rooting for me, turning the pages in some sort of pathetic hope that someone, somewhere or something could be the trigger to fix the mess of my own desperate existence. I always knew how the story ended and the same story in the sequel too but something made me keep on at it, relentlessly playing the game of hopeful deception, reading and re-reading the story of my life always thinking that: 'Maybe this time it could be different.'

In the depths of my despair I never truly wanted to die but each night the urge to never wake up the next day grew on me like a putrid mould. Rather than scrape away the rotten stench of self-betrayal I did what addicts do, I deceived myself, half or maybe a quarter believing that because I only use 'Drug A' maybe I'm not as bad as 'Those People' who use 'Drug B', I only smoke it not like 'Those People' who inject it. The mental gymnastics that go into this denial is pretty much a full-time occupation; minimization, justification and the 'othering' of other addicts without seeing that without intervention you are already or will soon become that dreaded despicable 'other'.

For me the biggest lie that I repeatedly told myself was that if I could only move away from where I was, then the change of environment would enable me to stop using substances. The desire for geographical location change was always strong in me, I wanted to run and run in the hope of eventually finding that happy place. Time and time again moving did not stop me using but still I continually chose to run; I've run from towns, cities, countries and even continents but each and every time I found the darkness of sanctitude that I always offered myself in these places.

By 2019 I was broken, I despised my life, my body was poisoned almost beyond repair but deep within the wreckage of that shell of a man I finally realised that it wasn't my toxified body that needed fixing. It was me. For the first time in my life I truly wanted to end that life and reach out for myself. My son was always in my thoughts and in my heart but I could never truly be with him until I found my own peace.

After a spectacularly honest appointment with my GP I was referred to addict services and life changing organisations called CGL and Emerging Futures. The support and treatment that was given to me at these places literally helped fix a completely broken person. I started detox in Autumn 2019 and continued into a community rehab program. The staff in those places are remarkable souls, they rescued me and rebuilt my life and they have rebuilt the lives of countless others, above everything else, they fixed me. ME!

Me's problem was never alcohol, never drugs, never other people's actions and most definitely never needing to move away. They made me realise that all along me's problem was *me*. Stripped bare I was the only constant in all *me's* problems.

I don't want the honest account of my life to ever represent drugs in a good way. The only reason that I didn't take the opportunity to kill myself with heroin was because I'm shit scared of needles. Thankfully I'm a lucky shitbag in that way and that was not to be my fate.

Life is different now; different in ways that I could never had hoped for. I now exist in an almost dream-state of consciousness where I truly am just happy to be alive. Amazingly my son has let me into his life again and spending time with him is simply joyous.

It also turns out that I did have a happy place after all, both in my head and back in Manchester. I feel lucky and grateful to have what I have. As you have read, I often selfishly crashed out and sheepishly meandered back into the bat-shit crazy circus that is The Piccadilly Rats. Their friendship and kindness and that of Ringmaster Garry in particular have saved and sustained me on a number of occasions.

The Rats are the gift that keeps on giving, I'm so proud to be one of The Piccadilly Rats.

POSTSCRIPT

Soundtrack: ABBA – *Knowing You Knowing Me*

Writing this book has been a tormented pleasure for me. My own personal life story *The Balloon* by MJ Pinkie (embarrassed pen name) is available on Amazon. If you take the time to dig out that particularly shocking memoir of a Wrong 'Un then you will note that I too have lived a life and learned my own lessons along the way.

Being an almost-reformed Wrong 'Un put me in exactly the right non-judgemental, open-minded head space that I needed to be in to start absorbing The Rats' Tales. In the same way Gaz had to micro-manage the unmanageables to get them to perform in the City Centre, I had to solve the same sort of puzzle to start extracting each of their own remarkable stories. From the start it became clear that this was no ordinary project and I was dealing with one of, if not the most, dysfunctional band in the world.

Ray Super-trumped him by dying but if it wasn't for that I would have to say that writing Garry's story has been the most challenging one to record out of them all. I'd ring him and he'd give me a headline for a chapter then he'd go Off Piste and then flip back further in time and give me another headline but he never hit me with the full body of any of the stories. After a few of these round-in-circles calls I took a deck chair to Market Street and sat next to him and his over the shoulders Pizza Hut sign on a Tuesday lunch time. I put my voice recorder on and let him waffle. The back to front encyclopaedia of the Rats started to flow as Gaz revealed some of his acting and comic talent as he mimicked each member of the band as he talked about them. When I got home to the wife my stomach was aching from laughing like I'd been in for surgery. I tried to play her back a voice clip of Gaz doing a Tommy impression, but she wasn't listening, and she did what women do, and said "how much time are you going to waste on this?"

The thing with wives is the bastards are usually fuckin' right and sure enough I spent months decoding that two-hour voice recording. I didn't get a single completed chapter out of it but I did get a list of about a dozen stories that I wanted to find out more about.

That became almost impossible because Gaz stopped answering his phone for a couple of months and when he did finally answer, he was one-word-answer depressed without telling me why. Unbeknown to me he had just got out of re-hab after his Boggart Hole Clough ordeal and gleefully chatting to me about Tommy's mankini was the last thing that he wanted to do. Rather than give up I decided to hunt down the other members of the group.

First I went looking for Tommy. Tommy Trouble is golden. To this day he does not own a mobile phone so I had to wander round town looking for him in order to pin him down and capture the account of his existence. He is as deaf as a post these days after standing in front of Gaz's amp for ten years so when I found him on Market Street I had to scream down his lug hole.

"I want to write your story Tommy, about your life."

"You daft sod" he kept saying to me.

"Tommy I'm being serious."

He just kept hugging me and trying to dig me in the liver.

"No Tommy I really do!"

Eventually I got him into a café and convinced him to meet with me the following day.

He never came.

Six days later he turns up at Piccadilly station where I work and pulls me out of a meeting.

"You bastard I've been looking everywhere for you," he tells me. I got him a brew and the poor sod waited an hour, sat happily in the station while I did what I had to do. As soon as I could get out of work, I scooped him up and reminded him that he wasn't waiting for a train.

His life story was short and simple and he's so proud of himself and the achievements of the band that without really trying he reduced me to mush. By the time I had finished shout-interviewing him, everyone in the Subway canteen knew about the life and times of Tommy Trouble. As we were wrapping up, he wrote his address in my notebook and put a heavy-handed remindful squeeze on my wrist to remind me come around to his house as soon as his story was written up.

A week later I drove by Trouble Towers and visited Tommy's impeccably kept council flat. I passed him his story and he passed it back and asked me to read it for him. We sat, I talked, he listened, he cried and I cried and then he asked me just like a little doughy-eyed boy, "Can I keep this Martin."

"It's your story Tommy, course you can," Then he rubbed my head in an over affectionately hard way.

My next life story victim was Heath. I knew nothing about him other than he played the drums and the bass and he had at some point in the past been made homeless but now he was fortunate enough to have his own place.

When I first went to a dingy Moston café to meet up with Heath t start absorbing his story I had no idea about what I was walking into. He told me that he'd never told his story to anyone before and this was massive for him. Unlike Garry he was able to chronologically detail his story in order from birth onwards and by the end of making the notes to create chapter one I could tell that his story was going to be an epic and emotional one. I thought finally I can crack on and get a bit of traction under this project. Then a waitress came, and I ordered him his preferred breakfast of sausage and beans. When the food came, he put a bit of black pepper on his sausage, took one bite then had to run for the bog where I could hear him retching. When he came back in a cold apologetic sweat he informed me that we'd have to wrap it up for the day before we had even really started but he was honest enough to tell me that he was about twelve weeks into a heroin and alcohol rehab. He was doing well and he had the full support of his son and that meant the world to him.

Over the next twelve weeks I interviewed Heath by phone, face time and in person and I was super privileged to observe the rebirth of a fabulous human being. The really mad twist on the Rats Tale is that in all the time that they spent together busking neither Garry or Heath knew that the other man had serious addiction issues of their own. So in the aftermath of Ray's death, neither knew that the other one was suffering so badly and to the extent that they were both in rehab at the same time.

After Heath's initial three-week detox stint in a

medical facility he returned to his flat alone and afraid, returning home felt like another loss. He had to do a week alone without any support before he was lucky enough to take up a place on a 12-week community rehab program, basically a day-release rehab in Ancoats.

Heath knew that he should arrange to see Garry and honestly explain his most recent and lengthy period of absence from the band but the truth was that he was in a much too fragile state to do so, he was too embarrassed to share the detail of his addict reality. Heath kept putting that phone-call off.

A couple of weeks into rehab he really wished that he had already called Garry. He bumped into someone from town coming back his way on the tram. Heath was shocked to the core when he was told that Garry had suffered a stroke and was brain damaged. Heath didn't really think to question that unkindly bolt of realism. The information was that awful that he never suspected that it might be incorrect. Surely nobody would make up something like that?

Heath put his own issues to one side and made the call. Garry's wife Diane answered and Heath blurted out "Can I come over and see Gaz?"

"Of course," she replied and a couple of hours later he nervously arrived.

Dianne answered the door all polite smiles and niceties and showed Heath into the lounge where a *very* short-haired Mr Stanley, who looked completely un-brain-dead and significantly younger than he had done five weeks previously when Heath last saw him, was lounging on his sofa watching TV like he didn't have a care in the world.

Without too much of a fuss he says "Hi Heath, have

a seat, fancy a brew mate?"

"Garry, some cunt just told that you were a vegetable, that you've had a massive stroke."

"What me and Diane do on this couch is our business mate." And before Heath could share the details of his long term absence said, "You'll never guess where I've been..."

He told his story and proclaimed himself a recovering alcoholic, an addict and a straight head going forward. Heath was in bits emotionally and he laughed and cried with Garry that day.

The man that Heath idolised for his togetherness was almost as fucked up as him. He didn't want that for his friend, but Heath recognised that the dream that he had always hoped for that was to one day be just like Gaz had finally came true in the most dramatic fashion. The fact Garry was part of their newly formed Recovering Addict Club was more than unbelievable. Heath went from thinking that his best mate was a brain damaged has-been, to learning that, he was now a lean clean fellow non-drinking machine. Going forward they could help and support each other but right in that moment Heath knew that he was only at the start of his recovery journey. He'd have to learn to walk before he could run both emotionally and physically as his body started to feel the effects of withdrawal from the substances that he had previously used as pain-numbing medicine. Heath had not felt real emotion for a long, long time and suddenly everything was amplified and he often found himself laughing and crying at the same time.

They tell people in detox that one of the great things about being clean is that you get your emotions back, but they tend to leave out that one of the worst things about being clean is also that you get your emotions back.

The next few weeks were all consuming for Heath but he still managed to make the effort to get over to see Garry in between his day-release rehab. They felt closer together and could just 'be'. They would sit and chat and watch TV and of course play music. Seeing the world without beer goggles was such an enhanced experience but it was very emotional time for Heath and he found himself welling up all the time. Garry got it and neither of them felt any embarrassment.

Two months was the longest period since the formation of the band that Gaz and some form of Rats' had not played in Town. Apart from Gaz having a breakdown and both himself and Heath being in rehab the big elephant in the room was would Gaz ever be able to perform again because his suicide attempt had cut through some of his guitar strumming wrist tendons. Heath never asked and then halfway through an afternoon episode of *Countdown* Gaz popped the question

"If the weather's good this Saturday, do you fancy going to play in Town for a couple of hours?"

Heath was scared shitless to play sober with all those people looking at him but of course they played and he cried his eyes out under that Rat mask as he saw all the happy faces through his peep holes.

Ray once infamously tweeted "fuckin' celebrities" and for the first time ever Heath felt like the semi-celeb that Ray had joked about. For the first time ever he was proud of himself. They got Alan out and made a bit of a noise but in truth Gaz's wrist were fucked but the first baby steps of a comeback were in place.

Gaz has become Heath's rock. The music and all that is important but to have somebody that he can talk openly and honestly to about both of their ongoing recovery journeys has been a massive plus for both of them, it's said that the therapeutic value of one addict helping another addict is without parallel and both men testify to this, just to be able to phone each other and say "you know what, I'm feeling like shit" and to be told "you know what that's okay I'm feeling the same" is both powerful and reassuring.

Gaz and Heath are in the "one day at a time" club. Throughout the whole of Heath's addiction he could never see a point where he would be abstinent for the rest of his life. That was and is too much of a distance to contemplate honestly but you know what, all he has got to do is stay clean today, forget about tomorrow. At the time of writing this Gaz has been clean for 365 days and Heath for 335 days and all of those days were just one day at a time.

Thankfully, as I am approaching completion of this barmy tale, Buster Rabcat's Spinal Tap prediction doesn't appear to have come true. He has not been seen in recent times and that is a bit of a worry but to my knowledge no other Rat has passed away between Ray's death and the completion on this book.

I'm pleased.

MR.
UNPOPULAR

Martin Pin Ball Gray

BUSTER RABCAT'S TALE

1: THE WHO NOT THE WHAT - WHAT?

Soundtrack: Rag 'n' Bone Man – *Skin*

The subject and big character featured in this final Rat Tale has, as you may deduce from his own Mr Man style self-portrait opposite, a bit of a self-esteem issue going on - in fact he detests himself. Everyone that meets him doesn't get it, but this man will freely admit that he is his own worst enemy.

The man is packed full of creativity, passion and energy. You would think a human being with these characteristics would somehow manage to hold themselves in reasonably high esteem, a mindset to celebrate a great attitude of being set up right and trying to make a difference in the world... but no; for Rabcat, his angst, anger and anxiety can't get past how shit the world is and, at this point in his existence, he is a complete prisoner to that mindset.

As the chief gatherer of all the Rats' life stories I was particularly looking forward to digging into this fella's past, mainly because he's a man of mystery. Back at the start of the project he gave me some good information about his time in the band but when I wrote up that particular piece of the narrative I was surprised to receive a sizeable bollocking from him because I took the piss out of his ethnicity. I copped it by email, then by phone as he was convinced that my writing style was offensive. He took my suggestive description of his drumsticks (chopsticks) to be a racial slur on my behalf. Of course I told him this was a load of bollocks as the pen trick was just a trigger to recognise his label. I agree with him that we are all just souls in a bag of skin. I don't see race and colour in terms of judging a person's soul but we are indisputably bagged up with labels on, be it Manc, Scouser, white, black or Oriental. That is what our eyes see and that is what our ears hear. He's right of course. That's why we are such a shit species.

Rabcat, like it or not, is a soul having an experience in an oriental-style bag of skin with a Scouse accent. What he doesn't register is that his particular temporary state of being, mixed up with his creative punk energy and a seriously cool, arty dress sense makes his own reverberation within the Manc Realm all the more impressive. He's rocking an undoubtedly high-end vibration.

Problem is he wants to be recognised for who he is, not what he is and I get that but this ain't a quantum physics lecture - it's the story of The Rats so it's hard to describe a human being without describing their skinbag and associated accessories.

Fair enough he enjoyed the secrecy and notoriety of the rat mask disguise and that was his thing but when The Rats were on the Judge Rinder Show, the Judge decreed that he lose the mask. I agree with Rabcat that it would have made much better TV to have kept the mask on.

I know that hit him hard and took the fun out of the project for him but to make for a great chapter in this book I would have liked to also remove his mask and get to know the ins 'n' outs of his whole life, his beginnings in this dimension within the matrix that he detests with such noble distaste.

As it happens Rabcat never chose to chip in his life story until now, just before publication, as up until now he was set on suicide and was convinced that the rest of the band would also spontaneously combust before publication day. He sees this book as part of their death curse and, no doubt, I'm the executioner but I think he seriously underestimates his own and his bandmates will to survive.

He's chosen to start his life story from his Uni days as he doesn't want to be known as whatever he was before those days if you catch my drift. Anyway for some reason he's happy to be identified as a student of all things so we'll start there...

Over to The Rabcat:

"Don't forget that I did speak with you earlier about not putting any needless (or tokenistic) references or cultural appropriations into any of your existing narrative, regarding my ethnic background when talking about me and how I came to become involved with the band, as I personally find that unnecessary and, as the great legendary King Monkey Ian Brown once said so famously: 'It's not where you're from, it's where you're at!'"

2: A WHOLE NEW UNI-VERSE

Soundtrack: Capital Cities – *Safe And Sound*

Newcastle was an alien place to Rabcat when he first landed there in September 1984, very different from his home city of Liverpool but surprisingly samey in lots of ways too.

Rabcat reckons cities built on rivers are a class apart from the other cities for some reason. Glasgow has exactly the same sort of dichotomy possessing an edge and beauty of its own, coupled with the friendliness and garrulousness of its natives much the same as Newcastle and Liverpool in that way.

All three cities are well known for being mutually respectful and admiring of each other - compared the perpetual rivalries you get between cities such as Liverpool/Manchester, Newcastle/Sunderland and Glasgow/Edinburgh. Maybe, as they say, it's something in the water: of the Mersey, of the Tyne and of the Clyde - proud maritime cities one and all, each with their high and low attributes, but all of them indisputably characterful and unique in their own boss, canny and wee ways!

Still, it felt a world away from Liverpool. It took Rabcat around ten months to realise that he'd done the dirty on Liverpool as he'd fallen slap, bang, wallop in love with this other dirty Northern city. The Tyne and surrounding area had seduced him on almost every level. He soon came to realise just how similar Geordies were to Scousers. (Note from the author - Shameless labelling of ethnic groups!)

The Geordie student experience was boy-to-man time for Rabcat. As a child and adolescent teenager he was quite shy and introverted but at Uni he started to express himself and be influenced by things that he had never previously been influenced by. How he reacted to these situations had a serious impact on shaping him into the person that he later became - a lone-ranging rebel.

It was a liberating time. It was also very politically

polarised time too as 1984 was the year of the Miner's Strike. Newcastle and the entire North East region suffered badly and students we were being indoctrinated into the prevailing political culture – of hard left, socialist ideals. It was no coincidence that Marxist propaganda and Che Guevara posters were also de rigeur at the time. To be anything other than Labour a supporter was to be declared a heretic and an outcast. Rabcat earned maverick status quickly by refusing to follow any dictum or trend. He was self-proclaimed, resolutely and proudly apolitical and atheist and even though he could sympathise and appreciate why, as students, his peers would be more left-leaning than right, no political stance made sense to him because he wasn't listening to the bullshit noise - he preferred to listen to the music of the time. He particularly hated it when political sloganeers or Bible-bashing zealots came to his hall of residence to demand that he listened to them preaching the Gospel of whatever. Rather than tell them to fuck off directly, he chose to politely let them fade into a state of futile loss as he nodded along with uninterested intention. He killed them with his patience.

Shit politics aside, Rabcat was blinded by the light of opportunity for growth within his new life and his new social life. His eyes were suddenly wide open as cultural and partying opportunities started to present themselves each and every day.

Discovering new bands and scenes was a student's rite of passage and the music side of the experience lit the Rabcat up. Arty bloke loaded his digs walls up with posters, some handmade, others bought from the cheap poster sales which were held every third day at the Students' Union.

Making new friends at Uni came surprisingly easy and naturally. He hung out in pubs, went to clubs to dance to all the latest 80s shit that was big at the time. Rabcat of that time hadn't realised how shit the world was and he didn't overthink situations like he does now so he was happy to get pissed and dance to shit music and just be. He had a Bono and a Tina Turner impression in his party repertoire and, at one time, just for a short time, he was almost an alcohol-fuelled exhibitionist.

Occasional tippling was Rabcat's only real vice and he gained a reputation as some kind of evil cocktail chemist as he liked to start a house party by mixing all kinds of incompatible liquids and unpalatable concoctions into party potions as some kind of endurance test done purely for the fun and, dare I say notoriety, amongst his peers.

Rabcat hated smoking so he never expanded his consciousness or got to burn holes in his favourite jumpers. He left the wacky baccy well alone. He also stayed away from the Class A menu on offer at the time. Talking Heads were flying the flag for creative Amphctamine use but Rabcat was happy fuelling up on Franken-cocktails to supplement the adrenaline that was flowing through him at breakneck speed amidst an almost constant state of party.

For the first time in his life (I think) he let himself go, becoming a hyper get go type of character, a stark contrast to the reserved, shy and withdrawn Rabcat of secondary school, sixth form, and even Art College.

A rocket of freedom and expression had gone off inside of him and without the shackles of later life he lapped up the party scene by night and drifted into daytime lectures more in body than in spirit. To this day he has no recollection of any meaningful lecture absorption.

He put little effort or application into a BA Honours course in Graphic Design, with an additional six month Animation Course in the Media Production Department. This led had an almost schizoid existence for the final six months managing about 6 lectures out of a total of 30 in all because he kept nodding off and falling asleep. For three years, he blagged and bumbled his way through the courses without really attending them proving himself smart in one way or another.

Rabcat is frugal. I don't know him well enough to say that he doesn't do extravagance, but I feel it. At Uni, he didn't overspend on anything, be it records or socialising or whatever else. The most expensive thing that he bought in Uni days was a nifty Hitachi twin tape-deck ghetto-blaster for £85 in early 1986. This replaced a small, tinny Toshiba single tape/radio that he had for his 18th birthday and looked after for 2 years before it went tits up. He OCD-tested *seven* other models under 14 day money-back warranty - each time exchanging the last one for a better model. He soon earned the title of Dixons Electricals Newcastle Branch most hated customer.

He also refused to shell out on clothing, second hand jackets, army and navy surplus, charity shops and the hip and trendy used clothing emporium FLIP were his go-to clobber vaults. Baggy over skin tight was his style, taking inspiration from punkier/indie kid/psychobilly/ skinhead looks that were all the rage back in the 1980s - the skinhead look figured particularly prominently in the working class Geordie capital.

Art student Rabcat's image statement was an

amalgam of all four scenes in used cheap Doc Martens and his look brought him confidence that he had previously lacked as a 2 Tone enthusiast wanting to look like one of The Specials, The Selecter or Madness. His hair was also a mission statement spiked up again in a cross between the four styles mentioned earlier - punk, goth, psychobilly and skinhead. He shaved his head bald at the back and sides then set the rest according to his daily vibe.

His threads were all over the place too as the non-conformist continued to mix it up camo/combat pants, cargos, chinos, baggy slacks, collarless military shirts, the occasional punk studded belt, or sometimes skinhead-style narrow braces in place of belts. Sometimes, he'd also design own t-shirts as well using dye paint which he'd simply just daub on with a paint brush.

Even though he had come out of his shell a bit, he was still a bit of a complicated character when it came to social interaction. His stock position, at least when he wasn't on the piss, was that of wanting to be unnoticed and unacknowledged but his expressional retro dress sense always brought attention and compliments that to this day he insists were unwelcome.

One outfit that he made for himself brought him plenty of unwanted attention. He painted a white T-shirt with a huge splodge of crimson red right by his heart and then loads of red rivulets/trickles running crudely down from it, so it resembled a massive gunshot wound in his chest with blood gushing down the front. On the back was a smaller splodge of an exit wound. Sick good.

This kind of morbidity crossed over into his official and unofficial Uni artwork and the t-shirt manifested into a dark poem and a catalogue of sick photo prints that one of the Bible Bashers was kind enough to help shoot.

Rabcat didn't let the slight embarrassment of having the sinister thought drive to create devious, dark and even perverse artwork stop him. Getting the God Squad involved in dark side doings was a revelation in itself.

The Christian prophesier from down the corridor would agree to photograph Rabcat in various deathly poses as he turned his room into something like a slaughterhouse from Hellraiser with black polythene bin bags and red paint-splattered wallpaper simulating blood draped on all three walls. Bible Boy never blinked, decent training probably if he was serious about a career in his own particular cult.

Piss-ups in student flats continued to come thick and fast and his learning and creative path ran in tandem with a strict sleep deprivation and prodigious liquid consumption program. Right through year 3 he hardly slept at all as he was always intensely hyper. Evenings on the lash were often followed by cartoon film animation sessions that he would later submit as coursework. He was skilled in being able to work and create while being pissed up. He'd work for hours then try and haul his arse into class having had little or no sleep. Even though he was skilled at painting drunk-induced mistakes did ultimately happen. One of the four short cartoons that he submitted for critique featured a guy playing a show tune on a Wurlitzer organ. Unfortunately when the film was played back to his fellow students the organist started to frantically bounce up and down but didn't appear to have any legs. A tragic lack of attention to detail. A true delivery of the Legless Art form in more ways than one.

On the party scene and within his social group, one girl stood out to Rabcat and most of his peers. Her name was Geraldine and everyone fancied her as she was really attractive as well as being a beautiful person in personality too. She was a Fine Art student with the most amazingly dirty laugh which everyone found so endearing. Everyone was desperate to get off with her.

She lived just up from his digs in the west end of Newcastle. One early morning Rabcat plucked up the courage to knock at her door when rolling in after being out all night. It was a bit of a Shakespearean scene as she answered the door bell by leaning out of the upstairs window and dirty laughing down at him in her own incredibly charming way.

"Are you here again?" she teased before letting him in.

They chatted easily almost as if she had been expecting him. "Shall we play a record?" Geraldine suggested with a glint in her eye, knowing full well that they'd wake everyone that lived in the flat up.

Geraldine cranked up "I Love Rock n Roll" by Joan Jett and the Blackhearts and when she heard her housemates starting to complain, she changed the speed on the old school record-player to distort the sound and make it even more annoying.

Rabcat found himself literally rolling around the floor, with Geraldine crying with laughter. Geraldine often kipped in the main room if the others were entertaining so a pull-out bed was there and ready to go. It was Rabcat's time to stake a claim for the Special One or at least create a romantic forever memory. As far as I can tell he didn't and innocent friendship prevailed. I have a feeling she wanted more than he imagined.

Everyone fancied Geraldine and Rabcat was probably guilty of underestimating his own allure. Not sure if he has any regrets around this but I certainly wish that he'd shagged her. He goes on to explain that it was quite awkward to hide his true feelings in her presence. From the outside looking in, why would you?

Two months later our man graduated gaining what Scousers call a Desmond - a 2:2 was a decent enough result considering. Geraldine was a year behind him but she ended up being a practising fine artist and experimental musician who played with the well-known London band Gallon Drunk in the 1990s and then later collaborated German collective, Faust. She was always gonna make a big impression.

I have a sneaky suspicion that it wasn't just Newcastle that stole the Rabcat's heart but after three happy years on the Tyne, it was time to head back south-west to La La Land.

3: GOLD OTHER

Soundtrack: James - *On Top Of The World*

Life soon returned to some sort of a not-a-Uni-party dull normality as Rabcat moved back home to his folk's place on The Wirral. He struggled to get into a normal sleeping pattern after living like an Art-House Vampire for the previous three years.

But before he got home, a chance visit to his Newcastle GP on the back of his earlier sleep deprivation made things a little more dull in the eyes of the uneducated as Rabcat responded to his Doctor's Health-Check-MOT-Questionnaire with a full confession, putting his hands up and admitting his guilt regarding his student party ways, Franken-Cocktail-warts-n-all.

The GP told him that his bad booze behaviours had risked his life suggesting that he was lucky that his major organs hadn't packed up telling him "You need to stop drinking". This kind of Witch Doctory makes no sense to me as he wasn't exactly Keith Richards or Pete Docherty. That said alcohol is a crap and dangerous drug. Rabcat took the kind and wise doctor's advice and has been teetotal ever since. No blood test, fuck all. I'm respectfully flabbergasted – only because I'm a cowardly fuck up without the balls to ever completely give up like that! Respect to The Rabcat – as long as he went on to have plenty of fun as a straight-head that is!

Jobs in the 80s were hard to come by and it took him around 8 months of sobriety before he got fixed up with a temporary three month placement in April 1988 working for a small design company in Liverpool. They specialised in doing stuff for Littlewoods stores catalogues. This was his first venture into work. It was a bit unremarkable as it was just standard artwork preparation for print and packaging but it was vital experience for him nevertheless. This was the age before computers and anything automated so it is pretty primitive by today's modern standards. His skills were already developed from Uni and it was a big relief to be up and running.

The placement didn't work out as the Boss in Rabcat's mind at least was a complete know-it-all, in his words: "He was a Nigel Farage-faced wanker". (Author's Note – Low Frequency Labelling violation). More than anything, his Boss couldn't spell and this annoyed the shit out of a very particular Rabcat who detested him as soon as he read his own name spelt wrongly in the small print of his original 3 month contract. As soon as he could, in late '88, Rabcat moved to a full time contract at Stockport Council to join their Graphic Design team. The new job was 45 miles away from the family home which meant it was time to uproot and move to the right side of the M62. For £32 pw rent he got a room in a shared gaff in leafy Heaton Chapel. He shared the house with the landlord and his bird.

Suddenly life was good again. He liked his new job and Manchester seemed like a really exciting place to be as the Acid House scene was just kicking off in the city. Rabcat was never gonna be a trip-head but he did start making trips to Yorkshire as he had been writing to a pen friend there for about a year before they started meeting up romantically. Pen friends were a thing back then before Tinder, Plenty of Fish and all that bollox came to be. Things were certainly looking up in general as chatting to strangers, Ice Pops and glow sticks were the new weapons of the Ecstasy rave generation – an almost forgotten vibration of love, kindness and optimism not seen since the sixties started to light up a previously gloomy post-industrial Manchester.

Not that Rabcat was ever likely to go completely with it and start getting off his tits on Ecstasy. Even so, he did time his move to Mancland rather well. Two hot summers in a row topped off by the Italia 1990 World Cup. There were few fighting footy fans at this one as the England fans must have taken all the E's that Rabcat missed out on with them to Italy as New Order sang England all the way to the semis without a single punch being thrown. Non-footy fan Rabcat got swept away that summer for two reasons: Firstly, by the beauty and euphoria of one of the best World Cups ever and secondly and more importantly, by the beauty and euphoria of Hanni, his pen friend who had rather sensationally become his first proper girlfriend... I think.

Before I describe their relationship, let me wrap up the footy talk. Being a non-conformist Rabcat couldn't support England post 1990, so he just pretended Euro 96 didn't happen and by Euro 2000 he'd joined the Orange Cladded Supporter Army of Holland after tapping into the Dutch party vibe on many leisure trips to his favourite European city, Amsterdam. (Lest we not forget: 4-1 SAS).

Anyway, Rabcat started to meet Hanni regularly in West Yorkshire which was bang in the middle of Mancland and Beverley, Hull. Rabcat's account of this relationship is sincere and clearly heartfelt. I'll summarise it as best I can. Hanni became his girlfriend and best friend, as close as family. They shared lots of intimate time and shared a love of music and the new indie scene that was taking off alongside the Rave scene of the time. Their relationship was deep and spiritual and they both readily agreed that sex was an overrated necessity. Their preferred level of intimacy was hugging and embracing and being at one with each other on a purely platonic basis. Their commitment to each other was based on trust as they shared their deepest and most private thoughts freely and easily.

Hanni had carried mental trauma from childhood, not from a physically abusive Stepfather but definitely from an unkind sort of father figure who deserted the roost too soon. Early into their relationship it became clear that one of Hanni's scars from childhood was an eating disorder. Their relationship stretched out over a couple of years and as well as meeting all across the

Yorkshire Moors, Hanni would come and stay near Rabcat's and they'd go to gigs. Rabcat was happy and content within the parameters of their romantic set up. Neither of them drank alcohol but they often felt a heightened sense of consciousness by just being together. Music was their shared passion.

As time went on, Hanni started to come by car and they'd share the driving as they explored every nook and cranny of the West Yorkshire Moors. They always shared light-hearted banter over all things music which often involved having a dig at all the 'Baggy Casualties' from the rave and Madchester scene and wondering whether or not a lot of that stuff was genius or absolute shite. One in car cassette tape that bonded them more than any other was "Gold Mother" by James. At the time James were already massive as a live band and as t-shirts sellers as their art effectively made them famous before they had even had their first hit.

Riding in the slipstream of the explosion of the great Madchester bands of the time, James threatened to be huge but somehow they ended up as a mere cult band in the shadow of The Smiths, The Stone Roses and The Mondays. That suited Rabcat who always championed the underdog. They both adored that album and played it over and over on their travels.

They shared an eclectic passion for the music of the time. When apart they would send each other mix tapes that they would compile obsessively, often trying to out-weird the other with strange and offbeat tracks from all kinds of oddball combos. These tapes were the love letters of their own particular love story. Self-indulgent expressions of a kindred spirit. Rabcat's soulmate found joy in the absurd but also exhibited a singular distrust of 'following the herd' and shying away from anything that was considered remotely normal. They shared a telepathic bond of mistrust for everything else other than themselves.

For Rabcat it was the happiest time, an enjoyable work life endorsed by music, travel and a true, loving relationship. One particular track on their favourite album "Gold Mother" was 'On Top Of The World – Don't Let Go' and that is a decent summary of their golden time. As previously mentioned 1989 and 1990 both enjoyed sensationally hot summers and almost every weekend seemed to be blessed by a warm encouragement to go out and explore. Their trips became more and more adventurous. They started crossing the border to visit Glasgow and Edinburgh, doing the Edinburgh Festival together twice. Travelling to gigs n festivals became the norm and they went everywhere together absorbing the rich beauty and culture of the land, the people and each other.

4: ANYTHING BUT THIS

Soundtrack: Everything But The Girl – *Miss You*

One weekend Rabcat and Hanni met up as normal to travel to a festival. Unfortunately, he instantly sensed a numbness and anxiety from Hanni that was highlighted in her lack of appetite. It transpired that she had had an argument with her mother the week earlier about trivial things of no real consequence. Her assurance, when pressed, was that her dulled mental state had absolutely nothing to do with their romantic relationship but that didn't take way the concern that Rabcat felt for his girl and, less impressively, for himself.

Hanni rarely ate what would be considered a real meal - she preferred to just snack on nuts, fruit and rye bread. She'd been a vegan from a very young age and she'd never touched meat since the day her real dad went AWOL on her. Worryingly, her snacking seemed to be at an all-time low and Rabcat expressed his concerns to her. Hanni reassured him, "I'll be fine, I can handle it."

He felt deeply disturbed and wasn't convinced by Hanni's supposedly reassuring words - but they did what they always did and cranked up the tunes as a form of escapism. Unfortunately this time round there was no immediate happy escape and everything seemed to be against them as Rabcat exploded into an unrelenting hayfever-driven sneezing fit that triggered a nose bleed. He had already sensed that he had upset Hanni by questioning the reasons behind her current state of distress and, an hour later, he must have annoyed the shit out of her as his relentless Hayfever fit refused to subside.

Their below par weekend continued at the festival as they both failed to plug into the vibe. It was all a bit too much and they left the outdoor music tent and the crowds for a bit and retired to a pub. Rabcat did the wrong thing for the right reason and tried to get Hanni to eat a proper meal at the pub highlighting the state of her unease and discomfort. She refused and he felt hapless for the first time in their 18 months together. He realised there and then that he cared as deeply for this woman as he did for his own family and, all of a sudden, it all felt at risk. He took the pressure off her by scoffing a plate of chips himself and let the weekend fizzle out without any further drama.

Putting it down to just a blip, he hoped for an

upturn when they next caught up with one another. He was more than pleased to receive a phone call from an upbeat Hanni a day or so later explaining that that she had eaten properly and was feeling a lot better with herself. She apologised for her irrational behaviour that day and Rabcat returned the apology for his handling of the situation. A shared nervous laugh put their first relationship low-point to bed and a happier, shared focus was supposedly set on the weeks to come. In late July 1991 Hanni sent him a 26th birthday card and, in mid-August, Art-boy returned the kind gesture by designing a home-made pop-up birthday card complete with moving parts to celebrate Hanni's Birthday. Tragically, he'd never get to deliver that card. Hanni had promised to drive over the following weekend but that was not to be. What happened next would, unexpectedly change Rabcat's whole life and his outlook on it forever. The day that everything changed irreversibly was August 4th 1991.

Hanni telephoned to tell him that she was feeling low. Everything had gotten on top of her. Rabcat was saddened to hear of her low mood but not too overly concerned as he knew that he would soon have the opportunity to help lift her mood on their next meet up. The call ended when Hanni said that she was going to go out for a drive to clear her head. Little did he know he was never going to speak to her again. Wherever that dark drive took her, she simply disappeared and sent her family and Rabcat into a bottomless pit of pain and fear.

There was no contact for three days, all that time Rabcat was worrying over her whereabouts. Imagine what it must have felt like for her mum, sister and boyfriend when those three days became weeks, then months then heartbreakingly - years. There was no indication as to which direction she had driven or whether there were any other people who had seen her in that intervening period. No trace of her or her car was ever found. Rabcat spent the next three years out of his head and body with worry and panic: wracked with guilt, doubt, bewilderment, anger and confusion. This set off the plunge into deep depression that consumed him for years. He found himself in a hopeless headspace where he felt guilty for his own depression when he weighed that against how Hanni's family must have been feeling without closure or any indication or evidence as to exactly how this came to transpire. The sudden disappearance of your most loved completely without trace. How does anyone deal with that sort of thing? Rabcat couldn't as he started to lose his mind.

As a result the period 1992 to 1994 were very difficult years for him filled with conflicting emotions of loss, anguish and despair which could never ever be fully tempered even when he started to make new friends. Gradually he started becoming part of new social circles to try and take his mind off all of the bad things going round and round his head but his thought processes were like an out-of-control fairground carousel which simply refused to stop - and in spite of all of his new friends' best intentions, he just couldn't turn it off as he kept obsessing over those last few hours over and over again.

Three whole fucking years of negative thought did a lot of damage to him. Eventually work-friends pushed him to visit his GP to seek professional help. Anti-depressants were depressing as fuck. The side-effects making him drowsy and lethargic, which for a manic, overactive guy was the absolute pits. Self-hate came into play and the usually squeaky clean Rabcat even had a brush with the long arm of the law when, as a cry for help, he started to steal erratically from magazine and record shops. HMV in Manchester was his regular place to indulge in a spot of casual adrenalin-fuelled kleptomania. He managed to make off with at least 10 CDs on different expeditions until one day, in January 1994, close to rock bottom, he finally got caught red-handed at the Lower Market Street branch of HMV.

Rabcat got nicked nicking another CD and was taken down to Bootle Street Police Station where he was questioned and interviewed. A search of his bag revealed more 'contraband', rather fittingly a full VHS Box Set of 60s hit series "The Prisoner" - the irony of it! - which he actually DID pay for, at the other HMV up the road - as well as a classic Blondie LP "Eat To The Beat" which he picked up from Vinyl Exchange.

Alarmingly the Dibble also found a polypropylene rope and a lot of antidepressants in Rabcat's bag. The conversation must have gone something like: "This guy is about to kill himself or he's about to enter The World's Strongest Man as it looks like he's fully equipped to man-tow a lorry". Maybe not, but they must have thought we've got a right one here.

A kind, patient and probably foreboding officer sat down and absorbed Rabcat's tragic story regarding Hanni, and Rabcat was quite rightly compassionately released without charge.

5: THE PRISONER APPRECIATION SOCIETY

Soundtrack: Ron Grainer - *The Prisoner*

Explaining to a police officer why he had gone a bit crackers perhaps made him realise that he needed to give himself perhaps a one or even a two percent break. He'd been through an experience that would break most people. He had become something mentally that was not kind or helpful to himself. He finally took stock and started to think about how he could forge a new way out of the rut that he found himself in.

Good people came to his aid and the new social circle that he sought out started to play an immeasurable part in bringing him back to life. By default or design, the right people appeared at the right times as he started to make friends all over Stockport and Manchester. These kind, cool Mancs became replacements for the tragic loss of his partner in a manner of speaking. They had to contend with medication and depression-driven mood swings that he carried forward from his experiences. Apart from the moods, Rabcat didn't do the necessary friendship-building bullshit particularly well as he was short on the confidence and probably the patience on the telephone 'n' all that but, face to face in real life, he was and is always electric company. He's a seriously interesting guy - so making the effort to go out and chat to people (stone-cold sober) in the right places made him a totally new life.

He hung out in hallowed haunts like The Cornerhouse, the old Green Room, The Abercrombie, The Salutation, the old Tommy Ducks, The Britons Protection, The Peveril of the Peak and The Lass O' Gowrie. He also socialised in the burgeoning Gay Village that had started to take root all along Canal Street at places such as Manto and the old haunts The Rembrandt and New Union, as well as the new emerging bars such as the Via Fossa. His new Bohemian chums would spend a couple of hours just chatting and laughing and slagging off all things music, art and film. It was a great time to be around in the days when coca-cola in a pub cost less than a quid before City Centre Mancland became outrageously expensive. Rabcat attended gigs around the city centre with some of these new pals at venues like The Boardwalk (which sadly closed the following year - 1995), as well as The Roadhouse, The Venue, Brick House, the Ritz, Jilly's Rockworld, Night and Day Café, The Star and Garter, the old Tiger Lounge and Fab Café, Joshua Brookes, the old Jabez Clegg. Sadly, many of these glorious places ("shit-holes" to some) have been consigned to history as a result of Manchester's unwelcome (to Rabcat) transformation during the whole of the post-Millennial decade into an increasingly expensive, soulless and aggressively over-gentrified metropolis. In addition to this, he also joined up with a new cult-TV appreciation society founded by fans of "The Prisoner" - the 1967 series starring Patrick McGoohan - based in Manchester that year.

There were appreciation societies for this series all over the UK dating back 20-30 years but the Manchester group had only just got going, so he signed up and became an almost founder member (love that word) and he spent the next four or five years hanging out with friends within this geek-squad.

Christmas time for Prisoner enthusiasts went down every year in August when they headed for Portmeirion in North Wales where the series was filmed for the annual "Six Of One Prisoner Convention". They'd dress up in the uniforms and re-enact scenes from various episodes with fans from all over the world. A complete release from the real matrix.

Rabcat did five years in a row at the gathering and remained a "Prisoner Six Of One" subscriber for the next eight years or so making and retaining many friends that also liked to be locked up in prison cells.

6: THE POWER AND THE GLORY

Soundtrack: Goldblade – *Do You Believe In The Power Of Rock & Roll?*

So between the Pub Scene and the TV Geekage, Rabcat had established a decent social circle and every credit to him. He'd been brave enough to walk back into society depressed, subdued and sober and he had discovered that he was still interesting enough to make and sustain friends. Full respect to him.

Every other Rat in this book let me interview them to produce their biog, Rabcat didn't so I've simply flipped his writing into my speak and highlighted the key parts of his story according to my translation. The downside of this technique is some detail that I'd like to share with the reader just isn't there – stuff like who taught Rabcat to play the drums?

Unfortunately, we miss out on the early stuff and start his drum story in 1996 when he chanced upon The Manchester Samba Band performing at the Lord Mayor's Parade and then also the original Gay Pride Mardi Gras down Canal Street. They had a terrific energy about them and a confident Rabcat simply went over and asked about how to join the band', a week later he found himself in Sankeys Soap fifth floor rehearsing space with fifty like-minded creative musicians. Eyes wide open, he was ready to start finding his groove and having the time of his life again.

The band was made up of people of all ages, social backgrounds, ethnicities and labels! Rabcat had actually been a frustrated drummer for at least 15 years and this opportunity meant that he now had a final outlet for all of the pent-up frustration and aggression he had accumulated over the years. He felt so liberated to finally have a blow hole through which to release the pressure of his existence.

Before he'd even really started to be part of this good noise movement, he already knew that he had found his true purpose in life - he was about to blast away the cobwebs of self-doubt, tragedy and introspection.

Within a few weeks of joining he was playing with not just one Samba band, but three and after a few months' time several other drum/percussion projects too. All of his previously dulled-down manic energy started to come back and be useful as he started to vibrate close to his true meaning.

If only Hanni could see him now.

Not one day went by when he wasn't playing or rehearsing with one drum band or another. The more he played, the higher his energy. The only drug he ever wanted in his life was adrenaline now and it was back gushing through his veins as he started go with the flow of life, rolling with the opportunities that kept on presenting themselves to him. He was more relaxed, more of a free spirit, taking the time to head into the city after work four or five times each week just to bash the hell out of some drums and have a good time. Suddenly, he knew hundreds of people and he was welcome.

He also reached out to the newly developing creative scene in Stockport getting involved in council projects working with youths at STOMP - The Stockport Music Project. He enjoyed that so much he even set up his own free-for-all improvised drum collective that he named !BASHER!

!BASHER! consisted of just six drummers all playing on kits in a circle and going batshit crazy, screaming through megaphones and making this god-almighty, atonal industrial racket for an hour or so. Rabcat loved it because no two line-ups would ever be the same, just him as a constant, with a Samba friend, Owen, and a selection of established band drummers and novices - it was just a case of creating a big fuck-off spontaneous noise just for the hell of it. And it felt good: a brilliant catharsis.

One of Rabcat's proudest moments was blowing the electrics up by placing the mics a bit too close to the amp on a particularly raucous thrash off. When the amp blew, the whole building fell into darkness. Rabcat is frugal so he wasn't going to let his bashing squad forfeit a two hour slot that they had paid for, so they carried on in the darkness. This kind of spirit must have made Rabcat some kind of cult hero amongst young the young musicians. He created good honest chaos. Being in seven bands wasn't the least bit exhausting for a fired-up, manic musician. His Uni endurance training helped and, without the alcohol, he found he could work full time, gig every night and go to clubs until the early hours and still feel great a few hours later in the office.

He was doing so many gigs and things each week

and often staying quite late for club nights as well, then getting the cab back home at 3 in the morning. He felt blessed to live in a city that had brought him back to life. Living in Manchester in the 90s as a creative person was an absolute joy. Cool as fuck! In 1999, Rabcat got to meet his childhood hero Glam Rock God, Noddy Holder, who famously fronted up the very noisy Black Country outfit Slade.

He signed his autobiography for him at Waterstones in Stockport. Surprisingly, Rabcat was a bit star-struck when speaking with him but that didn't stop him sharing some of his childhood memories around playing the Slade singles that he got for his 7th Birthday with the volume turned right down so as not to disturb my parents. Noddy laughed, sincerely agreeing that, "Yeah - we mixed them records so bloody loud with my huge voice, they even sounded deafening with the volume turned down!"

It was amazing to see how down to earth a true legend of the industry was and the experience focused a seriously talented drummer to get even better and make the most of his gift.

In 2000, he became involved with the punk rock band Goldblade who were already established on the Manc music scene and are rather impressively still going to today, more than twenty years later. The singer, John Robb, lived in Hulme was a well-known face. He was a journalist and TV presenter and an out and out Music Head. He accosted the Rabcat in Café Pop's basement one Saturday and asked him if he was a drummer. That was John's way of recognising that Rabcat had landed.

Rabcat was pumped because he had seen John interviewing various artists over the years backstage at gigs including one of his favourite bands, Saint Etienne. Goldblade's percussion man and second drummer in the band, Wayne Simmons, had left to become a full-time photographer and John had been tipped off through Samba circles that Rabcat might be the man... and soon he was in eight bands all at once.

Rabcat had never played in a well-known band before, not least one that had a reasonably decent pedigree – Goldblade already had a following, having been on the scene for at least four years. The band's rehearsal bunker was in Manchester on Whitworth Street underneath the Oxford Road Station viaduct arches. Here he met the rest of the band. He admitted to them that he'd seen them playing live before but hadn't really been a fan. (Typically straight but rather awkward Rabcat-ness)

They were cool with that and said, "No pressure – just bash along and see what happens." So he did and found Goldblade fun to jam with. Laughter filled the room as he played free and easy.

Band leader John said, "We have a gig at The Ashton Witchwood in two weeks' time. We want you there with us. It would be fucking mega to have the two drummers on it! You nailed it, one take, you played brilliant" so Goldblade's new line up was John (Frontman), Rob (main drummer), Keith (bass player) and Jay (lead guitarist) & Rabcat (Drummer 2). Rabcat was blown away – he'd somehow made it into a pure punk rock band. It felt like his biggest achievement to get his life back on track since the sad days of Hanni's disappearance. She would have been proud of him. He had probably become Britain's busiest musician.

These were his commitments:

- Manchester School of Samba - Brazilian / Latin

drum ensemble
- Cabassa Afro-Brazil drum community band
- SandBar Collective - African percussion jam group
- Sambangra - Samba / Bhangra fusion drum ensemble
- Wedding In Rio - Samba / Metal Band
- !BASHER! - Improv drum collective
- Stomp - Community music project
- Goldblade - Punk Band

It made for a spectacularly ridiculous existence where his real job and sleep was almost cheating. He'd come a long, long way in the ten years since the loss of his greatest friend. His life now had meaning again.

The Ashton Witchwood gig was a baptism of fire. During the band's first number *Do You Believe In The Power Of Rock 'n' Roll?*, a 200 miles per hour pure punk hurricane, Rabcat's co-drummer Rob suffered the ignominy of his kick drum pedal becoming disengaged and he spent a great part of the rest of the number on his hands and knees in maintenance mode as the song hurtled on.

Subconsciously, Rabcat did a double-time solo on the toms and snare just to make up for Rob's absence keeping the whole thing together with a series of truly furious vicious machine gun-like fills and accents, creating almost a speed-metal effect. Somehow it worked and the crowd went totally ape-shit and with just a few seconds left, Rob had re-attached his pedal and they were both able to bring the song to its thunderous, ejaculatory climax.

Buster Rabcat had earned his Goldblade stripes in just one song.

The band were astonished by his speed of thought

and action and his improvised solo ended up being adopted into the final recorded version of the song.

Landed!

7: DRUMS, DRUMS AND MORE DRUMS

Soundtrack: Zé Kéti – *A Voz do Morro*

Rabcat's Punk debut was in April 2000, but what happened the following month would eclipse any of his achievements so far. The UK was gearing up for its first ever nationwide 'Music Day' which was part of the larger Music Live Week. TV and radio stations broadcasted live shows from all around the nation as the whole country linked up together for one massive "Beat the Drum" event, followed by a whole week of related music events large and small. Manchester had by that point already developed the largest Samba scene in the UK outside London with no less than ten different bands in existence – Rabcat was now in four of them. Samba bands from all around the country assembled together in Albert Square outside Manchester Town Hall to perform a massive synchronised drum rhythm which would be relayed live all over the UK. It was unbelievable to see thousands and thousands of drummers all playing the same beat live on TV and the radio. The likes of this had never been seen in this country. It only lasted 20 minutes but it was beyond awesome. Pure magic!

The event made the national press and everyone involved felt proud to be part of this giant gathering. There were almost 1,000 drummers in Albert Square that day. This was a high point but Rabcat had no time to stop and celebrate as his workload and gig itinerary for the week was truly ridiculous. Music Week would stretch him as a person and as an artist to see how much he could get out of himself. May Spring Bank Holiday in particular was like a Guinness World Record attempt. It was the final day of the Music Live Week and he would attempt to play five different gigs with five different bands in five different towns across Greater Manchester.

His drumming pal Owen was his chaperone and fixer for the entirety of the day. He was the driver and also played alongside him in all the gigs except the final gig in Stockport.

First up was Oldham, a lunchtime set with Sambangra... then Wigan with Cabasa Carnival... then Bury inside the Met Theatre where he played with Wedding In Rio for a short set for their Latin festival... then a quick dash to Manchester Fallowfield to play an outdoor set with MSoS at Platt Fields Park... then to East Stockport to the Romiley Forum for the finale of the evening as part of the youth collective Stomp (22 strong for this one!). There was an audience of 200+ parents, and members of the general public and even BBC Music Live executives for this last event. Rabcat played drum kit and keyboards and it was quite a buzz – he was diversifying on instruments for the first time ever. Looking back he says it pains him that the event was never videoed – no smartphones back then. It was a magical time.

It took a while to come down from that week but later that summer he got back up close to that buzz as 1,750 drummers gathered in Castlefield Arena for The Manchester Samba City 2000. It was the most incredible drumming event ever seen in Manchester or anywhere in the country at the time.

By 2001 Rabcat's life had become a jubilant, frenzied noisy blur. His Samba Band involvements offered him a host of opportunities for travel abroad as all his bands toured the country, Europe, and even Brazil - though Rabcat always made sure that his paid work commitments came first. This prevented him from accompanying them on many of these trips but he did make it to Ireland four or five times, a trip to Holland and four trips down to London in consecutive summers (1997-2000) for the Notting Hill Carnival. He loved Notting Hill as the commute was epic. Samba drums beats would reverberate around the tube train carriages on the way to Ladbroke Grove for the Sunday Carnival Parade and the sheer cacophony either freaked out the passengers or got them into full on party mode! Rabcat loved to see innocent bystanders smile among the rhythmical, deafening din of his entourage.

The whole Notting Hill weekend was overwhelming; mobile sound systems, house and street parties, dance tents, amazing costumes, people, puppets, stilt-walkers, fire eaters, and, most of all, drums, drums, drums and drums thousands of them. It was an awesome experience.

In 2001, Rabcat had done thirteen years hard graft for Stockport Council but they tried to compromise and make it into something he describes as 'shit'. They started adding admin responsibilities to his role and even started micro-managing his toilet breaks telling him at what specific times he could go! Fuck that for a lark! Rabcat would decide when he needed to go, so he took the voluntary redundancy package that was available to him. He didn't really want to leave a job that he enjoyed and had in many ways been his recovery vessel but he wasn't one for having the piss taken out of him or kept in as directed by some Council Jobsworth so, that was that!

He got over it in magnificent fashion playing a support slot that same night as Goldblade opened for the mighty Motörhead at The Manchester Apollo. Standing stage-side watching Lemmy out there in his Stetson and trademark white cowboy boots, his neck craned upwards towards his mic, hollering and riffing his way through some of the meanest most bad-ass tunes, was beyond surreal. Playing The Apollo can't have been too shabby either. Rabcat's sometimes shit life had become a bit of a fairy tale and a couple of other gigs epitomised his privileged position. For example, in the winters of 1996 and 1997 when he headlined the stage of The Hacienda with the massed drummers of the Manchester Samba band and brass ensemble, ringing in the New Year on both occasions with superstar DJs Graeme Park and Mike Pickering. It snowed like fuck for the 1997 one! What a divine experience.

Leaving full-time employment was bitter-sweet as Rabcat had not long jacked in many of his samba band commitments because Goldblade were taking off and his work commitments cancelled out the availability to do it all; without looking back he threw himself into recording his first single and album with Goldblade.

Camera-shy Rabcat didn't relish featuring in the band's first video for their first single titled, *AC/DC* - their first with him as a member of the band. They filmed it entirely in their rehearsal bunker under the arches on Whitworth Street. It only cost them a few quid in camera batteries.

The single's record sleeve cover was a still taken

from this same video shoot. Rabcat made immortal, pictured hands and sticks held up aloft, head tilted back, enormous nostrils flaring. Their second video was filmed less than a year later and made it onto MTV. This one featured the band getting chased around Deansgate Locks by giant animated insects and bugs. The album came out in 2002 and was entitled, *Do You Believe In The Power Of Rock'n'Roll?* It was recorded in Liverpool's Motor Museum Studios which was owned by Andy McCluskey from Wirral synth legends OMD. Rabcat recalls the experience as 'Fun times'.

Touring the album was exhausting even for Rabcat. 150 gigs mainly UK but some in Europe where their following was growing. He tagged along for about a third of them. Festival appearances included the annual punk festival in Blackpool or Morecambe and Goldblade went on to support many legendary names of punk that Rabcat had worshipped growing up: The Stranglers, The Damned, UK Subs, Stiff Little Fingers, The Dead Kennedys, Penetration, X-Ray Spex, the aforementioned Motörhead, Buzzcocks, Neville Staple (ex-Specials and Fun Boy Three), The Selecter, The Beat, and then later bands that broke out in the early 1980s such as GBH, Discharge, Toy Dolls, The Business, King Kurt and also The Meteors.

They truly were heady daze.

The craziness and thrill of that never-ending UK tour wasn't just backing up legendary bands, checking out the salubrious clubs and the unassuming toilet venues was just as enlightening and memory invoking. Happy times indeed. By this point, he had long since left all his other bands and collectives behind as Goldblade were a total but justified, time hoover.

Rabcat had had his mental health issues previously but, thankfully, he had always managed to remain money-conscious and responsible and keep himself sustained in that way. Not doing so could have made things spiral quickly out of control as depression seems too often to magnify difficult situations. Rabcat avoided this by always trying to keep his main income-stream protected for this reason. He didn't recommit to Samba band action so he could focus on finding a new job. He got bits 'n' bobs; freelance graphics, IT workshops and so on, but nothing really to make him take his foot of the punk metal band pedal - although Goldblade's gigging commitments were far smaller than at tour time. Sod's Fuckin' Law!

8: GOD SAVE THE QUEEN

Soundtrack: Sex Pistols - *God Save The Queen*

Rabcat has a great deal of affection for The Netherlands, having visited Amsterdam in 1999 as part of the Manchester Samba Band to play a workshop and street festival. Rabcat fell in love with the city, and Haarlem the neighbouring city - both for their beauty, their canals and their culture - returning twice more within that same year and many times thereafter.

His 2000 visit took place during Euro 2000 – the European Football Tournament - where he stayed in Antwerp, Belgium, as well as Amsterdam. His adopted team, the Oranje, just missed out making the final as they were beaten by Italy. Almost begrudgingly, he started to develop a small interest in football initially triggered by Italia '90 but now, properly revived by the country in which he felt most comfortable.

It was another example of Rabcat's perverse and contrary nature; punks aren't really supposed to do nationalism in any form but, as previously highlighted, Rabcat always does his own thing. These days he keeps it real following lowly FA Cup thieves Wigan Athletic - nowt wrong with that!

The Dutch national team had been poor for a while but whenever international tournaments beckon, he was definitely in Camp Orange. Rabcat had plans to ultimately go over and work over there as he had long become enamoured with the Dutch way of life and everything to do with the country. He felt that maybe he would belong more in a country where being a creative free spirit was not looked upon with as much disdain and contempt as it is in the UK. Rabcat Politically Punkish Rant: "England, with its archaic mores, pathetic parochial society, truly outmoded and repressed traditions... oh, to say nothing of the despicable self-serving trough-licking pricks that call themselves politicians whose entire *modus operandi* is completely out of touch with common sense, reality, and the prevailing consensus and opinion of the people." And furthermore... "British public transport is total wank. There is no decent, reliable alternative to car travel. The Netherlands do it right. A proper public transport network and safe cycle routes."

As you can tell from that statement, he really rather despises the British Establishment but does quite fancy the Holland gig. Rabcat maybe should have taken a gamble and gone with his heart and just bailed to Holland as he found it hard to pin down another full time job in his chosen field on these shores. He didn't manage to do so for almost three years. He got by instead on freelance work for very little financial reward. It wasn't until early 2003 that his opportunity finally came knocking again as he landed a gig with marketing agency Red C right in the centre of town.

While working for Red C, Rabcat made friends with a colleague called Keith, who was also a drummer. Keith is still an active drummer playing in a punk band called 'Time for Action' with his brother, Neil, on bass and the former lead singer of Northside (Dermo). This band went on to provide the backing music for the short cartoon trailer promoting the (still as-yet-unreleased) documentary film starring Gaz Stanley and The Piccadilly Rats, "Small Music World".

Red C was a good job but it didn't last long as the company were skint and were soon dishing out redundancies; last one in, first one out. There were no hard feelings on this occasion but Rabcat was back again to square one and the frustrating piece-work situation that he kept finding himself in.

Thankfully it was time to record his second album with Goldblade. It was an exciting project, along with a new compilation CD for which Rabcat would get to design the artwork. The band also played a top gig at Manchester Castlefield Arena to launch the album that summer... that was a real blast. Unfortunately, Rabcat experienced an act of sheer ignominy as an attractive young lady mistook him for the bass player from Newport three-piece 'Feeder'. She asked for his autograph and after he signed, she gushingly declared how much she loved the albums 'Comfort in Sound' and 'Echo Park'. She thought Rabcat was the Welsh band's Japanese member Take Hirosa! To be fair he did have a similar bleached haircut. A quietly mortified Rabcat politely pissed on her bonfire and ruined her night. A lesser man could have had some right fun with that situation but Rabcat is a straight-shooting gentleman and he just fucked her right off.

Back in the real world, he took a job in a printers. The gaffer and his sidekick had outdated 70s mindsets and Rabcat found their oh-so-witty racial put-downs and derogatory ramblings deeply offensive. Working there was like starring in a puerile-pseudo-1970s sitcom. It was never going to work out. The place was badly run. The Gaffer would walk around smoking on the shop floor. The health and safety was laughable. Again this wasn't a good fit for anyone really but for a perfectionist like Rabcat it was his idea of hell. Racist incompetents were always gonna end up being told straight and that is exactly what happened.

One fateful morning, Rabcat stormed in the office and set about the boss verbally like he was smashing the shit out of his cymbals. He used swear words with real depth to them. The good guys in the office tried talking him round but he kept his dignity and was done. He walked out genuinely upset not just because he had been abused for three months but more that he had been forced to give up his livelihood because of somebody else's uneducated, incompetence and complete lack of respect. The boss was a true wanker and even took the time to follow him down to Admin to shout out that 'this chap would like his P45'. He was a childish fucker with no class at all.

This was a worrying situation for Rabcat as besides the financial worries and mental fatigue that came with exiting this job, he had also developed a chronic ear disorder called Ménière's Disease from which he had intermittently suffered since '95. It's a chronic ear problem that causes vertigo, spinning sensations and tinnitus which are all no-no's for a drummer. There is no known reason for the condition to appear but Rabcat puts it down to the depression and stress causes by Hanni's disappearance. This particular bout of the condition lasted for eight agonising months before it faded away – luckily, this coincided with the recording of his final album with Goldblade.

Rabcat also played a part in designing the cover and the single that was to be taken from the new LP, however disillusionment started to creep in due in some part to his ear problem which took the fun out of playing drums and gigging. He simply couldn't play to the best of his potential with his hearing so distorted as gigs sounded like he was listening to robots talking through synthesisers underwater.

Leaving his last job because of 'that prick' and feeling like he could lose his true vocation at the same time left a truly bitter aftertaste in his mouth. At the time he didn't know that this Goldblade album and single would be his last meaningful contribution with the band and that his career in the Design and Graphics Industry was also done. Rabcat had never stayed in one band or musical project for more than five years. His attention span doesn't stretch to that.

He never fell out with the guys in Goldblade - his gradual exit was amicable, there were no hard feelings or animosity. He'd just taken his foot off the gas trying to make an ill-fated career in the print game. This, combined with his ear problems, had helped him come to the decision that playing on Goldblade's fourth album

– his second - would be the very best way to put his fantastic experience and time with the band to bed.

The sessions for the new album were thrashed out at a studio in Wolverhampton. He put everything into fulfilling his and his bandmates' ambition to put down an album with the same kind of noise pollution depth inspired by 1980s German noise innovators Einstürzende Neubauten. Ah, if only...

Rabcat went on an all-out noise terror attack brandishing industrial power tools on stage and wrecking his drum kit in the process as the band got lost in the din. Rabcat particularly enjoyed drilling holes in the stage for manic percussion effect. Then, alas, he woke up again. With the very noisy album 'Rebel Songs' in the can, Rabcat had left his mark on the band and his time with Goldblade was over.

The band regrouped later but Rabcat felt that his work was done. He had creatively and physically maxed out and given his all. He felt that he didn't have anything more to offer his bandmates. His final contribution was helping design one final single cover and it became a battle of wills between Rabcat and lead singer John. Rabcat's idea for the single titled, "Psycho" was to have something really violent and nasty like a sinister looking murdering device, in this case a power drill as the main feature Psycho-style but John had an idea that he wanted this T-Rex like dinosaur on the cover instead. John didn't quite get Rabcat's lack of enthusiasm to somehow be brandishing a punk dinosaur. "If we are having a dinosaur, let's have it brandishing the power tool?" John wasn't having it and the terms of their compromise went with John's Dino on the front cover and Rabcat's power drill dripping with blood on the back. Both images were set against a bright yellow background with the title 'PSYCHO' in massive black letters beneath the dinosaur's feet.

It marked the end of four and a half years with the band and Rabcat had no regrets. He'd had an absolute blast. He'd had the opportunity to see so many legendary bands that he worshipped as a youth. He'd even had a small taste of rock and roll adulation - being asked for autographs always flummoxed to say the least. He was proud to have played in a band that were always ferocious live. Goldblade were pure punk rockers that gave off an electrifying energy that always used to return to the stage having passed through their wildly energetic fanbase. Rabcat describes feeling this return of energy transaction lifting himself and the band higher as they'd become almost delirious within their performances.

Vivid imagery of the glory of a well-spent youth is forever locked down in Rabcat's memory. Picture the whole band being stripped down to their waists in the stifling heat of wild performance - the steam rising up off their adrenaline pumped bodies like the spirits off their songs escaping off into the night.

As the gig ends with most of the band on their knees, exalted, their wide eyes and grins, a shared testimony of a band that never left anything in the dressing room.

9: GONNA MAKE IT

Soundtrack: Feeder - *Buck Rogers*

Despite his hearing problems, Rabcat found it impossible to completely step away from the music scene as a whole and he soon became a regular customer on the monthly folk music trains which ran between Manchester Piccadilly and Edale/Hathersage, Buxton/ Whaley Bridge and Glossop.

Soon after attending his first gig on a train he started to volunteer, helping out with running these bi-monthly events, making good friends and regular contacts with all of the various bands and musicians that played on board.

This became his longest-ever gig, finding joy in the light-hearted thrill of putting on community performances in such beautiful settings. This hobby spanned over a decade and over 160 events. He even carried it on after moving back to The Wirral, which was a hell of a commute. Even though he'd moved back to Merseyside, volunteering opportunities came up at Manchester Museum and then at the adjoining University of Manchester. He kept himself busy promoting the folk train events to students and even submitting the odd bit of editorial for the Uni's *MancUnion* student paper. He also got into lecturing, guiding first year Music History students through his specialist subject of British Post-Punk New Wave music and fashions of the late 1970s and 1980s at the Metropolitan University Music and Art/Fashion faculty. He really enjoyed giving these talks but, at the first sign of funding cuts, he chose not to hang around and beg for scraps of work.

On the outside, he stayed busy volunteering to put on street events, folk trains and free community street festivals but inside he was reeling, as between late 2007 and late 2011 he lost one half of his family. His mother tragically passed away in autumn 2007, and then four years later his father and middle sister followed in the same year - at either end of 2011. This destroyed him even more than losing Hanni in 1991. Rabcat wasn't mentally equipped for this level of trauma and his own physical and mental health suffered as he struggled to deal with the grim reality that many of his family were no longer around. He actually lost 11 close relatives, friends and family in the space of five years. It was the worst of times. Rabcat and his two surviving sisters somehow had to build a new life and it took a while before they had any semblance of normal day-to-day routine.

Rabcat overcompensated by totally immersing himself in all his hobbies in a way he'd never done before. Art, music, festivals, street events, nostalgic community festivals, record and book fairs and even country events – you name it, Rabcat did it – anything to keep the darkness at bay. He was like a bird having to keep manically flapping its wings so as not fall out of the sky. He had to keep on going at all costs, just to keep the dark thoughts and traumatic flashbacks at bay. He chose not to give himself the time to properly grieve as he knew it would finish him.

In his normal day-to-day life before these tragic losses, the unjust corrupted matrix of capitalist reality was already enough to keep the Rabcat in a permanent state of outrage and contempt for this life and this world as we know it. The loss of his family members forced him into a state well beyond this normal disdain. He experienced true unbridled heartbreak – an angst baking in his innards to gradually form a massive cataclysmic howl of anguish and pain that he still hasn't let go to this day.

He was in a really fragile state when a job provided a timely survival dinghy – an opportunity to become a tour guide at The Beatles Story Museum in Liverpool.

He started this new role on the 8th December 2007 – the same day that John Lennon was shot in 1980, exactly 27 years earlier. From the off he was proud to be talking music back near where he was born in Wavertree, Sefton Park, Liverpool. His family originally lived not far from Penny Lane. The thing with Rabcat is that he is dying on the inside each and every day but outwardly he speaks with such energy and passion it so hard not to think he is wonderful (he is) and should have a wonderful life.

He lit up the tour thrilling customers from all around the world with his passion and enthusiasm for all things Fab Four and Liverpool. That job possibly saved his life. He maxed out after five years stoically following his unwritten rules. Then he decided to move back to Stockport. Subconsciously the artist in him was again ready for a new challenge.

After everything he had been through, he needed love and laughter in his life more than anything else and soon after landing back on the Manc map, he stumbled into Gaz Stanley a couple of times the he fell under the spell of his new band leader and his lovable sidekicks.

All of a sudden The Rats had a superstar drummer and Buster Rabcat had a completely dysfunctional new family.

FINAL RAMBLINGS

Soundtrack: Faithless - *We Come One*

As I get older I've become no less of a fuck up of a man, but one thing I have learned in life is to unquestionably just go with the flow and get on with what is put in front of you. It's usually, if not always, put there for a reason. So when I became troubled by the experience of walking past homeless Mancs everyday, I didn't piss around wasting time thinking why I shouldn't just start cooking, feeding and chatting to those desperate expressions of the same consciousness as me. I just went with it and starting carrying pans of the best food I could muster around town.

This taught me how to be better at loving strangers. It gave me an understanding that strangers aren't actually a thing - The Human Species, as the old, skinny, bag of muscles called Maxi Jazz from the band Faithless so eloquently once shared: 'We Come One!'

That guy on the pavement is you, is us. So only part of you/us goes home after feeding and speaking to our reflections on the pavement. We come one. Once you get into that mindset then the doors start to open and magic starts to happen.

When Heath spoke to me from the pavement I listened. When he told me that he was a Piccadilly Rat the words washed over me in a way that I could register a meant-to-be connection. So weeks later when I came face to snouts with his whole mischief of a rat family I already felt that I was meant to be among them, as if they were almost kind of expecting me. I listened some more and soon I understood that I'd been placed amongst them to help them find themselves.

The story didn't flow at the start. It wasn't coming together at all as my always remarkably supportive wife watched on as the non-productive hours, days and weeks drifted into a writer's wasteland of nothingness as I kept staring at my batshit crazy initial notes from interviewing Garry Stanley.

Fortunately for me just as my creative juices were about to run completely dry, and as I struggled to put Garry's ramblings in any meaningful order, the evil bastards that run this world decided to lock us all up. House arrest was exactly what was needed to flip this particular had-to-happen pipe dream into reality. The Covid Plandemic gave me the perfect opportunity to carefully rinse The Rats of their life's stories as we cleared away the debris of their most colourful pasts. The almost impossible awkwardness of the project dissipated quickly as the flow cascaded upwards into a much more pliable domain.

Each member of the band spilt their own particular life beans and I encourage anyone and everyone to do the same. Life is one big lesson and taking the time to reflect on the lessons so far is such a beneficial thing to do. The fun thing for me as a writer is to attempt to translate why someone did something at a particular time whilst always aiming for their truth. Often this technique results in happy tears as the subject gets a decoding nudge as they realise 'I'm a fuck up for a reason.' or 'I'm not as much as a twat as I thought I was.' We are all just learning and every story is worth telling. What's yours?

That said, no project is easy and this one has had plenty of bumps in the road. Ray's story should have been much bigger but the poor sod died. His family had reservations about the intentions of the book before they felt the truth spot evidence and came on side.

Gaz, Heath and Rabcat all had buried demons to dig up, expose and lay to rest. Rabcat wanted no part in it initially but it has been a real joy to have him chip in his very personal account in injury time. Very unexpectedly he accepted my decoding of his tale in the most humble and appreciative way.

We Come One x